WRITE TO LEARN

WRITE TO LEARN

FIFTH EDITION

Donald M. Murray

Harcourt Brace College Publishers

Fort Worth   Philadelphia   San Diego   New York   Orlando   Austin   San Antonio
Toronto   Montreal   London   Sydney   Tokyo

Publisher Ted Buchholz
Editor in Chief Christopher P. Klein
Executive Editor Michael Rosenberg
Developmental Editor Laurie Runion
Project Editor Christopher Nelson
Production Managers Serena Manning and Melinda Esco
Art Directors Nick Welch and Melinda Welch

Cover Illustration: © Deborah Raven/Photonica

ISBN: 0-15-501986-4

Library of Congress Catalog Card Number: 94-74269

Address for Editorial Correspondence: Harcourt Brace College Publishers, 301 Commerce Street, Suite 3700, Fort Worth, TX 76102.

Address for Orders: Harcourt Brace & Company, 6277 Sea Harbor Drive, Orlando, FL 32887-6777. 1-800-782-4479, or 1-800-433-0001 (in Florida).

Printed in the United States of America

5 6 7 8 9 0 1 2 3 4   066   10 9 8 7 6 5 4 3 2 1

To Minnie Mae
who shares my words and my life

PREFACE

In writing—and rewriting—*Write to Learn* I have had the opportunity to learn my craft. For years I worried that my obsession with the craft of writing would make me too self-conscious as I wrote and therefore inhibit the spontaneous flow of language essential to effective writing. Many of my writer friends subscribed to the romantic notion that writing is a dumb act, that if you know too much about the craft you won't be able to write.

Writing, however, is not a dumb act. It is an act of the intellect, it is thinking with language, it is craft. The craft of writing is, first of all, a collection of all those attitudes and techniques that summon and nourish spontaneity. Craft frees writing so that we may write what we do not intend, and then craft always shapes it so others will understand what we have to say. The more I have studied my craft, the more my writing surprises me.

I write to learn, to discover what I have to say that I did not know I had to say in ways that I did not know it could be said. Every morning I arrive at my desk, a young apprentice to the craft, surprised at what I discover—by writing—that I am knowing.

It has been a blessing—a celebration—to write five editions of this textbook. Each time I have learned. The writing of this fifth edition has instructed me once more and I hope it will instruct you.

New Organization

I have added three new chapters that should make the book more helpful for students to use as they write, and more helpful for teachers to use as they teach.

Chapter 7, "Fit Your Process to Your Task," helps students apply their process approach to new writing tasks, and provides guidelines to such common writing tasks as the book report, the reflective essay, the research paper, the job application letter, and the narrative essay.

Chapter 8, "Go into the Writer's Workshop," contains a professional case history and three student case histories, one each in the task of description, analysis, persuasion, and in reporting research. A new student case history shows how a disciplined, academic research paper can also be a lively, graceful example of significant writing.

vii

Chapter 9, "Read as a Writer," shows how a writer reads 25 very different authors as they face a variety of writing tasks. It shows the student how to read more effectively and how to read to learn how they may develop their own writing.

Changes in the First Six Chapters

The first six chapters remain fundamentally the same. Chapter 1, "Write First," is designed to start the student writing immediately, and the next five chapters—"Focus," "Explore," "Plan," "Draft," and "Clarify"—take the student through the writing process.

Each page in these chapters has been reread and usually rewritten, based on my own continuing study of the writing process as a writer and as one interested in how writing is made. It has also been developed and clarified in response to the suggestions of students, classroom teachers, composition experts, and reviewers. Line by line, paragraph by paragraph I have tried to make this book more effective.

In Every Chapter

How the Computer Can Help

More than 60 percent of students at the University of New Hampshire write Freshman English papers on a computer, and the percentage is higher at many colleges and universities. This edition of *Write to Learn* offers students computer techniques that will prove helpful at each stage of the writing process.

Daybook Entries

I demonstrate how the daybook may be used to help students at each stage of the writing process.

Reading the Reader

The writer writes for himself or herself but keeps an eye cocked toward the reader. I show throughout the book how the writer can anticipate the reader's reaction and respond to it.

Tuning the Voice of the Text

Writers hear the voice or music of their drafts during the entire writing process, and this strand helps students listen and tune their voices as they draft.

Revising While Writing

The many forms of revision that take place before and during the draft are demonstrated throughout the book.

Inside Covers

There is a special index, "Help for Your Writing Problems," placed in the inside front cover and an added reference list of "Writing Techniques" placed in the inside back cover.

Using *Write to Learn* with *Read to Write*

Read to Write is a reader organized around the major components of the writing process, and emphasizes the relationship between reading and writing. Although *Write to Learn* is designed to be used alone or with other readers, *Read to Write* was written after *Write to Learn,* and each book supports the other. They have the same process and a similar attitude toward the act of writing.

The Instructor's Manual

I have written an instructor's manual to help the teacher with the practical problems of the classroom. It is based on my own experience as a teacher and on the experiences of instructors who have used *Write to Learn* in many different types of institutions and courses with students at varying levels of accomplishment. It is specific, practical, and designed to help both beginning and experienced instructors in realistic teaching situations. This manual can be obtained by contacting your local Harcourt Brace sales representative.

Acknowledgments

The longer I write, the more I realize that every book is written in a collaboration. Minnie Mae, who started mailing out the manuscripts I was burning when we were married, is my first reader and constant supporter.

Not enough is written about the professional relationship of writer and editor. Laurie Runion has been involved in the conceptual development of this edition as well as its chapter by chapter, page by page, paragraph by paragraph, sentence by sentence, word by word execution. She has suggested, commanded, demonstrated, supported, and corrected with perception, wisdom, and good humor.

Day and night, Christopher Scanlan of the Poynter Institute in St. Petersburg, Florida, and Donald Graves in Jackson, New Hampshire, are as close as the telephone and FAX machine. They always listen, laugh, and understand.

At the University of New Hampshire I have learned from and with many colleagues. Those who have especially stimulated and helped shape my thinking during the writing of this edition were Dr. Thomas R. Newkirk, Dr. Brock Dethier, and Lisa Miller.

The other members of my private writing community who appear behind my computer screen each writing morning shaking their heads no and yes, smiling or frowning, include Elizabeth Cooke of the University of Maine at Farmington, Dr. Thomas Romano of Utah State University, Dr. Bonnie Sunstein of the University of Iowa, Dr. Driek Zirinsky of Boise State University, Evelynne Kramer of the *Boston Globe,* and Dr. Lad Tobin of Boston College.

I have been given wise counsel by those who reviewed the last edition as this edition was begun and who read drafts of the fifth edition: Larry Burton, University of South Alabama; Sherie Coelho, Antelope Valley College; Eileen Donovan, Boston College; Gil Tierney, William Rainey Harper College.

I owe special thanks to the staff at Harcourt Brace: Michael Rosenberg, Executive Editor for English; Tina Winslow, Assistant Editor for English; Christopher Nelson, Project Editor; Serena Manning and Melinda Esco, Production Managers; and Nick Welch and Melinda Welch, Art Directors.

CONTENTS

CHAPTER 7   FIT YOUR PROCESS TO YOUR TASK   159

CHAPTER 8   GO INTO THE WRITER'S WORKSHOP   180

CHAPTER 9   READ AS A WRITER   224

CHAPTER 1
WRITE FIRST

Don't get it right, get it written.

JAMES THURBER

A promise: Write and your world will explode with meaning.

Your writing will reveal your world with an unexpected clarity and understanding. Creating your drafts, you will remember places, events, people, thoughts, feelings that you did not realize had been stored in memory. Writing will weave diverse elements in your life into a meaning you would not have predicted. Writing will make you ask questions that you have never thought to ask before and you will write answers that will surprise you. While writing you will feel and think more intensely than would have seemed possible before writing. You will see significance in the ordinary, drama in what had seemed routine. While writing, you will become more alert to your life than you have ever been before. Writing will make you aware.

Awareness is the first gift of writing.

We do not write with words but with information symbolized by words, life captured and examined with language.

To write well you have to increase your awareness of your past, present, and future, accumulating an inventory of special, revealing, interesting material. You build meaning by writing the words that capture this material and reveal it—first to you the writer, then to the reader.

To understand the relationship between awareness and writing, between writing and living, you have to plunge in and write. Write and your writing will instruct you.

The craft of writing begins when you put words on paper, read them, and discover you have said something more—or less—than you intended, then explore the difference with more words on paper.

1

Now is time to write: Writers write.

But write what?

Write what you become aware of as you write. Start thinking by writing. If I don't know what to write, I think back to an event, a person, a place that I keep remembering. I list whatever comes to mind. Nothing is too trivial, too stupid: specific details, phrases, sounds, fragments of conversation, colors, smells, tastes—anything. I want to see what is revealed when the compost heap is turned over.

I'm going to try to demonstrate how making lists works for me. Join me but don't copy me. My list will differ from yours, it should, and if I write another list tomorrow, it will differ from the list I wrote today. Create your own list from your own world.

I found myself going back into my childhood as I began putting fragments of language down on paper. Here is today's list:

Vassall Street
6 years old
grape arbor
Uncle Will's car up on blocks
back stoop
new house
painting the back steps with water
apple tree
can't play with neighbors
vacant lot
car radiator drained
secret place behind the garage
house of childhood
under the porch
Bible
sickly
fight with Walter Almeda

This list—written in private language—was meant to be read only by me. Each of those simple words or phrases gives off a personal meaning for me. "Sickly," for example, reminds me of my childhood illnesses and the long, dreamy weeks in bed convalescing in the days before miracle drugs; "under the porch" was where I first discovered girls were constructed differently from boys; the "apple tree" was the first tree I learned to climb; the Depression New England custom of draining the cooling system and putting a car up on blocks January through March, reminds me of my uncle's open Buick and the slow, windy, chilly Sunday afternoon drives in the days before a car had a heating system; the haunting image of myself "painting the back steps with water" reminds me of the imaginary games I played with Grandma Smith when I was very young.

I am going to use that list to find a FOCUS. The writer needs to focus as much as a photographer does. The photographer doesn't shoot without looking; the photographer looks, then takes a picture. The writer uses language to look at the world and find something worth exploring in writing.

To find my focus I look at the list and interview myself, asking questions that may help me see the possibilities hidden within my list:

- **What surprises me?**

  "Painting the back steps with water" brings back a whole afternoon filled with details: I can see the backyard, the people beyond the backyard, the water drying on the thick, worn back steps, see Grandmother towering over me.

- **Where's the tension?**

  "Can't play with neighbors" brings back the tension we had with our neighbors. We were Scots and Protestant; they were Irish and Catholic and that worried my family, and their worry became a mystery for me.

- **Where's the conflict?**

  Between the way I was supposed to behave and what I did "under the porch" and in the "secret place behind the garage."

- **What makes me feel happy, sad, angry, amused?**

  I remember my thrill at climbing the apple tree and seeing my familiar world all new.

- **What makes my memory itch? What do I keep thinking about when my mind wanders?**

  The scene of my painting the back steps with water.

- **What do I need to understand?**

  I need to understand the power of the image of my painting the back steps. I wonder what's so important about that afternoon painting the back steps with water.

Ask yourself the questions I did or any other that come to mind to find your focus. I'm going to focus on the scene on the back steps. And now that I have my focus, I'm moving to the next stage of my writing process and **EXPLORE** it.

A focus can be explored in many ways. You may have to go and observe your subject, interview someone who was involved, visit the library, and make entries in a notebook that you can read when it comes time to write.

In my case I began watching the movie of my childhood that is stored in my head. I traveled back in memory until I found myself near my childhood home and drove around the block several times, remembering how long a wobbly trip that was on my first two-wheeler (*that trip might make an essay*), remembering a bright blue Depression bike made out of leftover parts by the local blacksmith, the only African American in my Yankee hometown (*that might be a story, too*).

This movie runs when I go for my walk, while I wait for my wife in the car, during the commercials of a Celtics game, in all sorts of nooks and crannies of time during the day. Usually I make notes but I didn't need to in this case. In memory I visited the kitchen with the great, black cast-iron stove. It was my job to bring up the filled coal hopper from the cellar and keep a supply nearby for Grandmother. I went down to the dark, spider-webby coal bin and heard again the terrifying roar as a ton of coal slid down the chute from the truck. I went back up to the pantry where I grabbed the edge of a jelly bowl and pulled hot jelly over me, wasting, in a moment, an entire grape harvest. I could see the pattern in the kitchen's linoleum floor, the black soap stone sink, the ice box with the drip pan I hated to empty.

For days I lived in that house in memory, storing each memory against the time when I would write. I knew I had a rich abundance of material to draw on as I wrote. That's all I needed to know. It is time to **PLAN**.

There are many ways that I plan but the most common is to write as many first sentences as possible—three, five, eleven, seventeen—until I find one that interests me enough that I can see the sentence that will follow, sometimes even the sentence or paragraph beyond that. That's all and that's enough. I write to discover, to be surprised, to experience, to find out; I write to learn.

I find myself writing:

I return to the house of childhood and find myself alone on the bottom step of the back stoop, scratching words in the dust with a stick. I am the writer I will become.

conditions of writer alienation—can't play with Catholic kids Grandma, paintbrush, and water

That was all I needed to ignite a draft. The image is strong and compelling: a child writing words in the dust with a stick. But I am "inspired" to write even more by the sentence that follows: "I am the writer I will become."

That sentence sparks my note "conditions of writer alienation—can't play with Catholic kids"—and there is the tension that will ignite a draft. I know I want to find out what I have to say and I know it will involve the scene in the next note about painting the steps.

It is time to begin a **DRAFT.** Writers call the attempts they make to write *drafts.* They are experiments, sketches, trial runs. Sometimes the writer has to do many drafts—my personal record is eighty-six versions of a poem. Three drafts is common, but sometimes one draft is all the experienced—or fortunate—writer has to write. The writer also uses the word *draft* as a verb to describe the action of writing a version of a piece that may have to be rewritten—*drafted*—again: "I'm *drafting* an essay"; "First, I *draft* my articles"; "I *draft* to find out what I have to say."

Drafting is best done at top speed. Remember when you rode your first two-wheel bike? You had to pedal fast, even if the speed scared you because velocity made it possible for you to balance the bike. Velocity is as important in writing a draft as it is in riding a bicycle.

Writing with velocity keeps you ahead of the censor, the doubter within, the police grammarian, and the state-trooper speller who all apply premature criticism to a draft. Writers must first produce a draft, then they can be critical.

Speed also causes the accidents of insight and language essential for effective writing. You don't know what you are going to say? Good. You don't know what you are saying? Even better: Write to discover what you have to say. This counsel contradicts common sense. Each craft is that way.

Common sense told me to stand up and run from the German machine gun; the soldier's craft taught me that because machine guns rise as they fired, it is best to stay low and run toward the firing machine gun. Common sense—and some teachers we have had in the past—tell us to know what we have to say and that we should write it down slowly and carefully, not making mistakes. The experienced writer knows that learning is hidden in the mistakes, that we discover what we have to say and how we can say it from fast-written prose. Try it. You'll see it on your page and in my draft that follows.

I began with the scene of myself sitting on the bottom step painting with water. My commentary is thought out and was inserted after I finished the essay to articulate what I did instinctively—and at top speed, writing this draft in less than forty-five minutes the way you might write an in-class paper.

I sit alone on the bottom of the back stoop of the house at the corner of Vassall Street and Billings Road in Wollaston.

When I do not know where to start, I usually begin with description.

I can almost make out the words I try to scratch in the dust with a stick. Am I the writer I will become?

Changing the second sentence into a question makes an enormous difference. It creates suspense: The reader is invited to explore the subject with the writer.

I have the ideal condition for a writer: alone in a world made strange. We have rented a whole house in a new neighborhood and the family has undergone a change in fortune I do not understand. I have left behind the Airedale that terrified me on Grand View Avenue, but I know there will be new terrors here.

Now I know I have a piece worth writing. The first sentence of the paragraph puts my personal experience in a larger context: What are the conditions of creativity? That single sentence makes me be specific about those conditions in the specific terms of my life then. I also experience the surprise caused by velocity when I wrote "ideal" condition. I had expected sadness, unhappiness—but "ideal"? I find that interesting and have to write on to discover what it means.

Recently I drove past the house, circling the block to see if the significance of that haunting memory would come clear. The back steps were still there, and so was I.

The reader travels at my side.

I am alone, fenced into an unfamiliar backyard. As so often happens to us who are at the autumn of life, I am both in the car in this Sunday afternoon and back in 1930, within the mysterious world of half-remembered childhood.

At my age I see what is and what was at the same time, as if one photograph was printed on top of another. I share my double vision with the reader, placing both the experience and my reflections on it in specific time frames.

There is a boy next door, a girl across the back fence, a great variety of boys across the street, but I am told they are Catholic and I am Baptist and I am not to play with them.

I define the peculiar nature of my alienation knowing the reader will translate the prejudices of my childhood into the prejudices of their own childhoods.

I don't understand what those words mean but I know my family is serious about this, and something terrible will happen to me if I break their commandment.

Later, of course, I do, and find that they are not supposed to invite a Protestant—another word I do not understand—into their homes. Our parents' prejudices do not become ours, but I am left with a sense of alienation, of my own difference, that is another condition of most writers.

I show the reverse prejudice but decide not to go on—in this draft—to explain how I found the alien mothers often more affectionate than my own. I emphasize my feeling of difference, another condition of most writers.

But this day, on the bottom step, I have not broken my parents' law and Grandmother, seeing me sitting alone, suggests I paint the back stoop. She gives me an old paintbrush and a can of water and I paint the steps.

Looking back at those two simple sentences, I realize how long it took me to learn my craft and simply reveal a scene. No flourishes, just ordinary words revealing an ordinary scene that will, through the writing that follows, become extraordinary.

I easily enter the world of make-believe and paint; Grandmother returns to admire the painting I have done. But even at the time there was something special about the task and perhaps that is why I remember each stroke of the brush, how the wood darkens and how soon it fades.

I remember my innocence—my ignorance—when I wrote this. Now it seems inevitable to me, but at the time I was only describing a feeling—a hope, a guess—that there was something significant in painting the back steps with water.

I suspect there was an end to innocence that afternoon. I had made a choice between the world of reality and the world of imagination. I chose imagination.

This is the crucial paragraph in the draft. If a draft works for me, I push what I am writing to a deeper level of meaning about halfway through. I go further than I—or the reader expects—finding an insight that intrigues and lingers in the mind after the reading is done. This insight—generated by velocity—is the reason I write: to discover meaning in experience.

I would soon be 6 and I knew there was only water in the can and Grandmother knew I knew and yet we could share, that afternoon, the satisfying illusion of a job well done.

I keep the essay rooted in the specifics of my experience, allowing its importance to rise from them.

I would soon start first grade at the Massachusetts Fields School and it would not go well, perhaps because my imagination made it possible for me to enter the book and become a character, often a character new to the story who traveled his own path through the book, a path the teacher could not see.

Effective writing creates a conversation with the reader. The reader asks what happens because of your decision to choose imagination. And I say,

"Oh boy, I'm glad you asked that question" because I, the writer, want to hear my own answer.

When the teacher pointed to a map, my imagination ran up the pointer and into the map, exploring under the canopy of the rain forest, unable to hear the teacher's questions. When we studied the Revolutionary War I became a boy of Boston, in 1775, three-cornered hat and all, a busy printer's apprentice, unavailable for class discussion.

I make my school experience active. I do not tell about it, I show it, revealing it to the reader who may then remember his or her own classroom hours.

Looking back I wonder how I got through school at all; I attended school but rarely remained in the class. Imagination provided my text.

In writing this essay, I am discovering a new answer to a question I keep asking myself: Why did I do so badly in school, dropping out of high school twice and finally flunking out?

I lived—and still live—in the geography of memory and fantasy, what may have been, what may yet be. I am still the small, lonely boy painting the back steps with water, and I wonder if in giving me water and a paintbrush, my grandmother hadn't given me the gift of imagination that has been my trade ever since and causes me to remember that afternoon so many years ago with such clarity.

I weave back to the opening scene, to what followed school and suggest a reason why I remember that image so clearly.

Now it is time to **CLARIFY.** I read the draft out loud and, as a reader, making small changes to make my meaning clear, ran it through the spell checker on my computer, had my wife read it, then sent it off to Evelynne Kramer, my editor at *The Boston Globe,* and the next day she called. She liked it, but she was not sure what it meant. I paid attention to her reaction; I have learned to respect, trust, and depend on her. If she was not sure what it meant, readers certainly wouldn't be sure.

You may not have a computer with spell check, a wife who is a good reader, or a professional editor, but you can be your own editor, reading what you have written over as a stranger to be sure what you have written will be understood. If you are lucky, you may be able to find a good test reader, a person who can read your early drafts as readers will read your final ones. That person—a classmate, a roommate, a friend—will help you see the strengths as well the weaknesses of your draft and will help you recognize what needs to be added to make the paper clear to a reader. They may be critical but they should be supportive. My own condition for test readers: They make me want to write when I leave them.

I read it over and agreed with my editor. I had been too close to the subject and started too abruptly. I decided I had to step back and put the story in a context the reader could understand. First I made a statement, and then I gave a number of personal examples in the second paragraph that I hoped would spark memories in readers' minds.

Here is the new beginning as the essay was published:

All My Roads Lead Backward

Each of us is haunted by images from our childhood that have a mysterious attraction we cannot completely understand.

One image I often remember—and dream—is the green crusted pilings at Salem Willows that slide upwards as I sink, almost drowning. And the brown wallpaper of the small downstairs room into which I was locked, the day I could not go to the Brockton Fair. The huge tire and drive chain of the Mack dump truck rolls toward me on Billings Road. The hammer after it left my hand and my uncle falling, that is all.

Over sixty, reflecting back on the life we have lived, we examine these haunting images, perhaps even returning to the place where they occurred in the hope of discovering meaning—or at least the reason they are so immediate after all these years.

In one recurring scene I see myself sitting alone on the bottom step of the back stoop of the house at the corner of Vassall Street and Billings Road in Wollaston.

▪ DISCOVERING THE WRITING PROCESS ▪

Now you and I have experienced a writing process. There is, however, not one writing process but many. Each person's process may change as the writer's own thinking style evolves, when the writer faces a new writing task, or the writer becomes more experienced with a particular writing task.

The process we used is:

Focus
The writer chooses a way to look at the subject, focusing on one aspect of the topic.

Explore

The writer researches the subject either formally or in the informal way I did in memory, seeking out the specific details from which the writer can construct a meaning from the confusion of information.

Plan

The writer sketches a trail map for the draft, usually finding a lead or starting point, then some landmarks that may appear along the way.

Draft

The writer drafts quickly to outrun the censor and cause those instructive failures that reveal the meaning of the subject, surprising the writer—and the reader—with an unexpected insight.

Clarify

The writer clarifies the meaning by revising (reconsidering the form and its structure) and editing the language (reading each line aloud) so the reader will understand what the writer has learned about the subject through its writing.

Writing is both an art and a craft. The process is not something to be followed rigidly, step by step. There are times when the writer may begin by drafting or exploring to find a focus. As Eudora Welty says:

> The writer himself studies intensely how to do it while he is in the thick of doing it; then when the particular novel or story is done, he is likely to forget how; he does well to. Each work is new. Mercifully, the question of *how* abides less in the abstract, and less in the past, than in the specific, in the work at hand.

We all know why writing often goes off track—"I began at two A.M. Sunday night after, you know, like a weekend," "The dog ate my notes," "I found out how I shoulda written it after I finished." To improve your writing, concentrate on when the writing goes well: Write down the conditions and the processes you followed during your best writing experiences, the attitudes you had as well as the techniques you used, a record of the environment in which the writing took place.

▪ WRITING IN A DAYBOOK ▪

The environment in which much of my most creative writing takes place is the daybook in which I write to myself. The daybook competes with the computer as my most valuable writing tool. Even the name *daybook* is important to me. For years I tried to keep a journal. I imagined I was Gide or Camus. But I wasn't either of those writers, and what I wrote was not perceptive but pompous, full of hot air, hilarious to read, and utterly useless to me as a writer. At other times I tried to keep a diary, but then I found myself recording only trivia—the temperature, or whom I met, or what I ate.

I don't know where I heard the term "daybook," but a number of years ago I found myself using the term and writing every day—well, almost every day—in a ten-by-eight spiral notebook filled with greenish paper, narrow ruled, with a margin line down the left. This worked for me. I write on my lap, in the living room or on the porch, in the car or an airplane, in meetings at the university, in bed, or sitting on a rock wall when resting during a walk. A bound book doesn't work for me. I find a spiral book convenient and easy to handle; and since I write in all sorts of light, indoors and out, I find the greenish paper comfortable. I chose the size because it fits in the outside pocket of the bag I carry everywhere.

The organization is simply a day-by-day chronology. When I change the subject I write a code word—novel, poem, talk at St. Anselm's, children's book?—in the left-hand margin. That way I can look back through the book and collect all the notes I've made on a single project or concern.

I often write in the daybook during the first fifteen minutes of the day before I eat breakfast; then I keep it near me all day long. If something occurs to me I make a note during a television commercial or in a meeting, or while walking, or in the car.

How I use my daybook varies from time to time. Since I now do most of my writing using a computer, my daybooks have pages or paragraphs I have printed out and pasted in so I can read, reconsider, and play with the writing during spare moments. All the writing in the daybook is a form of talking to myself, a way of thinking on paper. Much of my "spontaneous" writing can be tracked through years of daybooks in which I have thought and rethought, planned and researched, drafted and redrafted its movement from interesting fragment to possible draft.

Here are some of the items you might see in my daybook:

- Questions that need to be answered
- Fragments of writing seeking a voice
- Leads, hundreds of leads, the beginning lines of what I may write
- Titles, hundred of titles
- Notes from which I have made lectures, talks, or speeches
- Notes I have made at lectures, talks, or speeches of others; also notes I have made at poetry readings, hockey games, and concerts
- Outlines
- Ideas for stories, articles, poems, books, papers
- Diagrams showing how a piece might be organized or, more likely, showing the relationships between parts of an idea

- Drafts
- Observations
- Quotations from writers or artists
- Newspaper clippings
- Titles of books to be read
- Notes on what I have read
- Pictures I want to save
- Writing schedules
- Pasted-in copies of interesting letters I've received or written
- Lists, lots of lists
- Pasted-in handouts I've developed for classes or workshops

I don't have any single way I use the daybook. Anything that will stimulate or record my thinking, anything that will move toward writing goes into the daybook. When a notebook is filled—usually in about six weeks—I go through it and harvest a page or two or three of the most interesting material for the beginning of the next daybook. When I'm ready to work seriously on a project I go back through past daybooks and photocopy those pages that relate to the subject I'm working on.

The daybook stimulates my thinking, helps me make use of those small fragments of time, which on many days is all the time we have to write. There is no sign of struggle. I'm not fighting writing, I'm playing with writing. If it isn't fun, if nothing is happening, I stop and wait until the magic begins. The daybook also keeps my writing muscles in condition; it lets me know what I'm concerned with making into writing; it increases my productivity.

If you decide to keep a daybook, make it your own. Don't try to follow anyone else's formula. And don't write it for another audience. It's a private place where you can think and where you can be dumb, stupid, sloppy, silly; where you can do all the bad writing and bad thinking essential for those moments of insight that produce good writing.

Your daybook might not—should not—be like mine. It may be a file stored in a computer. From time to time, I have kept a computer file called JOURNAL. The poet Mekeel McBride's daybook is a bound sketch pad in which she draws and paints as well as writes. I envy her and have tried it but it doesn't work for me. I know other writers who use file cards, tiny pocket notebooks, huge accounting ledgers, scraps of paper stuck in file folders in a drawer, a paper compost heap that flows from desk to floor. And some writers keep only mental daybooks in which they make notes of the world and rehearse the writing they intend to do, trying out one approach and then another in their minds. There is no one way and no correct way to write well; there are many ways and it is your job to find what works for you and be ready to switch when it stops helping you write well.

Fear.

I don't like that word. It is a strong word but the person who says it is weak.

Or perhaps strong enough to admit it.

Fear.

The shadow companion who rises with you when you get up in the night. The person you meet unexpectedly when you turn the corner. The twinge of pain in the left arm, the morning when you can't remember a proper noun. The reality that rises from the obituary page.

Fear.

What we try to avoid, deny, ignore.

Fear is physical- a queasiness, a shakiness, a dizzyness, a kind of feaver

Fear increases the symptoms of what is wrong, magnifying them.

As men, we have been taught to deny ourselves. Someone recently mentioned the "wounding" men do to each other in joining the squad, the

This is an example of daybook free writing in which I explore a topic that is on my mind—in this case *fear*—to discover what I feel about a passing thought or emotion.

> team, the management group. The
> "kidding" may be harsh but we
> learn to take it, ignore how we feel,
> and we learn to dish it out.
>
> Ignoring our true feelings—hurt, anger,
> aching, fear—may serve us well in
> getting ahead in a corporate world
> out on football field competition but
> it doesn't help when we have to
> confront our weaknesses—how we feel—
> and analyze it.
>
> The very act of reading ourselves, in
> males of my generation, feels feminine,
> although we all know what is the
> toughest sex.

Although this eventually became a *Boston Globe* column, I try not to have a restrictive intention or expectation while free writing. I simply write quickly to see what I have to say and to discover what form it may take. It may become fiction, poetry, or a column. While this did become a column, it also fertilized some ground in which poems have grown.

The Writer in the Newsroom

1/6 NE Press

④ · Voice

⑤ ③ · Line/rehearsal,/mystery?

⑥ · Many Leads
③

· Discovery [attitude: Will Discover full
meaning of story in its writing.]

? ⑦ · Experiment w/ form/
angle of vision} to Reveal

⑧ · Velocity - Discovery Draft

⑨ · revision - 3 readings

· Write Out Loud

② · [after Reporting] (writing will make
you a better reporter)

① · importance of writer in the newsroom

· Time for writing.

On this page of the daybook, written in a restaurant while waiting to meet someone for lunch, I worked on a talk I was going to give 12 days later to a New England Press Association Convention. This is the way I usually prepare a talk, a magazine article, a business memo, the chapter of a textbook. I list the elements that may be appropriate as they come to mind, then manipulate them into a meaningful shape, cutting some, adding others, and reordering—and reordering and then reordering.

The list, ordered and reordered, is as important to the creative act as it is to the supermarket shopping trip. As these entries demonstrate, I make use of fragments of time and put the ideas into a savings account so I can withdraw them when I have an hour or two in which to write.

I usually begin my day by being one of the first customers at The Bagelry, where I consume a bagel and a large, black coffee and solve the problems of the world with an early-rising friend. He didn't show up on this snowy morning so I took one of the paper bags on the counter and started brainstorming my memories of snowstorms when I was young. I am never bored—not if I can get my hands on pen and paper.

When I finished breakfast, I folded the bag, stuck it in my pocket, and took my walk. During my daily exercise, the ideas I had scratched down continued to bubble away in my conscious and subconscious. When I got home I sat down at the computer and drafted a column that was published under the title "All Hail and Snow." The next day I wrote a poem that was ignited by my brown-bag notes and it soon divided into two poems as I continued to explore my worlds of snow.

The playwright Marsha Norman says:

But I'm really writing all the time, I'm afraid, even when I'm not at my desk. You'll notice there are little pads of paper everywhere? It works for me to write down the things I want to know. Regarding a character, the progress of a scene. . . . Even before I begin to write, I will say, "These are the things I must know before I start to write." I'll simply make the list of questions. Over the course of the next couple of weeks or months I'll get the answers to those questions. Even when I do rewrites, I just make a little question that says, "How is another way to say this?" Then I will put the paper away. It may be on the back of a grocery list, but once I write the question down, I never forget it. I do have a prodigious memory, and that helps. So I don't need to keep track of all these pieces of paper, I just need to have them around. The answer will end up on some other piece of paper. Gradually, in the course of getting ready to write, those pieces of paper collect, and pretty soon I have a whole box of them.

Throughout this text, in each chapter, I indicate how you can use the daybook to stimulate and support your writing. Translate what I say to whatever form of written, drawn, or mental note taking and rehearsal helps you.

The method of capturing, connecting, and developing ideas is not important but the act of capturing, connecting, and developing is.

■ FINDING YOUR OWN WRITING TERRITORIES ■

When we wrote at the beginning of the chapter we explored personal territories. Willa Cather said, "Most of the basic material a writer works with is acquired before the age of fifteen." Some of your best writing may come from these territories as did my essay on painting the back steps.

These territories—or themes—are the ones I keep returning to when I am alone. In mining these territories I have found a lifetime of writing. They are:

School and writing. I was always fascinated by pen and paper, obsessed with the mystery of how words and lines could create and clarify a world. I read books, studied pictures, and did badly in school. I did not learn in the way that the "bright" kids learned and thought I was dumb. My motivation to become a teacher and to write books about writing and the teaching of writing came from my personal struggles in the classroom; I wanted to understand how writing was made so that I could help students like myself explore our world through writing.

Family. Like most families, mine had difficulties—problems, tensions, conflicts—I could not understand when I was young. Much of my writing today deals with family: my grandparents and parents who are dead, my daughters, their husbands, and our grandsons; the daughter we lost when she was twenty. I keep writing about family to celebrate and to understand.

Sickness, aging, and death. I had a sickly childhood. The grandmother with whom I lived became paralyzed when I was very young and I helped take care of her until I went to college. I wrote many magazine pieces about health issues and now I write a weekly column for *The Boston Globe*—"Over Sixty"—that documents my own aging.

War. I was in combat as a paratrooper during World War II and am still trying to deal with the internal conflict of pride and shame experienced about my own months in combat. The Pulitzer Prize I received was for writing on military affairs and my columns and poems constantly find their way onto the battlefield. The novel I am writing explores the affect of war on those who appear to survive it.

List the subjects that make you itch. What do you think about when you are driving alone in the car, taking a walk, tuning out the people you're with at dinner or a party, doing errands or the laundry, while listening to a boring lecture? What keeps you awake nights? What do you avoid thinking about but can't help thinking about? Donald Barthelme said: "Write about what you're most afraid of."

Of course much of the writing you do in school or at work concerns territories dominated by teachers or employers. It is important to try to make the territory your own, to turn the assignment so you can write with confidence—and an abundance of specific information on which you can draw. I was recently assigned to write a story on the home office. I put my own office in this context and compared it to a few of the male "dens" I visited in homes far more affluent than mine.

▪ FINDING YOUR OWN MYSTERIES ▪

Our best subjects come from the mysteries in our lives or in the topics we are exploring with language. Grace Paley said, "We write about what we don't know about what we know." Many of us know a parent, uncle or aunt, teacher or neighbor who had their lives changed by the Vietnam War but often we do not know the details or the nature of the change. Their personal history is a mystery that might help us to understand them—and the nature of war—if we could explore that mystery.

Seek and confront the mysteries in your life to find writing subjects. The mysteries may be personal: Why did I return to a spouse who abused me?

What was the affect of my parents' drinking on my life? Or they may be impersonal: What makes it possible for a heavy metal plane to fly? Why does one product sell while a similar one sits on the supermarket shelf?

Some of the mysteries that have led me to write:

- How can I feel both pride and shame at my combat experience? This unresolved mystery has produced columns and poems as well as the novel on which I am currently working.
- Why didn't I do well in school? How might school have been made meaningful to me? This led to articles and books I have written on teaching.
- How is writing created? This has fascinated me from grade school to today and has led to nine published books about writing.

The mysteries may be small or large, personal or impersonal, but they engage our minds, presenting problems we need to solve, providing us with unexpected answers as we watch our words appear on the page or screen.

Techniques for Discovering Subjects

There are many other ways to discover the mysteries that will produce effective subjects. Play with them to see what works for you.

Brainstorming

One of the best ways to discover what you already know is to brainstorm. When you brainstorm you write down everything that comes into your mind as fast as you can. You don't need to be critical; you do want to be illogical, irrational, even silly. You want to discover what is in your mind. You want to be surprised.

Here I have brainstormed about my childhood to see what other topics I may have that need to be explored in writing. I'll start with the geography of childhood and see where it leads me as I list as fast as I can, not worrying if I am silly or stupid.

Brainstorm beside me in the margin of the text. There's plenty of white space. You may discover a subject you want to explore through writing. My list is personal; I'm writing about *my* childhood. Your list doesn't have to be. Brainstorm any topic, personal or impersonal, with which you have some experience to see if there's something you wish to explore.

Now to brainstorm:

- **geography of childhood**
- **the block**

- the vacant lot
- empty stores
- cellar hole
- under the porch
  - playing doctor
  - sex mis-education
- behind the garage
- dogs, Airedale, Chow, scared
- uncle
- Grandmother collapses
- alien WASP—white Protestant in Irish Catholic neighborhood
- school
- nearsighted
- sat in back row
- glasses
- "four-eyes"
- turn the other cheek, beaten up on playground
- Muddy Ducks
- fights
- seriousness of games
- Red Sox, Bruins
- snow
- sleighs
- Uncle Will's car up on blocks in winter
- his Buick
- the Sunday drive
- almost drowning
- fear of water
- sickly childhood
- days in bed—good
- reading
- friends who lived in walls
- fantasy
- temper—threw hammer at uncle, he fell
- Grandmother's paralysis
- day I pulled hot jelly over me
- wood stove
- mystery of basement
- "   " attic
- den
- brown, color of my childhood

That took eight minutes. It's possible to brainstorm for a much longer time, but I find short spurts—fifteen minutes, ten minutes, five minutes—are more productive. You can also brainstorm together with another person, or a group of people. The important thing is not to censor what you say, not to judge it, not to really understand it—but to let it come.

This brainstorming list is printed simply as it came. I didn't prepare for it, except by living with my grandmother until I went off to college. I had to let it come.

After you have brainstormed, look at what you've written to see what surprises you or which items connect. These surprises and connections remind you of what you know and will make you aware of meanings you hadn't seen before.

It is important not to worry about how the brainstorming list is written. Don't worry about spelling or penmanship or sentences; it is a time to write in a sort of private language of code words that stand for particular meanings in your own mind. When the phrase "turn the other cheek" appeared on my brainstorming list it reminded me of all the years—from grade one until grade six—when my mother would instruct me not to fight but to "turn the other cheek." If I really believed in Jesus, she said, the fists of the other boys would be held and they would not smite me. Apparently, I was never able to believe enough because their fists kept hitting me and I lived in fear, humiliation, and guilt at my lack of faith. All that and much, much more would pour out if I wrote about that in a column, novel, or poem; but the simple phrase "turn the other cheek" would be enough to hold it in reserve for another writing period.

I brainstorm before I write important letters or a memo. I brainstorm class lectures and novels. I brainstorm articles and poems and textbooks such as this. I also brainstorm before I decide to buy a car or take a job or choose a vacation. Brainstorming shows me what I know, what I need to know, and what the connections are between what I know and don't know.

Looking for Surprise. I look at the list to see what surprised me. Whatever you are brainstorming—an academic paper or a job application letter—first go over the list to see what surprises you, to find out what discoveries you have made.

The surprise doesn't need to be enormous. I am surprised by:

- **under the porch**
  - **playing doctor**
  - **sex mis-education** ◄┐
- **behind the garage** ◄┘

I don't remember what happened behind the garage and that's enough of a mystery for me to start to explore my childhood world when I first became aware of sex—I thought the facts of life ridiculous when I first learned them and, in fact, they are.

I also note:

- seriousness of games
- Red Sox, Bruins

That is all it takes to remind me of the importance of being a sports fan in a town like Boston. It was one of the few subjects that connected me with my father and my uncles—the world of men—and the emphasis on sports and competition probably marked me more than I know. If I write about that I may discover its importance.

An old theme for me but a new twist:

- sickly childhood
- days in bed—good

What have we lost because of miracle drugs—convalescence. I am nostalgic for the long, lonely hours of fantasy and the reading that helped make me a writer.

Looking for Connections. Next I look for connections between the items on my list and draw lines connecting them, creating little bunches that may lead to a subject:

- the vacant lot
- empty stores
- cellar hole

Child's delight in playgrounds created by construction and business failures in the Great Depression.

- alien WASP—white Protestant in Irish Catholic neighborhood
- turn the other cheek— beaten up on playground
- fights
- seriousness of games
- almost drowning
- fear of water
- sickly childhood

Might explore the terrors of childhood.

- school
- nearsighted
- sat in back row
- glasses
- "four-eyes"

Might reconstruct the school world of a nearsighted kid when you got beaten up for wearing glasses.

Mapping

Another form of brainstorming that often works is mapping. In mapping you put the subject or topic you want to think about in the center of the page, and then draw lines radiating out from it when another idea occurs to you. These lines branch off, capturing the fragments of information that you have unknowingly stored in memory.

Here is a map of thoughts I have about my childhood:

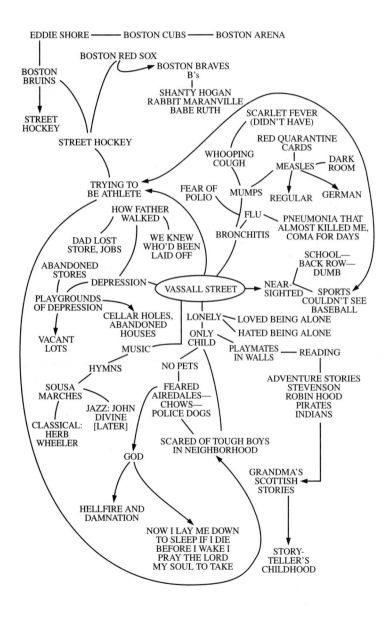

How Mapping Leads to Writing. That map took less than ten minutes to create, the same as the brainstorm list, but it produced different information. I rediscovered the red quarantine cards that were placed on the door when anyone had scarlet fever or measles; this might lead me into the territory of childhood disease before miracle drugs. The map also made me aware of how much I learned about the world came in the form of stories—from the Bible, from Grandma and the uncles, from the street, from the classroom. And then there was the role of music, my family's hymns and Sousa marches, my jazz and the beginning of my interest in classical music—I could write a musical geography of my childhood.

Making a Tree

Another helpful technique to discover what you already know and don't know you know is to draw a tree that reveals the branches that can grow from a single idea:

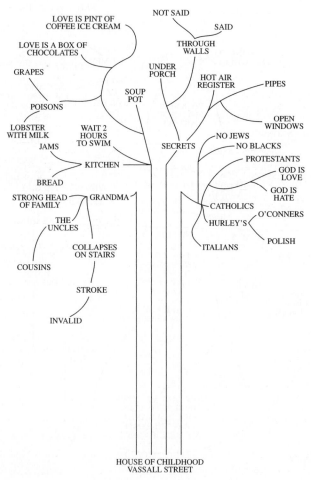

This is a way of breaking down the subject or a way of letting the subject expand. Some writers who use trees successfully place the central idea at the top of the page and let the tree grow down, whereas others place the central idea at the bottom of the page and let the tree grow up. Both produce excellent results.

This tree took five minutes to create, and it produced some new insights. I discovered the larger complexity of religions with which I grew up and their contradictions, the food myths that were important in my childhood, and the role of secrets in our family.

Free Writing

Another technique I have found productive is free writing. To free write, sit down and let the writing flow; see if language will start to reveal something that unexpectedly interests you—an event, person, place, idea, feeling. Suspend critical judgment, as you do when brainstorming or mapping, and look for something to happen.

I'm never sure that *anything* will happen when I free write. But it really doesn't matter. Some days the writing comes, and some days it doesn't. If free writing doesn't work right away I'll try brainstorming or mapping, or staring out the window, or turning to another project, or getting a cup of tea, or taking a walk, or otherwise creating an interruption. It is important in doing creative work to step back from the draft, the canvas, the score, the lab experiment—just far enough to gain perspective, to allow the subconscious to percolate. But in a few minutes I'll return to my desk, and *something* will work.

Now I'll free write, aware that my free writing looks more polished than the beginning writer's. It is. I refuse to fake it for the purpose of an example, but don't worry if your free writing is a lot sloppier than mine. It should be.

I don't think I was ever alone in that house of childhood. Mother was a woman of the streets, shopping, always shopping, chatting with friends, having lunch with them. She hated housework and cooking; she loved going out. And yet, although Grandma was there singing hymns in the kitchen; and Uncle Will was at his desk, keeping the books for one customer or another; or Father was at the dining room table organizing sales slips from the store and Mother was in the living room reading a woman's magazine; I remember being alone in that house. I had hiding places. My own room, under the dining room table, between the bushes and the house, behind the sofa, at the top of the stairs in the dark, in the empty coal bin.

I must have been a strange little boy, always listening, always making up stories, always trying to understand the tensions between the four adults with whom I lived. They were all so self-centered they gave me a lot of room—space, we'd call it today. I drove by the house and it is smaller, much smaller, than I remembered. I suppose I was never more than a few feet from anyone, and yet that loneliness is real. And the silence. We did all our hurting with turning away, what was not said, was our favorite weapon.

That few minutes of writing certainly took me where I did not expect to go, giving me a whole new vision of my childhood on Vassall Street.

Velocity in free writing is important; write fast so that you say what you do not expect to say. And note that free writing isn't really free. It starts to take you somewhere, to tell you what to say and how to say it. After free writing look back to see whether you want to follow any of your paths, to explore them so the writing stops being private and can go public to readers. Decide whether you want to share with others what you are discovering. If you do, you'll find that the more personal the writing, the more specific and private, the more it will spark memories and ideas in your readers' minds.

Free writing is just as valuable a technique to use as a starting point for a term paper, an historical essay, or a review of scientific literature. It's a way of thinking in which you can preserve the flow of thought.

Interviewing Yourself

Develop your own "itch list" to help you find a subject. Here are some of the questions I ask myself to discover what I want to "scratch" next:

- What has surprised me recently?
- What do I need to know?
- What would I like to know?
- How are things different than they used to be?
- How will things be different in the future?
- What have we lost?
- What have we gained?
- What do I know that others need to know?
- Who would I like to get to know?
- What's not happening that should?
- What's happening that shouldn't?
- Who would I like to see at work?
- What process do I need to know?
- What process would it be fun to observe?
- How can I switch my position so I will see my world differently?
- What have I read, heard, thought that confuses me?
- What connections are being made that surprise me?
- How are peoples' behavior changing?

- How are beliefs changing?
- What makes you mad?
- Sad?
- Happy?
- Worried?
- Frightened?
- Content?
- What do I expect to see, hear?
- Why?

■ STARTING THE WRITING HABIT ■

The myth: Published writers—screenwriters, playwrights, novelists, poets, nonfiction writers, short-story writers, as well as composers and artists—lead lives of Bohemian excess, smoking stuff, drinking stuff, and chasing stuff all night long.

The reality: Writers write; the artistic life is a life of discipline. Gustave Flaubert said, "Be regular and ordinary in your life like a bourgeois so that you may be violent and original in your work." Flannery O'Connor testified, "Every morning between 9 and 12 I go to my room and sit before a piece of paper. Many times I just sit for three hours with no ideas coming to me. But I know one thing: If an idea does come between 9 and 12, I am there ready for it."

Sounds simple, doesn't it? It isn't. Getting the writing done day in and day out, despite interruptions, phone calls, obligations, duties, responsibilities, inertia, exhaustion, poor health, bad weather, invited and uninvited guests, too much drinking, too much eating, or too little eating, wars, storms, births, deaths, marriages, divorces, travel, letters that come and letters that don't come, and a million other problems, is what separates the writer from the hope-to-be writer.

Time

We have two kinds of writing times: fragmentary and insulated. Fragmentary time is the few minutes you have before a class begins, sitting in a doctor's office, waiting for a friend to show up for lunch, waiting for a bus, or during the commercials while watching TV. Insulated time is the half-hours, hours, hour-and-a-halfs, two hours you are able to shut out the world—in your room, the library, an empty classroom. Obviously, we have much more fragmentary time than we have insulated time, and it is important that we make use of both kinds of time.

The focusing and planning I do is performed mostly in small fragments of time that can be measured only in minutes, sometimes in seconds. This writing is done in my head and in my daybook. It isn't a question of hours but of minutes.

Try it yourself before class begins, waiting for a friend at the Student Union, during a commercial break on television, waiting for the campus bus, during a coffee break at work, or as a short break from studying; see how long it takes to brainstorm five essay titles, write a lead paragraph, draft a description, focus on a definition, sketch an anecdote, or even outline an article. I suspect you will find that when you thought you worked ten, or fifteen, or twenty minutes, you've worked two minutes, or four, or ninety seconds.

If you make good use of those fragments of time then you'll be able to write when you have a stretch of uninterrupted time. For most writers an hour is good, but not good enough. Two hours is plenty; three hours is heroic. During those times unplug the phone, lock the door; do not read, plan, edit, nap or eat—just write.

The time of day is important. Most young writers start writing late at night and end up writing in the morning—the early morning—when their minds are fresh and the world is less likely to intrude. Goethe said, "Use the day before the day. Early morning hours have gold in their mouth."

The time of day, however, is not as important as habit. Most productive writers—there are exceptions—establish a routine and write at the same time every day. They know the time and the people around them know the time. Alberto Moravia says:

> When I sit down to write—that's between 9 and 12 every morning, and I have never, incidentally, written a line in the afternoon or at night—when I sit down at my table to write, I never know what it's going to be until I'm under way. I trust in inspiration, which sometimes comes and sometimes doesn't. But I don't sit back waiting for it. I work every day.

Do not attempt long, exhausting writing sessions. Few writers are productive in that way. Most writers write regularly for one to three hours every day and those are considered full-time writers. You may have to try for an hour a day or half an hour. Philip Larkin says:

> I don't think you can write a poem for more than two hours. After that you're going round in circles, and it's much better to leave it for twenty-four hours. . . . Some days it goes, and some days it doesn't go. But over weeks and months I am productive.

Once you have produced a draft, fragmentary time can serve you again. I find it better to edit in short bursts. If I edit more than fifteen minutes at a run I tend to be kind, far too kind. In these slivers of time, early and late in the day, I can cut, insert, reorder, and perhaps decide that I need another draft when I have a few hours of isolated time.

Place

It helps to have a place where you go to write. It should be a place where you can leave your work lying out and come back to it later, where you have your tools at hand and you have the climate that you prefer.

Ross MacDonald said, "I took my lifelong tenancy in the bare muffled room of the professional writer where I am sitting now, with my back to the window, writing longhand in a Spiral notebook." I like to look up from my writing and see a view. Other writers, such as Ross MacDonald, turn their backs to the view. I need music when I write; other writers need silence. Create a place of your own where you can shut the door and be alone.

That's an ideal many students can't achieve because they have families or roommates. Joyce Carol Oates says, however, "If you are a writer, you locate yourself behind a wall of silence and no matter what you are doing, driving a car or walking or doing housework, which I love, you can still be writing, because you have that space."

It isn't easy to create that internal space but it can be done, as Lois Duncan points out:

> Now I keep a typewriter with a sheet of paper in it on the end of the kitchen table. When I have a five-minute lull and the children are playing quietly, I sit down and knock out a paragraph. I have learned that I can write, if necessary with a TV set blaring on one side of me and a child banging on a piano on the other. I've even typed out a story with a colicky baby draped across my lap. It is not ideal—but it is possible.

Donald Graves has been able to write in a dormitory room with pneumatic drill construction going on next door or in a small summer cottage filled with family, friends, and dogs by using earphones and listening to Beethoven at top volume to insulate him from the surrounding world.

Find ways to detach yourself from the world and go to that place where you can "hear" the writing. Depending on your personality, that place may not be the ideal artist's cabin high in the Rockies. I wrote most of one novel in a park, either sitting in the car or at a picnic table far out of the range of my mother-in-law's voice. I like to write in coffee shops and diners where no one knows me, and where there is a stimulating but unobtrusive background life that I can observe or ignore. When I was an undergraduate my favorite writing places included the top row of the empty football stadium, a pleasing assortment of rocks on the Atlantic coast, a special table in the library, and an empty classroom late at night. Find the places where you can hear your voice as it speaks from the page.

Conditions That Invite Writing

I have to cultivate the conditions that will encourage writing. I do this by look-ing at what conditions existed when the writing came easily, when I was ready to write and the writing flowed almost effortlessly. Yes, there are such days.

Expectation

I expect to write. My attitude predicts my performance. The swimmer who goes to the starting block prepared to lose, will lose; the writer who does not expect a draft will not write one. I have to recall when I have written easily before, that the draft will come.

Demand

External. A deadline helps—a line beyond which you are dead if you don't deliver. No excuses. I am lucky because I start the week with a Monday morn-ing deadline on my column. All week I know that I will sit down Monday morning and produce a column, and I do. My editor expects it; I expect it. An external demand that requires a finished product can make all the difference between a published writer and a wish-I-were-published writer.

Internal. I also have an internal demand. I need to write to understand the life I have led and am leading. Elizabeth Bowen explains, "Writing is a kind of double living. The writer experiences everything twice. Once in reality and once in that mirror which waits always before or behind him." Compare it to what happens to you when you go over last weekend's party in your mind or in conversation with a friend, re-creating what you did and didn't do, should have and should not have done or said to find out what it means. I write to discover who I am and what the life I am leading means. I *must* write.

This doesn't mean just personal writing. Lawyers write briefs to find out how past judicial decisions impact their cases; business people write reports to discover where profits are being made or lost; insurance investigators write to find out if the company must pay a claim; scientists and engineers write to find out what experiments taught them and what future experiments need to be performed.

Rehearsal

Sometimes I come to my desk stupid, empty, drained of anything to say and then, if I just plunge in and write blindly, I may receive a good piece of writ-ing that surprises me; but most times I come to my desk having rehearsed what I may say, the way I would rehearse an employment interview. I go over fragments of language, strategies of development and communication in my conscious and subconscious mind. I talk to myself, I dream, I imagine what I may say, sometimes making notes, often just letting the random fragments of writing circulate through my mind. It is all brought together as I start to draft.

Forgiveness

To write, I have to write as well as I can write today, accepting the fact that I cannot write as well as I'd like to or as well as I imagine other writers are writing. I keep rereading the wise counsel of poet William Stafford:

> I believe that the so-called "writing block" is a product of some kind of disproportion between your standards and your performance. . . . One should lower his standards until there is no felt threshold to go over in writing. It's *easy* to write. You just shouldn't have standards that inhibit you from writing.

> ★   ★   ★

> I can imagine a person beginning to feel he's not able to write up to that standard he imagines the world has set for him. But to me that's surrealistic. The only standard I can rationally have is the standard I'm meeting right now. . . . You should be more willing to forgive yourself. It doesn't make any difference if you are good or bad today. The assessment of the product is something that happens after you've done it.

Velocity

To balance a two-wheeler I have to pedal fast, and to outrun the censor and to cause the accidents of insight and language that mark good writing, I have to write fast.

Ease

I try to write with ease, relaxed, allowing the words to flow through me naturally. If I do this, the draft will instruct, telling me what I should say and how I should say it. The evolving draft will take its own course, exploring experience as it is relived. If I am patient, receptive, open to surprise, the draft will tell me what I have to say. E. M. Forster said: "Think before you speak, is criticism's motto; speak before you think is creation's" and "How do I know what I think until I see what I say?"

Write easily. Relax. Allow the writing to pass through you. Do not force, strain, intend, but receive. The cliché says, "Easy writing makes hard reading" but the experienced writer knows the opposite is true—graceful, fluid writing makes easy reading.

All of these conditions and attitudes help get me to start writing. They aren't all in place every day but enough are so that I begin each day writing, and that writing gives me the wonderful surprise of hearing what I didn't know I knew. That's what keeps me writing.

▪ WRITING USING A COMPUTER ▪

Every writer knows there is magic in tools. Writing comes out of the little blinking cursor on the computer screen, the ink, the pen, the typewriter, the paper, as much as the brain.

I have a closetful of once-favorite tools, and travel with a supply of favorite pens and notebooks, the ones that have poems and stories in them.

The computer, however, has become the greatest tool of all. Every writer I know works on a computer. Electronics makes writing, rewriting, and editing faster and easier.

I was not an easy convert to computers and can understand those who fear them. I am not handy with gadgets and particularly dislike machines that appear to be smarter than I. Yet when I bought my first word processor, I was able to use it to write in twenty minutes.

Writers, after all, don't need to know how computers work. I don't know how a fountain pen, a telephone, the TV, my CD player, or my diesel station-wagon works, but I can use them. What writers do using a computer is simple: We put down words, move them around, get rid of them. Even I can do that.

Let's see how the computer helps me write:

Process	**Benefits of Using a Computer**
Focus	
My writing begins with the discovery of a central tension.	1. Makes it easy to play with notes and ideas for writing so that I can discover an effective focus. I enjoy writing and the computer increases the fun of writing by making it easy to write.
Explore	
A continual conscious and unconscious search for revealing specifics.	2. The computer allows the writer to tap into many sources of information, to record notes efficiently and organize them in a way such that they are retrieved easily and inserted in a working draft.

Process

Plan

I first write the opening sentence or paragraph that establishes the subject, my point of view toward it, the voice, and the order of development.

If I outline short pieces, I list fragments; on long nonfiction articles and books I often write the heads first and then draft each unit, not necessarily in order.

Draft

I believe in velocity in writing and bicycling. It is essential to create energy, to outrun the censor, and cause the accidents of insight and language that are vital for effective writing.

Clarify

Revision is circular; the writer moves back and forth through the writing process as one change makes another change necessary.

Benefits of Using a Computer

3. Encourages drafting and refining of many (5, 15, 25, 50, 75) leads.

4. Helps order file material and reorganize text before, during, and after drafting.

5. Makes it easy to develop a dynamic outline of heads and subheads that evolves as I write and discover what I have to say and how I should say it.

6. Makes the speed I believe is essential for my writing possible.

7. Allows me to make errors in early drafts and to correct them easily later when the meaning of the text has been discovered. Permits the failures essential to good writing.

8. The ease of expression encourages me to speak normally and to tune that voice to the needs of the draft.

9. Makes it possible to shape and reshape the draft, a process important to me that needs investigation.

10. Allows me access to the easily read printed text so I can discover what I am saying as opposed to what I intended to say.

11. Integrates drafting with revision and editing, a matter of extreme importance in the discipline of thinking we call writing.

Process

My first revision is often done in small chunks, after drafting six or seven paragraphs.

I also revise by layering or overwriting, reading and laying down another layer of draft right over the last one. The draft tells me what needs to be done and I do it right then and there.

I spell check and submit to my wife, who corrects spelling, typos, punctuation, and errors in logic or grace.

Submit

I am a writer. I submit clean, professional copy and seek the helpful response of my editors.

Benefits of Using a Computer

12. Makes it easy to perform the circular act of revising and editing in small units during drafting, something I did not do before I used a computer.

13. Allows me to write over an existing draft, an essential part of my process that was the product of using a computer.

14. Allows a clear reading of the final draft so that errors may be discovered, and allows a poor speller such as myself to use a spell checker that can help some of the time.

15. Allows me to submit an attractive text in a typographical design that clarifies and supports my meaning.

16. Combined with a fax/modem, makes an immediate response from an editor possible so we can collaborate immediately to improve a text.

17. Increases productivity many times. I have seven books in development, and I move between them and my other drafts in a matter of seconds. The computer connects all my writing projects.

Productivity is essential to learning any craft, and by writing I am learning to write.

Learning to Use a Computer for Writing

Many of you will have already learned how to use a computer in school or at work. If you haven't, take advantage of the programs offered at the computer center on your campus and try using its computers for your writing. In today's society, it is essential that you be computer literate. This doesn't mean you have to be an expert, just that you have hands-on ability at a computer.

Buying Your First Computer

Most schools have a discount program for students who are buying their first computer. The major computer manufacturers all know that the computer and software on which you first learn will probably remain your favorite, and they want your business.

One thing to consider is the support you will receive from manufacturers and dealers. Technology changes quickly. The first computer I owned was the standard in the field when I bought it, but three years later it was obsolete and the manufacturer was no longer making parts for it. Buy a computer made by a company that is well established and offers service.

What I Wish I Had Known

The computer is dumb. It does nothing on its own. It works on the basis of relatively simple commands. You can reveal those commands and go back and eliminate a command you didn't mean to give or forgot to take back—that is usually my problem.

Learn to type because that skill will make all your writing using a computer or typewriter a thousand times easier than it would be if you hunt–pause–peck–pause–hunt–pause–peck–pause . . .

Back Up! Back Up!! BACK UP !!!

Back up what you write. Copy what you have written on one disk to another disk. It is easy to make a quick copy and important to get in the habit. You can lose everything you have just written if there is a drop or surge in power.

Selecting Your Other Writing Tools

You can, of course, write without using a computer. Will Shakespeare and others did quite well without fancy software programs. Make your own checklist for selecting your writing tools and be sure that you have tools with which you are not only comfortable but allow you to have fun.

I keep lap desks handy in the living room, on the porch, in my office. The ones I have are built on bean bags or fit across the arms of a chair. These make it possible for me to set up shop anywhere at home or in a vacation cottage or motel.

But don't forget that the writer really writes with brain and eye, memory and experience, form and language. No machine produces an insight, a perception, an idea, a concept, a theory; no machine orders and reorders random information into meaning; no machine documents or provides evidence; no machine produces the right word, the inspiring phrase, the clear running sentence; no machine produces an individual voice, which is heard by an individual reader.

▪ WRITING AS A READER ▪

Writers are their own first readers.

S. E. Hinton says, "I advise writing to oneself. If you don't want to read it, nobody else is going to read it." The writer develops the ability to step back and see if the draft can be read and understood, if it is both interesting and clear.

Edmund Blunden elaborates: "I don't think I have ever written for anybody except the other one in oneself." "The other in oneself" is the reader who can detach himself or herself from what has just been written. This seems hard at first. I do it by imagining a particular person I know and respect. That person is intelligent but does not know or necessarily care about my subject. I have to attract and hold that reader. I role-play the reader, get up and walk the way that reader walks, talk like the reader, and then sit down and read like that particular reader.

Reading what you have written should make you laugh when you get pompous or write to impress instead of to inform; uncomfortable if you find yourself writing "down" to the reader; disgusted if you are writing what you do not know or believe. As Toni Cade Bambara states, "First and foremost I write for myself. . . . I try to stay honest through pencil and paper." Ernest Hemingway put it differently: "The most important essential gift for a good writer is a built-in, shock-proof shit detector."

Stand back and read your draft as a stranger but always be your own first audience.

▪ HEARING THE VOICE OF THE DRAFT ▪

Voice is style and tone and more. It is the human sound that arises from a written page. Voice is rhythm and beat, inflection and emphasis, volume and pause; it is the manner in which the author speaks; it is the flow of what is spoken; it is the emotional content of writing, it is energy and force; it is the presence of an individual writer speaking to an individual reader. Voice is the most important, the most magical and powerful element of writing. During writing and revising the writer hears the voice of the draft and tunes it to the meaning being developed and made clear.

One way to hear the voice of the draft is to speak aloud while writing. Then you will hear the tone of what you are saying, the background music that communicates mood and emotion. You can do this by "silently" speaking what you were writing as I am doing now. Then you will be able to hear what you are writing—and be able to tune the voice of the draft to what is being said.

Voice is magic but not mysterious. From another room, you can recognize the voices of those with whom you live; you know if they're mad, sad, having a good time, asking, rejecting, commanding, pleading. As a writer, you can accomplish the same thing through your writing. You establish a voice that arises from the page. Read aloud—and I mean right out loud—the following first sentences of the following passages to hear the voice of the text:

The Joy Luck Club
Amy Tan

My father has asked me to be the fourth corner at the Joy Luck Club. I am to replace my mother, whose seat at the mah jong table has been empty since she died two months ago. My father thinks she was killed by her own thoughts.

Amy Tan's voice takes you right into her world. Her father's command establishes a new relationship with his daughter who is "to replace my mother" (his wife). The next sentence explains why this new relationship and the last sentence creates a mystery because he does not have a conventional 1990s American cause of death such as cancer or heart disease. The narrator's voice is direct, simple, spare of emotion, neither resentful of her father nor sad for the loss of her mother, but the voice of young observer of life who is recounting an event that has significance to discover its full implications.

Prospect
Bill Littlefield

Scouting was a funny thing for me to get into, the way both Alice and I felt about travel. But I'm damned if the business wasn't full of guys who didn't like to fly, even though there was an awful lot of flying involved, and guys who said they hated to drive, too, though sometimes they'd drive all day and all night. There were guys who said they got stomachaches when they had to sell a boy's parents on the idea of him signing, and others who claimed they'd rather go to the dentist than fill out all the paperwork their clubs required. But we will put up with almost anything for the chance to do something that offers us joy. And when you get older you will fly, or drive, or stand on your head to be in the presence of that thing, which is a fleeting thing.

This is garrulous voice of an old baseball scout retired in Florida. We hear in this voice an old man who has spent his life sitting in the stands chatting with other old baseball players.

The Remains of the Day

Kazuo Ishiguro

It seems increasingly likely that I really will undertake the expedition that has been preoccupying my imagination now for some days. An expedition, I should say, which I will undertake alone, in the comfort of Mr. Farraday's Ford; an expedition which, as I foresee it, will take me through much of the finest countryside of England to the West Country, and may keep me away from Darlington Hall for as much as five or six days. The idea of such a journey came about, I should point out, from a most kind suggestion put to me by Mr. Farraday himself one afternoon almost a fortnight ago, when I had been dusting the portraits in the library.

Now we hear a radically different voice, the formal voice of a British butler, created by a young writer recognized as a master stylist.

The Merry Adventures of Robin Hood

Howard Pyle

In merry England in the time of old, when good King Henry the Second ruled the land, there lived within the green glades of Sherwood Forest, near Nottingham Town, a famous outlaw whose name was Robin Hood. No archer ever lived that could speed a grey goose shaft with such skill and cunning as his, nor were there ever such yeomen as the sevenscore merry men that roamed with him through the greenwood shades.

This is the old-timey voice of one of my childhood's favorite books. It is a traditional storyteller voice that attempts to imitate the voice of a minstrel, preserving oral history.

The Things They Carried

Tim O'Brien

First Lieutenant Jimmy Cross carried letters from a girl named Martha, a junior at Mount Sebastian College in New Jersey. They were not love letters, but Lieutenant Cross was hoping, so he kept them folded in plastic at the bottom of his rucksack. In the late afternoon, after a day's march, he would dig his foxhole, wash his hands under a canteen, unwrap the letters, hold them with the tips of his fingers, and spend the last hour of light pretending.

O'Brien, perhaps the best of the Vietnam novelists, uses a reportorial voice, somewhat detached, that allows him to reveal the horrors of war—in this case a soldier's loneliness and distance from the woman he loves.

Beloved

Toni Morrison

124 was spiteful. Full of a baby's venom. The women in the house knew it and so did the children. For years each put up with the spite in his own way, but by 1873 Sethe and her daughter Denver were its only victims. The grandmother, Baby Suggs, was dead, and the sons, Howard and Buglar, had run away by the time they were thirteen years old—as soon as merely looking in a mirror shattered it (that was the signal for Buglar); as soon as two tiny handprints appeared in the cake (that was it for Howard). Neither boy waited to see more; another kettleful of chickpeas smoking in a heap on the floor; soda crackers crumbled and strewn in a line next to the doorsill.

Another storyteller's voice that re-creates an oral tradition on the page. No reader can escape the power, energy, force of this voice by one of our most respected writers.

Wildlife

Richard Ford

In the fall of 1960, when I was sixteen and my father was for a time not working, my mother met a man named Warren Miller and fell in love with him.

Richard Ford, another of our most respected writers, creates a sentence of utter simplicity that reveals, in a few words, a very complicated story that would be told—and explored—by the sixteen-year-old narrator.

Each of the voices is different but each is true to the author and to the story the author is telling. They each make me want me to listen, to read on.

Each writer has an individual voice that comes from such influences as genes; ethnic, religious, and regional heritage; social and economic class; and educational background. The important thing is to take that personal voice and tune it to the meaning of the text. All of the above examples of voice serve the meaning of the text. Think of a musical score that tells you when to be scared, when to laugh, when to be sad. The music of written language does the same thing: It tells you what to think and feel.

▪ QUESTIONS ABOUT WRITING ▪

I keep writing about the same subject. Should I have many subjects that I write about?

In school, you have to learn to write about many different subjects in many different forms. When removed from formal requirements, most writers find they return to a few traumatic experiences, the ones that have marked their lives. Usually those are the mysteries of their teenage years. I write about death and disease, marked by the paralysis of my grandmother and the death of my daughter decades later, which taps into that deep well of feeling and fear I experienced when I was young. I started publishing in a fourth-grade class-room and began collecting quotations about writing when I was in high school. I went overseas when I was nineteen, and am still trying to understand what I saw and what I was able to do. We each have one or two or three sub-jects that are so important to us that we keep exploring them all our lives. My mother-in-law in a nursing home, ninety-six years old, muttered about the fact that her mother had sent her to live with relatives when she was only eight years old. She was still trying to figure out if her mother loved her more or less than her sisters eighty-eight years before.

You're being awfully personal. Do I have to write about that kind of stuff, take off my clothes and dance around in public the way you do?

I hope not. It embarrasses me sometimes; I don't always feel comfortable run-ning around in my birthday suit. And I don't always do it. I do it when it's the best way to help others or to say what I have to say. My knowledge about writing comes primarily from personal experience. I'm also a pretty open per-son. I need to share my life with others and have them share their lives with me. It's my way to live, but it doesn't need to be yours. Most writers I know are much more private than I. You don't have to be an intellectual or emo-tional nudist to be a writer.

But on second thought, all writing is revealing, and your distance and de-tachment may reveal more than you think. If you write about rape only in terms of statistics, you may reveal yourself as someone who is detached, disin-terested, and unsympathetic to the individual human pain of a rape victim as much as you would reveal yourself if you write about such a topic in personal, emotional terms.

I don't like what I'm finding out.

Me, too. If it's too uncomfortable, stop writing and move on to something else. That often happens. Writers write to learn. What they discover may not be what they want to discover—the football hero writing about what it's like to play big-time football may confront the fear of injury he's never before admitted. I recently started to write a memorial poem for my daughter who died at twenty and found I was expressing a natural anger felt by many survivors at those who left us before their time and return, in memory, to haunt us. I was embarrassed to admit my feelings, but when I shared the poem with a few readers they said it articulated a feeling they had but had suppressed. It is the vocation of the writer to articulate the thoughts and emotions of others, especially those that are usually hidden, suppressed, and unspoken.

My teacher won't let me write about what I want to write about or think what I want to think. Should I talk about this with the teacher?

Be sure you are right by talking with your teacher. If you still feel that way, do what you have to do to pass the course, but also become a secret writer. Most writers have had to do that. I did. And the writing I did for myself increased my fluency in my other writing, was good therapy, and even gave me a career. The writer has to find the audience for the writer's work. Most writers trim their sails to the demands of the audience. The most courageous ones create their own audience. That's a dangerous and painful course, but most great artists, composers, and writers were booed when they faced a public who expected what they were used to seeing and hearing.

Do I have to play "Follow the Leader" and march through the process exactly as you describe it?

No. Follow the writing; follow the language. It's helpful to have a plan or a way of working, but as John Fowles advises, "Follow the accident, fear the fixed plan—that is the rule." Writing should be an exciting, adventuresome activity. It should be full of surprises, unexpected opportunities, twists in the trail, surprising views, new challenges. You can always vary a method of working and go back to it when you need to. A writing method should never make a writer follow a discipline of writing that ignores the evolving life of a draft.

What if I skip a step?

Try it. I certainly skip steps from time to time. More than that, I start in different places, perhaps with planning, perhaps with drafting. Whatever works is right. But when the writing doesn't work it helps me to go back to a procedure that has helped make meaning in the past.

Sometimes I know I have something to say. It's all there in my head and I just have to write it down. Is that wrong?

Wonderful. Get writing. You have probably rehearsed your topic, consciously and subconsciously saying it over and over to yourself, so you don't need to draft and revise to discover the meaning. This often happens when there is something important in our lives. We keep thinking about it, and we think in language, and when we come to write about it, it's all there.

My writing process is really different from yours. It's so different I'm not even sure it's a process. It seems more like a mess.

If your writing says something clearly and accurately, don't worry about it. If you hit a home run every time you go up to the plate you shouldn't change your batting stance. Pick the best piece of writing you've done, and then remember the stages you followed in creating it. That's your writing process. This isn't based on a perfect piece of writing, it's based on your best piece of writing.

If you run into writing tasks in which the process doesn't work, then you may want to try a process suggested by one of your classmates, your teacher, or this text. You will probably not be able to follow another person's process exactly, but you'll learn ways of adapting your process to the writing job before you.

I don't have one writing process, I have different ones, depending on what I'm writing.

Sounds good to me. I adapt the process to the writing of columns, book proposals, novels, humor articles, personal and business letters, textbooks such as this. I do not write them the same—a column may take forty-five minutes, a textbook a year or more. The pace is different, the length, the thinking task. Each project adapts the process to its own needs.

I don't believe you when you say that you don't know what you're going to write when you sit down at your desk.

You won't believe it until it happens to you. But I'm not a complete blank. I have a hint or an idea, a pretty good guess, and later in the book I'll be showing you how to develop those guesses. And there's always room for surprise. The best pieces of writing are a lot different from what I expect: The stuff I don't expect is usually the best stuff. John Galsworthy said:

> I sink into my morning chair, a blotter on my knee, the last words or deed of some character in ink before my eyes, a pen in my hand, a pipe in my mouth, and nothing in my head. I sit. I don't intend; I don't expect; I don't even hope. Gradually my mind seems to leave the chair, and be where my character is acting or speaking, leg raised, waiting to come down, lips opened ready to say something.

That's the way it feels to me. Not just in fiction, but in nonfiction as well, in writing textbooks, in writing this textbook, in writing this answer. I listen to the question, and then to my answer.

I'm worried about being too disciplined in my work habits. I might lose my spontaneity. I mean, I want to be really creative.

John Kenneth Galbraith has said, " . . . when I'm greatly inspired, only four revisions are needed before . . . I put in that note of spontaneity." The spontaneity comes from the writing, not from thinking about writing. It arises from the spontaneous combustion of ideas and language as they meet on the page.

It is a romantic notion that creative people—scientists, engineers, artists, musicians, businesspeople—get their best ideas while staring out the window. They don't. The ideas come on the job from the job.

▪ WRITING ACTIVITIES ▪

1. Turn on a tape recorder while you write, and talk out loud about what you're doing. Don't worry about talking in complete sentences. Just talk to yourself, the way you probably do talk without realizing it. "Let's see . . . mmm . . . I wonder if . . . perhaps I'd better go back. . . . No, I guess I'll keep going on this draft . . . can't quit now . . . maybe I should get a Coke. No, stay here. Let's see, I've got to start this stronger, maybe use a better verb. . . ."

   After you've finished your draft, listen to the tape as you read your draft, then make notes on what you're doing so that you can discover how you write. It may be fun to have a friend or two do the same thing, and then compare each other's versions. That way you can learn new tricks of the trade, and share yours.

2. Find a painter, carpenter, composer, cook, scientist, stone mason, engineer, play director, journalist, potter, some other creative person who will let you observe them while they work. In doing this, you can see another process and discover its relationship to the writing process.

3. Work with your librarian to locate books such as *Writers at Work—The Paris Review Interviews,* published by Viking, which reveal the creative process. Write your own description of the process as they describe it, and see how it may help reveal insights about the writing process. Follow your own interests and read interviews with actors or coaches, or successful businesspeople, or scientists, people who have found a way of making a breakthrough.

4. Perform a skill with which you're familiar, such as playing the guitar or climbing a rock wall, and think about how what you're doing might be applied to writing.

5. Start a writing process log or daybook, picking out a notebook that feels comfortable to you and is the right size so that you can have it with you most all the time. Doodle in it, write in it, paste things in it, record

observations and thoughts, ideas and drafts for titles, leads, ends, middles. Create outlines and diagrams. Don't worry about neatness or correctness—this is a place to have fun. Talk to yourself, think to yourself, find out what you are seeing, hearing, feeling, thinking and what it means.

6. Find a classmate who will allow you to watch him or her write, noting all the writer's habits, moves, behavior. Switch places and let the other person observe you. Interview each other to discover what the writer thinks he or she is doing while writing.

7. Take an interest of yours or a subject you are studying in another course and read biographies, autobiographies, diaries, letters, profiles, interviews to discover how a person has followed the trade—done the job—of being a painter, a prime minister, a physicist, a basketball star, a business innovator, an inventor, a coach, a minister, a philosopher, a composer, a sociologist. See what connections you can find between what they do and what writers do.

8. Make a work schedule for the course, figuring out how you can write each day, breaking the assignments down into bite-sized chunks. Remember that habit helps: If you write at the same time, in the same place, with the same tools, you'll find it easier to maintain your discipline. Talk to joggers or executives or good students to find out how they manage their time.

9. Draw a picture of your writing process to see what it reveals about how you work *when the writing goes well*. Ask classmates to do the same thing. See what tricks you can learn from one another.

10. List the conditions that you need in order to write, then create a plan that will allow you to work under those conditions.

11. After you've written a piece, tape-record it and play it back so you can hear the voice appropriate to what you are saying. Play it again with your draft in hand so you can mark how the voice may be tuned, sped up, slowed down, made clearer, developed better, be less or more emotional, whatever is needed to make the voice support what is being said.

12. In your notebook, list those subjects that you keep thinking about, the mysteries in your life, the issues that obsess and concern you, the things you don't understand that you need to understand, so that you will discover the territories you need to explore in writing.

13. Take a piece by a writer you enjoy and read it aloud to hear the voice of that text, then examine the text to see how the writer makes music rise from the page.

14. Go through a piece of your own as I went through my column in the beginning of the chapter and note what you were doing and why, what you should do and why, in the margins.

15. Start keeping a record of how your writing process changes during the term.

16. Write now! Sit down and let the draft flow to see what you have to say.

17. Describe a process you use in a job you know or observe someone at work on a craft, then write out a sequence showing how similar steps might become a writing process.

18. Observe a newspaper reporter, a technical writer, an advertising writer, a science writer at work and create a writing process you or your classmates might use to satisfy an academic assignment.

19. Take a piece of writing you like and imitate its form and voice in writing about an interest of yours—scuba diving, playing in a band, working a customer for a good tip.

20. Dictate a first draft into a tape recorder, then transcribe it to see how you can make the reader hear your spoken voice.

21. Describe your writing process last year and describe how you can change it to make it more effective.

22. Keep a notebook beside you and record precisely what you do at each stage of the writing process, then type it up to see where you could improve it.

CHAPTER 2
FOCUS

■══════════■

*. . . if there is one gift more essential to a
novelist than another it is the power of
combination—the single vision.*

VIRGINIA WOOLF

All week long I know I am going to sit down Monday morning and write a
column for *The Boston Globe* that is similar to the personal essays I once wrote
in Freshman English. Readers often ask me how I can come up with new ideas,
week after week.

In trying to answer my readers' questions about how to find a subject, I
examine my process and discover three principal answers:

> *One*—I am constantly aware of my world and my reaction to it as we dis-
> cussed in the last chapter;
> *Two*—the things I observe, think, and feel combine in a fragment of lan-
> guage I call a **focusing line**;
> *Three*—all I need is that focusing line as a starting point, I don't need—or
> want—to know what I am going to say because the adventure of the
> draft will reveal what I have to say and how I will say it.

The focus is the point at which writers concentrate their attention. When
we take a picture, we focus on the spot where the most interesting or revealing subject may be captured in a photograph. It is the same with writing. The
writer may focus on an event, a moment in a person's life, a decision, an act, a
discovery, a cause or an effect, a problem or a solution; this is the place where
writers feel they will find significance by writing.

What the Focusing Line Can Give the Writer

We are all terrified when we begin a first draft and step off into the unknown, but the focusing line makes this step less terrifying. The focusing line solves a great many of my writing problems in advance. Let's look at one of the lines above and see how it helps as I begin a draft:

As I look back on my life, I visit the geographies that contained my world.

Possible Direction

I have a strong indication of where my mind might travel in writing a draft.

Research. I could choose to research my childhood neighborhood and examine the political, economic, and sociological changes in that area.

Reflection. I could think back on my childhood and how that geography affected my life.

Description. I could map my childhood world in words and see how one's vision of an area changes as people age: My first trip around the block was more exciting than my first trip to Norway.

Limitation

What I write will not be about my high school neighborhood, the battlefields on which I fought, the neighborhoods in which my children spent their childhood. The focusing line helpfully excludes.

Point of View

This can be thought of in two ways:

Angle of vision. The point of view determines the place from which the writer and the reader observe the subject. The angle of vision includes everything that can be seen or known from that point. I may, for example, write from the point of view of an eight-year-old who has not yet questioned the prejudices of his or her parents, or I may write from the point of view of an adult who is critical of the prejudices of his or her parents. Sometimes point of view refers to first, second, and third person; I, you, he/she.

Opinion. Point of view is also used to describe the opinion the writer has of the subject. It is important for the writer to have an opinion of the subject—my parents made the new neighborhood a fearful place because of their prejudice, an attitude the child found unjustified.

Voice

Voice is the word music that reveals and supports the meaning of the piece. We all respond to what is said to us and, especially, *how* it is said to us.

Voice is the *how*. The focusing line, to the writer's trained ear, often contains the music of the piece: "I hated the ordinariness of war" has a music different from "Fear became ordinary, wounds became ordinary, death became ordinary in war."

Form

Form is the type of writing: fiction, nonfiction, poetry, screenplay, argument, memo, lab report, book review. It includes the tradition of the type of writing; the reader knows what to expect from a story, a poem, an argument. In the line "death became normal, living abnormal" I may see an essay and in the line "hope died, then fear died" I may see a poem.

Structure

Structure is the way I may get from the first line to the last; it is the trail of meaning I will follow as I produce a draft. Structure may take many forms. It may be in the form of a narrative in which the action and reaction between the characters creates a chronological structure that pulls the reader forward; in argument, the logic of one point leading to another may drag the reader toward the writer's conclusion. The focusing line "In digging a foxhole I uncovered the skull and helmet of a soldier from an earlier war" may lead the writer and reader back through history.

Opening

The focusing line is often the first sentence or paragraph of what I write: the lead *leads*—draws, entices—the reader into the writing. A line "My neighborhood had fences to keep out those who were different" might develop in the following lead: "Recently I visited the Land of Prejudice, the geography of my childhood where fences did not make good neighbors."

Do I consciously march through all those elements when I have a focusing line? Not always. But sometimes it helps to take apart what the cabinetmaker put together, to discover how he or she knew those pieces of burled wood could become a corner cabinet.

▪ OTHER WAYS TO FOCUS ▪

In addition to the focusing line, here are some other ways to find a focus.

The Steinbeck Statement

John Steinbeck used to write down what a book was about on a single three-by-five card. He might write a 500-page draft but his focus would be on that sentence or two on the card. I have found it a valuable technique to do this when I have trouble with focus. That statement includes and excludes. It keeps my eye on target.

BUT—and don't forget this "but"—the statement will have to be revised as you write. You may know what you hope to write about when you begin but all writing is a voyage of discovery. You have to make course adjustments, refining and revising your statement as you discover what you have to say.

Beginning by Ending

Many writers—including Truman Capote, Raymond Carver, John Gregory Dunne, William Gibson, Joseph Heller, John Irving, Eudora Welty, Toni Morrison—claim to know the end of a draft before they begin. They all have a destination that may be changed by the writing but destination gives their first draft focus.

It may be helpful to write a dozen or so last sentences. Once you choose one and know where you are headed, you may know where—and how—to begin.

Finding a Controlling Image

When you started to write as a child, you sometimes drew a picture first, sometimes wrote the caption first. You worked back and forth calling both drawing and writing, writing. I believe writers still work that way. I see what I write, and many times the focus of my writing is in an image: my grandmother ruling the family from her sick bed; my first dead soldier and his look of surprise; the kitchen table that was always set at the end of a meal, ready for our next silent meal.

Pay attention to what you see with your mind's eye—or with your real eye—as you research or think about what you are going to write. The focus may lie in that vision. You may have a controlling image that will supply a landmark to guide you through the writing.

Anticipating the Reader's Need

The focus of a piece of writing may come from the reader. In writing memos to a dean when I was English Department Chairperson, I knew what the dean wanted to hear and how he wanted to hear it—documented with statistics. My job was to focus a wandering, discursive discussion of our department needs in a way that the dean would "buy" our argument and give us the fiscal support needed.

Put yourself in the reader's place to see if you can understand what a particular reader needs to learn from the text. That may be your focus.

Moving the Angle of Vision

When writing, the writer invites the reader to stand at the writer's side so the writer can point out the view and comment upon it. The place where the writer stands gives focus to the draft.

Then, once the reader is at the writer's side, the writer moves the point of view or angle of vision, taking the reader along as the view changes and the understanding of what is being seen increases. Where the writer and reader stop keeps the writing in focus.

Adjusting the Distance

Distance is a key element in writing. Distance is how far the writer places the reader from the subject. Many writers always write close up, others always stand back at the same distance. Movies and television have made us all aware that the camera puts us on the mountain ridge watching the cattle rustler and moves us in close to see one steer rolling its eyes in terror.

Move in close up and you'll see in detail. The lens frames the revealing action, response, or object. You'll gain immediacy and intensity but can lose context, what the detail means. Stand way back and each detail is in context. Pun intended: You see the big picture. The frame extends so that you have a broad view but you lose intensity.

The trick is to stand at varying distances, each appropriate to what is being said. The writer moves in close to increase intensity, moves back to put what has been seen into context; the writer stands back to establish context, then moves in close to make the reader see, feel, think, care.

There is no ideal distance from subject. The craft is to always be at that distance which helps the reader see, feel, and understand. The skilled writer uses a zoom lens, adjusting the distance so that the reader experiences intensity without losing context, has enough detachment so that the reader has room to respond, is close enough so that the reader is forced to respond.

Play with distance as you focus and draft—describe your grandmother's hand as you held it in the nursing home, describe her in the group picture of the family arriving in America when she was the little girl in front—to see how it will help you explore your subject and communicate it.

Asking the Research Question

In the academic world, the focusing line becomes the research question. The sociologist, historian, physicist, economist, literary critic, health ethicist, philosopher, biochemist, and members of every other intellectual discipline need to learn how to ask good research questions. The research question is central to the term paper, the master's thesis, the doctoral dissertation, the grant proposal, the paper at an academic meeting, the scholarly article and book.

The research question should:

- *Be significant.* Its answer should provide new insight or knowledge. *How does the brain affect learning to write?*
- *Be limited.* The answer should be able to be found within the time and other limitations of the research—a semester, summer school, a thesis or dissertation year, a sabbatical. *How did four stroke victims at the VA hospital relearn to write?*
- *Demand a specific answer.* The question should evoke an answer that is neither vague nor general, but specific and informative. *What were the three most important turning points experienced by the four stroke victims at the VA hospital as they relearned to write?*
- *Be in a specific context.* The question should be connected to existing knowledge that will give a reader information the reader needs. *What are the implications for third-grade students with learning disabilities in the three most important turning points experienced by four stroke victims at the VA hospital as they relearned to write?*

Making a Thesis Statement

The thesis statement is a fully developed focusing line: "Toni Morrison reveals the tensions of small city, Midwestern life for everyone, not just African Americans."

The advantage is that the thesis statement provides focus for the research and the writing. Academic writing has historically been argument in many disciplines and the thesis statement provides the writer and reader with a clear debating point. It encourages, for example, the reader to say, "Whoa, I'm not so sure Toni Morrison does that. Let's see your evidence."

Many teachers demand, for the reasons above, a thesis statement before the paper is researched or written. The great danger is that the scholar will only look to document that statement when, in fact, they might discover a different critical view.

In that case the writer should submit the revised thesis statement to the instructor: "Toni Morrison's novels document how different the small city, Midwestern experience of African Americans is from their white neighbors."

▪ STARTING A NEW WRITING TASK ▪

The writing process you are learning can be adapted to any writing task and to changing conditions. As we proceed through school and beyond new classes, new jobs will demand new forms of writing: memos, reports, fund-raising letters, poems, case histories, theses or dissertations, sermons, police reports, book or literature reviews, grant applications, letters of sympathy, job or graduate school applications, screenplays, scientific or laboratory reports, legal briefs or judicial decisions, marketing plans.

Some of these tasks will require a long text or a short one, will be straight text or be coordinated with a complex graphic design, will be written alone or with a partner or a committee, will be done in a day or less or a month or more.

In every case you will be able to adapt your experience with the writing process. I've adapted that process to write radio scripts; ghost political and corporate publications; create short poems and long books; write memos, applications, reports, and all sorts of other writing tasks. You build on what you know how to do.

Making an Assignment Your Own

The best strategy to deal with any writing assignment effectively is to make it your own. The skilled writer shifts the ownership of the assigned piece of writing from the teacher or employer to the writer. There are guidelines for doing this.

Reading the Assignment Carefully

Go over the assignment several times to be sure you know what is expected. If the assignment has been given orally, write it out and read it over. Be sure you understand the purpose of the assignment, not just *what* you are expected to do, but *why* you are expected to do it. The reason for the assignment will often help make the assignment clear. If you don't understand it, read what you have written to the instructor.

Asking Questions

If you have studied the assignment carefully and still do not understand it, ask the teacher or employer for clarification. It may be appropriate to ask to read good papers others have done in the past or examples of published writing, which practice the lessons being taught by the assignment.

Standing Back

Once the assignment is clear, walk away from it. Study the assignment from a distance to see what comes to mind. The assignment should be given to your subconscious, which will play with it, making connections with what you know, have seen, experienced, thought about. An assignment always increases my awareness. I'm told by an editor to do a story on street people and I'm suddenly aware of the bag ladies, the young man mining the dumpsters in the alley, the woman talking to herself on the street corner, the late-afternoon line at the mission or soup kitchen, the early-morning turnout of drifters at the church dormitory for the poor. I note how they dress, I record the wary looks they give people, the way they make themselves invisible, the layers of clothing they wear, the bottles ineffectively hidden in small paper bags, the shaking hands, the shuffling step. Little of this is conscious, I've just been made aware, and I see connections with experiences in my past—the refugees who clogged the roads leading from the battlefields they were fleeing and to which we were advancing—and with what I'm reading, perhaps Steinbeck's account of those fleeing the Dustbowl during the Depression for California or John Berger's report on the guest workers imported to North European countries from Southern Europe.

It is often helpful to stimulate this essential circling of the subject by using the techniques in Chapter 1 such as brainstorming or free writing. Don't just attack the subject the way you've attacked similar subjects but collect and recollect information from which you can discover the most effective way to deal with this particular assignment.

Being Self-Centered

Look at the assignment from your own point of view. Don't look at an assignment from a point of weakness, saying to yourself that you know nothing about the topic. That is rarely true. Of course you should do the academic work required by the assignment—read the book, survey the voters, perform the experiment, observe the patient—but go beyond that. Look at the assignment from a point of strength. Think what you know that may connect with the subject. You may have had jobs, for example, that will allow you to make a special connection with a character in a book who has moved to a new and alien place, discovered he or she is adopted, or is sent to a nursing home the way your grandmother was. A history assignment may connect with a literature course; a paper in business administration may make use of what you studied in a computer course. Look at the subject from your own point of view so that you shift the position of authority from the teacher to yourself.

This does not mean that you have a license to be prejudiced, to present unsubstantiated opinions, to be unfair. What it does mean is that, in the process of thinking about the topic and writing about it, you take advantage of what you know. If you are writing about the care of the elderly, you may use your experience in working as an aide in a nursing home, your family's guilt about sending a parent to such a home, your neighbor's reasons to stop working as a nurse for the elderly. Such information may give you a way to approach the subject or to document a viewpoint in your final draft.

Limiting the Subject

Don't try to cover the history of medicine for the elderly in Western civilization since 1600 in five pages. Instead, limit the subject—perhaps concentrating on one nursing home, one disease such as Alzheimer's, one day or even one patient. Limiting the subject allows it to be developed properly, so that one single point can be developed and documented in a way such that it satisfies the reader's hunger for meaning and information.

Remember the significant relationship between the words *author* and *authority*. Whenever possible, try to become an authority on the subject on which you are writing. You can do this by taking advantage of what you know, by researching the subject, by exercising the muscle between your ears and thinking about the subject before you write: Thinking through writing for each draft should be a way of discovering meaning.

■ FOCUSING IN THE DAYBOOK ■

My daybook encourages the play that is essential in finding focus and allows it to happen when I'm waiting for my wife in a parking lot, watching the Celtics on TV, waiting for a friend to show up for lunch. I use the fragments of time to perform the brainstorming, mapping, listing, and other activities described in this chapter.

Here are some examples of focus-seeking play in my current daybook:

Poem?
> in war he's at home
> at home he's at war

This fooling around will become a poem.

The toy I remember best from my childhood was an empty Quaker Oats box. I hated porridge but loved my drum, my castle tower, my wheel, my echo box, my cave.

This did become a column.

When you age, your nose gets bigger—and your ears. We all become more of what we are.

This fragment became a television commentary.

On the ten o'clock news
a soldier peers over the edge
of the TV screen . . .

This did become a poem.

■ FOCUSING USING A COMPUTER ■

The computer allows me to write fast and velocity is vital as I seek a focus for my subject. I can produce a flow of writing and then pluck from it the word, phrase, line, or paragraph that provides the focus. After that, it is easy to manipulate the other words I've written so that they line up and support the focus.

When I'm working on one thing that stimulates my thinking, and ideas for other subjects come to mind, I can make quick notes easily using my computer that can be filed and read later. The computer also makes it easy to bring quotations, charts, figures, text, all sorts of information together and then manipulate it so that it reveals a pattern of meaning.

■ FOCUSING FOR THE READER ■

Readers are attracted by a well-focused subject—a piece of writing with a clear vision of the subject. Some of the elements that tell the reader that the piece of writing is focused are as follows:

Angle of Vision
It is clear from where the football story is seen—the press box, down in the field, in the locker room, on the practice field, in a prospect's kitchen when the recruiter visits.

Information
Give the reader revealing specifics—before steroids the linebacker weighed 234, afterward 267; the wide receiver was injured on the first play, but he had a full scholarship and played the whole game; five times the tight end cut left, the last time he cut right and caught the pass that won the game.

Economist John Kenneth Galbraith says:

> I would want to tell my students of a point strongly pressed, if my memory serves, by Shaw. He once said that as he grew older, he became less and less interested in theory, more and more interested in information. The temptation in writing is just reversed. Nothing is so hard to come by as a new and interesting fact. Nothing so easy on the feet as a generalization.

Opinion
The writer is fair but has a strong, well-documented point of view toward the subject. Steroids are bad for the player, a scholarship shouldn't mean that a player should play when injured, the experienced player works out strategic patterns during a game.

▪ HEARING THE UNWRITTEN VOICE ▪

From the moment a subject occurs to me, I listen to the voices within the potential draft, and listen to the fragments—the lines—that pass through my mind and across my daybook page.

I have trained myself to hear the voice of the final draft in a fragment of language, the way an archeologist can examine a pottery shard and describe a civilization. The voice doesn't just lead to how the writing will be presented, it tells me what the as yet unwritten draft may be. It tells me what I think about the subject when I write about it. Voice leads to focus.

Let's take a simple topic—the house of childhood—and read these fragments aloud to hear what they might tell me, the writer:

- The house of childhood
- Secrets in the house of childhood
- My escape from the lonely house of childhood
- Brown. That was the color of my childhood
- The lonely house of childhood
- I miss the lonely house of childhood
- We hurt with silence in the lonely house of childhood
- I never thought I would escape the silence of my childhood
- Silence made me hear the voices in the walls of my childhood home
- We feared God, Grandma, Catholics, the Irish, Scarlet fever, the bill collectors, and funny foreign eyes in the house of my childhood
- My house of childhood, so large when I lived there, seems tiny now
- I am still the boy who could not ride a bike, was told not to play with Catholics, feared the silences that filled the house of childhood
- Silence filled the house of my childhood
- I always listened from other rooms, learned the language of walls . . .

The music I heard in that last line made me write the following lines in my daybook that seemed to be looking for a poem:

I always listened from the other room,
learned the language of walls,
read silences, the shut door,
the dark. . . .

Later I wrote:

I learned the language of walls:
whispered argument, point
counterpoint, quiet.

I wove silence
into story. . . .

Different drafts appear in the next daybook until I got to the one I showed
to my poetry group that began:

Born onto a sea of narrative,
he thought stories were sound clouds.
shadows with voices . . .

The next day I wrote the poem through beginning:

~~When~~ **Night stories crept upstairs**
~~he~~ **where he captured them in the hall,**
[he] hid them in his room . . .

During all that play I was listening to the voice of each poem and looking
for the focus: how stories were discovered by a child and how that influenced
his life. I did it by play, ending up with the following poem:

The Storyteller's Childhood

When stories crept upstairs
he captured them in the hall,
hid them in his room, wove
them wove them into dreams.

He watched family stories travel
under the wallpaper, emerge
at the seams, found others escaping
faucets, chattering in water pipes.

Some stories exploded when he opened
the furnace door, others lay folded
in trunks, some had been framed
but could be heard if he was alone.

In winter, stories were etched
by frost on window pane; in summer
they came as shadows of bird wings
that woke him as they past.

Some of the best stories were left
on morning pillows, others were told
by silence, escaped in a pause, grew
from the rich loam of never said.

Outside he found neighbor stories
caught in the privet hedge or played
out in pantomime against the drawn
shade. He stole stories humming

on telephone lines, trapped secrets
dogs shared in barking gossip, heard
confessions from the open windows
of passing cars, read stories

from faces, the way his father slowly
walked from the trolley car stop,
held the key before he turned
it in the lock. If he brought

bon bons that night their bed
would squeak. The boy crept out,
patrolled dark streets, stealing
neighbor's secrets before they woke.

It could just as easily have been an essay:

My grandson lies quiet, attending to what I cannot see or hear. I wonder if he hears the voices in the walls I heard, joins the secret family that had a dog with a curling tail—we had no pets—escapes into a world of make-believe that was—and is—as real as the life I have lived.

As close as we are as a family, there is something private about the human condition. We may be the animal that most of all needs secrets. . . .

▪ REVISING BEFORE WRITING ▪

Don't think exclusively of revision as what you do *after* a draft is finished. Every idea you reject or accept is a demonstration of revision. Focus is an act of revision as we choose what to focus on and what to ignore.

Each draft of the poem was revision, yet I was only trying to get to the beginning point of focus, to discover what the poem would focus on and reveal to the reader.

When you choose one subject over another; identify an angle of vision; select a genre; write a line, a paragraph, a page in the head or on the paper, you are revising, shaping what may be said, may be drafted.

▪ QUESTIONS ABOUT FOCUSING ▪

Do I have to have a focus? Can't I just write a draft and see what happens?

Sure, if you have a lot of time on your hands. Think of focus as a potential destination. You may decide to go out to the lake. On your way you pass Chip's house and he suggests you go to the mall and at the mall you meet the Richards twins and you go to a movie. You wouldn't have gone to the movie with the twins unless you had started out for the lake and passed Chip's house. Focus gets you going. The focus may change but it helps to focus—to have a target—when you start to write.

What if what I want to say has been said before?

It probably has, but don't worry about that. It hasn't been said by you. Your own particular background and way of thinking and speaking may make it different. But the difference isn't the important thing. The important thing is to have a well-explored subject, a piece of writing that is so well made it will stand up and speak to a reader. And remember that at this stage you can't be sure just what you're going to say. You may have a focus—you know the island you want to explore—but haven't done the exploration yet. A good piece of writing will almost always be different when it is finished from what the writer thought it would be when the writing process began.

What's most important?

What the reader needs to know or what you would need to know if you were the reader.

What if what I think is most important isn't what the teacher thinks is most important?

You have to be able to support your idea of what's important with convincing evidence. That evidence will be lined up and presented to the reader during the next stages of the writing process. But, of course, this depends on the teacher. Some teachers believe there is only one right answer, and you may have to find that answer to pass the course; but most teachers are willing to be persuaded if you have a specific focus supported by concrete evidence.

Everything seems equally important.

Ah, that's the challenge. You have to find the key, or just decide arbitrarily for this piece of writing that one element is most important. You can write about two or three things that are equally important, but then you have to find a way of making the combination of them most important. For example, "Most law school professors agree that there are three qualities an effective courtroom lawyer needs," or "There are four equal forces that came together and led us into the Vietnam War."

My focus seems too personal.

Most good writing starts from a personal point of view. The writer thinks and cares. The writing, however, shouldn't sound too personal. You need to get out of the way and let the evidence speak for itself.

The reader is persuaded by information, not by being told what to think (remember how long it was since you really enjoyed a sermon?). As you move from focusing to clarifying, you will be providing the information to the reader. The starting point may be personal but, in many cases, the final draft will be written in such a way that the reader will be convinced by the objectivity and the fairness of the prose.

What if my focus isn't the right one?

There isn't usually a right one, and that's something that's hard for most beginning college students to accept. William Perry of Harvard has done studies that show college freshmen want to find an absolute right or wrong. That's natural, but college is not a place where you get precise answers; it's where you discover how to ask good questions. We live in a complicated and complex world, and although for some there are absolute wrongs (if I were president, I would make it a capital offense for anyone to eat a smelly, gooey, soft-boiled, poached, or sunnyside-up egg in a public place—but I would face pressure from egg lovers, the police and courts who would have to enforce the law, and the egg lobby), most issues are complex.

In writing there ain't nothing that is absolutely right or wrong. I just used incorrect English, on purpose, to make a point and get attention; it therefore became correct. In writing, what works is right. You can write correctly and produce unreadable prose. You can write incorrectly and communicate. This is one of the things that makes writing hard—and fun.

Before I began this essay I didn't think I had anything to write about, now I've got too much. Help.

That's a good problem, like having too much money in the bank or too much power under the hood. Select one topic and explore it. Which one? The one you remember when you walk away from the list, the one you catch yourself thinking about when you didn't think you were thinking.

▪ FOCUSING ACTIVITIES ▪

1. Brainstorm by thinking of an important event in your life, when you were scared or happy or unhappy or angry; or brainstorm by thinking of an issue, argument, or opinion you want to develop, and put down every detail you can think of as fast as possible. To find the focus circle the detail that:

   • surprises you the most
   • makes you feel uncomfortable

- makes you emotional
- makes you think
- suddenly connects with other details
- makes you ask a question
- reveals a problem

2. Map by using the same event or topic to see which different things are recalled. But don't worry if the same things keep coming up at first. Just go as fast as you can. Some things will be the same, and some may be different.

3. Free write: Write as hard and fast as you can without worrying about grammar, spelling, mechanics, penmanship, or typemanship. The important thing is to get a flow. You may even want to tape-record to hear what you have written. The important thing is to let language lead you to discover what you know and what you need to know. The draft will begin to develop a focus, to return to the same theme and that may be your focus.

4. Work to make yourself more aware. Go to a familiar place and list as fast as possible fifty specific details, or a hundred, or two hundred. The more you list the more things you'll see you haven't seen before. It may be fun to take a frame or cardboard tube and see what you can see in a small framed area. It may be profitable to take one sense at a time and record what you can smell, hear, taste, and touch as well as see, focusing as if you were using a camera.

5. Make an authority inventory, listing all the things you're an expert on, that you have focused on: the jobs you can do, the things you can repair, the places you've lived or visited, the problems you can solve, the hobbies you enjoy, the people you know, your family background. Each of us is an authority on many things, and our best writing usually comes from what we know and care about.

6. List the things you'd like to know. You may see how you can satisfy your curiosity about whales or how laws are made or why the police get violent or why animals are used in laboratories.

7. List the things you need to know: how to appeal a university decision, how to apply for a scholarship, how to get a better summer job—all the hundreds of things we need to know. You may find a good topic and its focus.

8. Role-play to find a focus. Watch a situation—a crowd growing unruly, a person making a speech, an ambulance responding to an accident, a person being hired or fired—and imagine yourself in that situation. Figure out how you would act and react, think and feel. This will give you some interesting questions to ask. Seek out a person who is involved in the situation and interview him or her.

9. Take an assignment you have been given and list five ways you could make it yours by responding in terms of an area in which you are an authority.

10. Make a movie in your mind of an important experience. Then turn it into a novel, a poem, a government report, a TV series, a short story, a talk to the Rotary Club luncheon to discover how each genre helps you view the same subject in a different way.

11. Interview other writers in the classroom and outside to find out how they get ideas. Read books and articles on creativity to discover what others have said about the creative process that could help a writer find ideas or topics to explore. Interview artists, successful business people, doctors, lawyers, police officers, nurses to see what sparks their good ideas.

12. Become a stranger to your familiar world. Visit from outer space, become your great-great grandmother, a Russian or Chinese student, look at the familiar as if it were not to see subjects you need to think about and explore, perhaps in writing.

13. Take a camera and shoot a subject close up, at a middle distance, far away. Study the photos and decide how you would write at different distances. Try it.

14. Take a subject and list the mysteries within it, the points of myth, legend, gossip, speculation, tension, and conflict to see if you can find a focus.

15. To find your focus, try to list the most important things you are going to try to say in your draft on one side of a three-by-five-inch card.

16. Say, in one sentence, what you want readers to do after they have read your piece.

17. Read an article, speech, short story, poem and identify the one sentence or line that best reveals the writing's meaning.

18. Go back in memory to an event, place, or person of importance to you: Write down the one detail that reveals the most. Then list the details that flow from memory because of that one revealing detail.

19. Think of the most important thing that was ever said to you. Put it in context.

20. Look for the single word to describe the room you are in right now.

CHAPTER 3
EXPLORE

■══════■

*The writer . . . sees what he did not
expect to see. . . . Inattentive learner in
the schoolroom of life, he keeps some
faculty free to hear and wonder. His is
the roving eye. By that roving eye is his
subject found. The glance, at first only
vaguely caught, goes on to concentrate,
deepen; becomes the vision.*

ELIZABETH BOWEN

Writers are explorers we send out to describe our public and private worlds.
They use language to capture the not yet thought in words not yet said. They
make the unknown known through language; they make the unspoken heard
through voice. They live at the far and close edges of our lives, revealing what
we have not seen—or not understood—in the world around us and have not
seen within us.

Writers do this exploration all the time: It is their blessing and their curse.
They examine what we overlook; they reflect on what they see—and their reactions to it. They are blessed in never being bored, always aware of the drama
of the ordinary and the internal drama as we try to accept and understand
what they have seen. They are cursed in always being aware of what is painful
in life and aware of their pain in observing it. The biographer and historian
Catherine Drinker Bowen says, "Writing is a kind of double living. The
writer experiences everything twice. Once in reality and once in that mirror
which waits always before or behind him."

67

The explorer first seeks information. Writers write with information—the specific, accurate information that the reader needs. Readers read to satisfy their hunger for information—specific, accurate information they can use. The writing act begins with the accumulation of the raw materials of writing. The act of writing gives that information meaning: Writing is thinking.

In Chapter 2 we explained how the writer explores the external and internal world to find a topic; in this chapter we will show the writer/explorer at work developing the information from which the topic will be understood by writer, then reader.

■ EXPLORING WITH THE
WRITER'S EYE ■

Central to exploration is the writer's eye. The writer's eye sees what is, what isn't, what was, what may be. An athlete's eye is inherited. The eye doctor I visit treats many players on the Boston Celtics basketball team. I asked him if their eyes, not just their height and the way they can jump, was different from the rest of us. He held up a finger far out of my peripheral vision and explained that all the Celtics could see the finger that was out of my range of vision.

The athlete's eye is genetic but the writer's eye must be developed. You can train yourself to see **revealing specifics**. A revealing specific is a detail, fact, quotation, word, phrase that gives off extra meaning. The politician on the platform may pay close attention to all the other speakers, then looks away, paying no attention when the next speaker is a woman. It is an accurate detail and a clue to his attitude toward all women. The screaming of the basketball coach that confuses his own players, the students who sit together at lunch and the ones who want to sit with them but don't, the trustees' decision to spend money for a hockey rink but not for faculty salaries are all revealing specifics.

The writer's eye collects the concrete information readers' like: a statistic, a fact, a direct quote, a specific act. Concrete details give a draft liveliness and authority—readers believe, often in error, the more specific detail the more authoritative the author—it seems to ring with authority just because it is specific.

The writer's eye gathers information, using all the senses: the way the overhead light glints off the surgeon's scalpel, the eyes that reveal so much—and so little—above the surgical masks, the smell of medicine and sterilizing steam, the brass taste of fear, the feeling of helplessness a patient experiences when lashed down on a surgical table, the comfort of the nurse's touch.

And, lying there, with part of your body asleep but your brain wide awake, you hear what isn't said, see what doctors don't do as well as what they do, the looks that pass from doctor to nurse to technician, you feel something of what it must have been like to have surgery before modern anesthesia, what surgery may be like with the further development of the laser. You see what is, what is not, what was, what may be.

The writer's eye sees patterns. Specifics have to add up, to lead the reader toward a conclusion, to answer the tough question, "So what?" You see the way the police stop the driver of a Lexus that goes through a red light but treat her with courtesy. Then you see the police stop a battered Chevy for the same offense, make the driver get out of the car, slam him up against the hood while another officer calls in to see if the car is stolen or if the driver has a record. You are aware of the skin color of the second driver and begin to remember your father's prejudiced comments at the dinner table, how the teacher laughed when an African American showed up in an elective math class—"No special treatment here, Carlos," what the history textbook said about the Holocaust. You connect all such specifics into a pattern of prejudice.

E. M. Forster said, "Only connect," wise instruction for the writer who deals with context and implication. Specific details are not enough by themselves, the way the police handle a suspect must be connected with a pattern of police brutality, training, prejudice, whether or not the treatment is appropriate or excessive.

The writer sees past, present, and future. My mind turned backward in a recent column, when I wrote of looking out at snowy woods and seeing snowball fights when I was a boy and fire fights during the Battle of the Bulge in World War II when I was a young paratrooper, my first sled rides with Uncle Will, and a snow hut I built as a boy. I walk by a new building on campus and see within it the memory of the old building that was torn down on the same spot. Cows turn into parked cars and I see the future shopping mall destroying the farm. The writer is always looking backward and forward, studying the present to discover the cause of events and to imagine their effect. The writer lives in a changing world, seeing what is, what was, what may be. As Robert Cormier says:

> What if? What if? My mind raced, and my emotions kept pace at the sidelines, the way it always happens when a story idea arrives, like a small explosion of thought and feeling. What if? What if an incident like that in the park had been crucial to a relationship between father and daughter? What would make it crucial? Well, what if the father, say, was divorced from the child's mother and the incident happened during one of his visiting days? And what if . . .

The writer's eye instructs, it sees meaning where the writer did not see meaning. Writers write from what they don't know as much as from what they do know. In Chapter 1 I didn't know the meaning of that afternoon when I painted the back steps with water. I wrote to see what writing would teach me.

As I write about my war experiences—how much distance there had to be between us when we dug in along the front line, how we kept from getting to know replacement soldiers because most of them would be wounded or die, how we could not admit our terror to those around us—I begin to remember how lonely infantry combat was, how little comradeship there was at the front lines. Language defines, develops, and changes my world.

And the writer's eye provides the abundance the writer needs during writing. When you write about a person, place, or event important to you, you begin to remember details you didn't know you had stored in memory years before. I start to describe my first car and remember the high, crooked gear shift, the feel of the accelerator; I hear the rasp when I apply the hand break; I smell the oil and gas and exhaust and the city smell in the wind that strikes my face. The more details I write, the more I have to write. This marvelous eye gives the writer a resource for revealing detail. What is most magical to me is that my writer's eye saw all sorts of specifics I was not aware of until I wrote.

Take a piece of paper and return in your mind to an important experience in your life and list the details you remember using all your senses. Soon your writer's eye will reveal what you didn't know you saw at the accident scene, in the locker room, on the first day of school in a new town, last Saturday night.

▪ SEARCHING AND RESEARCHING ▪

The Internal Search

School teaches us to look in the library, on CD-ROM, in the laboratory; but the writer must first look inside at what is stored in memory. By writing we make use of all that we have lived, felt, thought, know, if we respect and make use of what we have unconsciously stored in memory.

Remembering

The first place from which to collect is memory. You have recorded far more than you may realize on most subjects. You may also have put an old subject in a new context. When I visit a new high school I always remember North Quincy High School and failing and dropping out and, finally, flunking out. I collect information about the new school, first of all, in the context of my own autobiography.

Start your collecting process by listing (in your daybook, journal, on a piece of paper) code words and revealing specifics that remind you what you know about the topic. In remembering high school I might list:

Mr. Collins, the principal
Bench outside his office
Day I goosed a teacher by accident

Miss Gooch who had to jump to answer phone on wall
Teacher who took a swing at me because I was a Scot
Stack of forged hall passes I found when we moved
History report on Bismark
Jobs more interesting than school
Class of 45+ students
Teachers condemned to teaching
Chicken game we played when writing in class
"Stardust" played last at ALL dances
Grade of 65, not a C or a D
I thought rich kids were born with slide rules

This is a private list as yours will be. These are notes to yourself that may start a chain list of memory. The more specific the items, the more memory will be triggered.

The External Search

The external search extends the internal one, reaching out to library and computer online sources, authorities that can be reached in person, by mail, by phone, on internet. It includes all the normal techniques of the scholar with the on-the-scene and interview techniques of the journalist, sociologist, anthropologist.

Reading

There are as many ways to read as there are to write, yet most people—prisoners of habit—usually read in the same way, at the same pace, no matter what the reading task. Never let school give you the impression that reading always has to be work, a purposeful job of collecting information. Reading can often be play: It is one of the best ways to leave the real world and escape to the imagination.

Reading Fast. Many people say that they read slowly but remember what they read. The research I have read—and my own experience—denies this. Of course there are times when you have to—or want to—read slowly to savor or decode a text, but speed itself can be a benefit to reading. When you read fast it is an effort that concentrates the mind. You pay attention, your mind doesn't wander, you enter into the text and are carried along by the logic, the emotion, the music of language. Many times you have to read fast in order to allow all the threads of the text to weave themselves into meaning. Read too slowly and you see only an individual thread or two, not the pattern evolving. Try it. There are many schools that teach speed reading but you can do it yourself by forcing yourself to read at the point of discomfort.

If you are a slow reader, try the following. Don't read each word individually but make yourself read in groups of words or lines, not single words. Move right ahead. See what happens.

Afterward, you may have to go back and read it again or study one passage carefully, but then your attention will be concentrated on what you know you need to understand, and I suspect you will remember more than you expected to remember.

Skimming. To collect information efficiently, the student has to get through many books, articles, and reports to discover what needs close attention. Here's a checklist that may help organize your reading by skimming:

- The **title** should relate exactly what the book or article covers.
- A book's **table of contents** and an article's **abstract** may reveal its subject.
- The **author's biography** may help you discover the relationship of the writer to your topic as well as the author's authority to write on the subject.
- The **index** will lead you to discover specific references.
- The **bibliography** will open up other sources to explore.
- Scan the text itself to find revealing **section headings** or **key words**.

The reading writer needs to develop these techniques that, of course, may be applied to scanning newspapers or microfilm or files the writer finds through computer online research.

Interpreting. Once your eye has caught a key word or specific revealing detail, interpret its meaning by putting it in the context of the piece you are reading or writing, or both. A college brochure may boast, for example, that 60 percent of its student athletes actually graduate. One reader may be impressed by the statistic, whereas another may be appalled at the high percentage who fail to earn a degree.

Meaning never resides in isolated facts, but in a context. It is the job of the reader to try to determine the information within the writer's context and then to incorporate that information in a context that is appropriate and accurate.

Immersing. Fast reading can produce immersion in the text where you lose yourself in the mood, the poetry, the sweep of the account that puts you on a street in a strange city, in the hospital waiting room, in combat. By reading fast, you get the feel of a subject and the sense of the writing itself.

Connecting. Fast reading reveals information that connects with other information in the text, in other texts, in your notes and drafts, in your mind.

Remember that you are writing to discover meaning and to allow specific pieces of information—represented by words—to arrange themselves in many patterns until there is one pattern that reveals significance.

Interviewing

The interview, in which you question an authority, is one of the basic tools for collecting significant information. Most people are shy about interviewing. It helps to remember that the person being interviewed is placed in a position of authority, and most people like to be considered as an authority, to tell someone what they know.

An interview can be informal, as in casual conversation, or formal, where you set up an appointment, research the subject carefully, and have prewritten questions to ask in order to probe deeply.

Before conducting an interview, find out as much as you can about the person you are going to interview by preparing at least four or five principal questions that must be asked in order to obtain the needed information. These are the questions most readers would ask if they were there. Think of the reader; ask the reader's questions.

It's important to *listen* to what your interviewee has to say; don't go on asking the banker about interest rates after she has said the bank is closing. The interviewee may surprise you by what he or she says, and you have to decide, on the spot, which lead to follow.

Most interviewers take notes by hand, but it is more and more common to use a tape recorder. Always ask permission to use a tape recorder when conducting a telephone interview because the subject can't see the recorder. Face to face, when the recorder is visible, it is a courtesy, not a necessity, to ask permission to record. Most people prefer a taped record to an interviewer's notes—some even insist on using a tape recorder. You should, however, practice taking notes by hand, capturing the essence of what people say, even if you use a tape recorder. Sometimes the tape process doesn't work, and if you're not taking notes yourself you may become lazy and miss his confession: that his wife was popped into the kiln.

It's always best to conduct an interview in person; then you can see the facial expressions, the body language that emphasizes or contradicts what is being said, the environment in which the person lives or works, the way the person interacts with others. If you can't interview someone in person then you may have to do so by telephone, or even by mail.

How the Interview Can Lead to Writing

When you are researching any topic, from criminal justice to World War II to urban blight to environmental hazard, don't forget to use live sources, and talk to the people who are involved. They will not tell you *the truth,* they will tell you *their own truths,* and then you will have the challenge of weaving all the contradictions together into a meaning.

Using the Telephone and the Mail

Organizations are good sources of information. The library contains directories of organizations that help locate groups whose main function is distributing information on one particular side of a public issue: They are for or against abortion, distributing condoms to fight AIDS, allowing individuals to own hand guns, saving or developing wilderness areas. These organizations will send pamphlets, brochures, or reports and answer your questions.

Governments—local, county, state, federal, and even international organizations such as NATO and the United Nations—consist of many groups that will provide you with reports, speeches, laws, regulations, proposals. Your local members of Congress can help you find the right agency and the specific office in the agency to contact.

Using the Library

One of the greatest sources of material is the "attics" that exist in almost every town, city, and state in the country, as well as in schools, universities, and the nation's capital itself. These attics collect books, magazines, newspapers, pamphlets, phonograph records, films, videotapes and audiotapes, photographs, maps, letters, journals—all the kinds of documents that record our past—and we call them libraries.

Every library has a card catalog and/or computer file that identifies what is in the library's collection and gives its location. Belong to more than one library if you can. When I was free-lancing, I found it a good investment to purchase cards in four library systems. Libraries are an elemental source for a writer, as important as wind is to a sailor.

If you are not yet familiar with your library, most college libraries have tours that will show you how the library works. Take the tour. Most libraries also have pamphlets that help you locate what you need to find. Study such materials. And most of all, use the library. Browse. Wander. Let the library reveal its resources to you. And if you need help, ask for it. Cultivate a good working relationship with your librarian. Librarians are trained to be of service, and all of us who write are indebted to their patience and skills in finding information for us.

When you locate a reference in the library, it's important to make a note of all the essential information contained in that book so that you can use the library easily the next time, and so that you can list the book in footnotes or bibliographies. Even if you write something that doesn't include footnotes or a bibliography you should know the source exactly: where you got the material so that you can respond to questions from editors or readers.

Usually you record the author's last name first, then first name, then the middle initial; the title of the work, underlined if it is a book, placed within quotation marks if it is an article; the publisher, the location where published; the date; the number of pages; and, for your own use, the library reference number together with the name of the library.

The purpose of such notes is to tell you exactly where the information source resides. It's also important to keep a record of the books you found worthless, so you won't go over them again, as well as the ones that are particularly valuable. Most research doesn't result in big breakthroughs, but a slowly growing understanding of the subject.

Observing

Don't overlook one of the writer's primary sources of information: firsthand observation. See how many of your five senses you can use to capture information, and to communicate that information to your reader.

If possible, go to a location important to your topic. It may not be where your writing takes place—you may be writing about the proceedings of the Continental Congress in which our nation was conceived—but you will understand that process better if you visit a legislature, a city council session, a town meeting.

Awareness Increases Awareness

As you train your writer's eye, you will discover how much you notice: the way an old lady dresses for her weekly trip to the supermarket; how candy and gum are placed so they can be grabbed by children riding high in their seats in the supermarket carriage; how the dignified, well-dressed man palms a candy bar and the look of shame on the face of the young boy who is with him. I am never bored because my eye makes the world interesting, exposes the extraordinary in the ordinary, the significant in the trivial.

▪ EXPLORING IN THE DAYBOOK ▪

I explore my world in the daybook that is always with me. I note revealing specifics, quotations, references, facts, thoughts of my own on the piece I am researching, but more important, on whatever passes by that interests me.

I make notes in the margin—"col?"; "WTL,Ch.3"; "Poem"; "Novel"; "Ohio talk"—that allows me to find these chronological fragments. I am amazed at how material accumulates. I paste in news stories; computer printouts of my notes and drafts, references to books I must look up or sources I should write or call; leads and outlines and rehearsal drafts that may reveal voice.

And the more I write down, the more I remember. The act of writing something down reinforces memory and frequently I do not have to look up what I have written. It also stimulates my observing/recording skills, making me more aware than I was before I began the daybook custom.

▪ EXPLORING USING A COMPUTER ▪

The computer has changed the entire world of international research. The problem used to be, "Where can I get the information I need?" but now it is, "How can I handle the abundance of information that lies just behind my keyboard?"

Libraries are now computerized, networked with other libraries and with data sources that may be in another city or another country but just seconds away by a modem that can send information over telephone lines. Librarians, media center experts, and computer specialists can help you tap into these services and you should make this a part of your education.

I have developed my own files of information—for example, writers' quotes—that I can draw on right in the middle of a paragraph since my work is stored on a hard disk. I have past notes as well as other pieces of writing all stored away, ready to be retrieved in seconds. My research notes go into the file and are usually placed where they may appear in a draft so that the text is written between them and they become a sort of pre-outline. Each day I use my computer to record and retrieve information.

▪ EXPLORING AS A READER ▪

Throughout the process of exploration you've certainly been aware of one reader: yourself. You have found some information that interested you and other information that didn't. You have seen things that relate to other things and things that had no apparent relation. In all this process you have been role-playing, consciously or unconsciously, the audience.

Many times this audience is specific. You write something that will be read by a teacher, a classmate, an employer, a friend, someone who needs to know the information, someone you want to persuade or educate or entertain. In some modes of writing, the audience is paramount. This is true when you're writing a memo asking for financial support from a college administrator, or when you're writing an examination for a teacher. In other forms of writing, the personal essay or the poem, you may be at first writing for yourself, and later realize that others would be interested.

The intended audience should help you write. Being aware of who may read what you write gives you additional eyes with which to see the subject. The reader's eyes help you collect and select, and will be with you throughout the writing process. Being aware of the audience does not mean that you change what you see, avoid what you think is important, or in any other way pander to the reader. Your job as writers is, above all, to be truthful, accurate, fair, even if the message you deliver does not please the reader.

▪ HEARING THE VOICE WHILE EXPLORING ▪

The writer is alert for the voice of the material that may become the voice of the draft. There is music in every piece of research you discover. Listen for the dancing avoidance in the presidential statement, the ponderous beat of the scholarly tome, the rage in the voice of the dispossessed, the smug song from the fortunate, the drumbeat of damnation in the legal brief. Quotations from live interviews, phone calls, books, articles, memos, reports, papers help tell you of the significance of what you are hearing.

Voice is a clue to meaning the way movie music underlines the action on the screen. Often in writing you pick up the voice that is appropriate to the draft from what is said by the research. And don't forget to listen to the voice of your own notes. You may, for example, make notes on how animals are tortured to test cosmetics and hear the anger in your voice that will be tamed and made effective in your final written argument.

Never forget that writing is music, the melodies you hear rising from the page are vital to earning the reader's trust and to communicating the meaning of what you have to say. The music of your drafts—your voice—also helps instruct you in the early stages of writing, telling you what you feel and think about the subject.

▪ REVISION AND RESEARCH ▪

Don't wait until a draft is completed to revise. As you explore and find more material—substantiation, contradiction, doubt, qualification, new meanings— we keep changing the first vision of what we may write.

I have a clear focus: I am going to write how terrible war is but all the material I find and remember that day is about a good wartime experience, a time when I am alone on a mission on a beautiful snowy day in the Ardennes in Belgium.

I change my focus and write about a good day at war. I describe the loveliness of the Christmas card woods, tell how a lone German came into a clearing at the same time I did, how we shot at each other and missed, waved to each other and went on our way. In recounting that experience, I discovered—and revealed—a horror of war: Good people who appreciate beauty and have a sense of humor can attempt to kill each other. In some ways, our good-humored salute to each other is more terrifying because we had fired on each other with live ammunition. We had tried to kill. We are not monsters but young men caught up in war. The focus of my writing was revised as I explored the subject and collected raw material for my writing.

Much of the excitement in writing comes from having an opportunity to explore those subjects you want—or need—to find out more about. Exploring both satisfies and stimulates your curiosity: The more you find out about a subject, the more you realize there is to explore. You will have a rich inventory of material that will make your writing easy and will also satisfy the reader.

▪ QUESTIONS ABOUT EXPLORING ▪

When do I know I have finished exploring and am ready for the next stage in the writing process?

You'll never know. You'll always feel there will be a new and wonderful piece of information in the next book you read or the next interview you conduct— if only you had the time. Some writers get so involved in research that they never become writers. Most professionals stop when they already know the answers they will hear as they ask the questions. In other words, they aren't finding much new. When that happens, it's time to write.

And, of course, there's the deadline. You have to figure back from when the writing is due and allow time for clarifying, drafting, ordering, and focusing if you're going to have a good piece of work.

Who is an authority?

The best way to find the authority you should interview is to ask the people in that business who's the best. Ask nurses in the hospital, police officers on the force, teachers in the school, scientists in the lab who you should talk to find out about your subject. They work with all the authorities and they are authorities themselves.

How do I know who's telling the truth; if a fact is a fact?

By checking. It's a good idea to have three sources for any important data. It's not so much that people lie as that they're uninformed; they believe what they're telling you, but it may not be true. As a researcher you have to keep your common sense in good working order. When you are suspicious about a statement or a detail, pay attention to that hunch and check it out.

I'm shy; I don't like talking to people.

Most good reporters are shy. I used to hide in the closet when I was a kid and company came to the house, but it got uncomfortable sitting on a pile of shoes. I still get a funny feeling in my stomach when I go out to interview people. I was just reading an article about the most famous reporters in the country and they all shared a common difficulty—making the first phone call.

Realize that interviewing someone is very flattering for the person being interviewed. If you arrive saying, "You're the greatest living authority on cockroaches," you won't be able to shut up the delighted authority.

What if people won't give me information?

Give them a reason to give you the information. Flattery, as above, is a good reason. If that doesn't work then you have to find a good reason: Do they want to educate the uneducated (you)? Do they want to persuade? Do they want revenge? Do they want to raise money for their cause? Do they want to defend themselves? There are many reasons why people will give out information, and you have to find the one that will unlock the information you need.

I've got too much information; I've got more notes than I've got dirty socks. It's a mess.

Good. Strong pieces of writing come from an abundance of information. Walk away from your notes. Sit down with a pad of paper and write what you've learned from your research, the things that have surprised you the most or that seemed the most significant or that connect. What you remember will usually be what is most important.

Read the next chapter. It tells you what to do with a mess of contradictory, interesting, confusing information.

I keep getting lost. How can I keep track of what I'm learning while I'm doing?

I like to take a few minutes at the end of each day and make a quick note on the outline or trail I've been following. Sometimes I do this in terms of what questions I still need answered; other times I keep a short list of key items: "What I Know" and "What I Need to Know." On a book I often have a draft table of contents that I keep changing as I explore the subject.

What are the qualities of a really good piece of information?

That of course depends on the story, but here are some elements:

- It is accurate.
- It connects with other pieces of information to help create a pattern of meaning.
- It reveals significance.
- It surprises.

■ EXPLORING ACTIVITIES ■

1. List all the specific information about your topic, writing down anything that comes to mind. Put a question mark after those you are not sure of and keep listing. Discover how your writer's eye has collected so much you did not know you knew.

2. Make an authority inventory, listing all the things you're an expert on—the jobs you can do, the things you can repair, the places you've lived or visited, the problems you can solve, the hobbies you enjoy, the people you know, your family background. Each person is an authority on many things, and the best writing usually comes from what a writer knows and cares about. There is a significant relationship between the word *author* and the word *authority.*

3. Interview someone else to find out what that person is an authority on. Dig in to find out how the person became an authority on the subject. What makes the person angry, satisfied, happy, interested, sad, or laugh when he or she talks about it?

4. Go to the library and find out what sources exist on a subject that interests you. The people who work at reference desks are very helpful in showing you all the places in the library that there might be information on a specific subject.

5. Go to the library or computer center to discover the computer resources available and learn how to retrieve material from at least one source for the topic your are researching. Report to the class on available computer resources.

6. Practice scanning—quick reading—to find out what interests you by reading a book that covers the subject in its broadest terms. For example, if you're interested in one variety of sea gull, check out a book about birds and go through it quickly to see what you can find out about your sea gull.

7. Practice making quick notes by watching television news and taking down the essential details.

8. Collaborate with one or two other classmates to research a limited topic. It's interesting to learn from others how they approach a subject differently from you. Each writer has his or her own way of exploring a subject, as well as a different background that changes his or her angle of vision on a subject.

9. Look up a piece of writing on a subject you want to research and try to figure out where the writer got the information. Some books have interesting appendices in which the authors discuss the problems of research they encountered, and how they solved them.

10. Try to apply the research techniques in this chapter to a problem in another field so that you can see how these techniques can be adapted to a problem in social work or hotel administration or physics or history. Ask a professor to share some of his or her research techniques with you, and report on these to the class.

11. Role-play. Observe a situation—a crowd growing unruly, a person making a speech, an ambulance responding to an accident, a person being hired or fired—and imagine yourself in that situation. Figure out how you would act and react, think, and feel. This will give you some interesting questions to ask. Visit a person who is involved in the situation and ask the questions.

12. Practice looking for the detail that reveals—how the doctor walks calmly when there is a crisis, how the expert teacher uses silence to control a class, how a politician uses first names, how an expert programmer plays with a computer. Try to catch the action in a few words that reveal.

13. Write down, as fast as you can, a list of all the details you remember from last week's activities. Use all your senses. You'll be surprised at what you remember, and you may find things you want to explore more deeply. Doing this kind of collecting will also make you more aware in the week ahead. And the more you see, the more you'll have to learn by writing.

14. Write your own case history to discover how you work and how you may work more effectively in the future.

15. Take your writer's eye to a familiar place—the dorm, your kitchen at home, a school hang-out, the fast-food place where you used to work—and see how many pieces of information you can collect in a hour: a hundred? two hundred? more?

16. Use one sense and one sense only—sight, hearing, smell, taste, touch—to describe a familiar place.

17. Transport yourself to another century or another culture and record your world as if you have just discovered it.

18. Create a box by putting four pegs in the ground 12 inches apart, then connecting them with string. See how many forms of botanical or zoological life you can observe in that square foot.

19. Follow Donald Barthelme's advice: "Write about what you're most afraid of."

20. Imagine you are your parent and write a description of yourself.

CHAPTER 4
PLAN

Has a drinking song ever been written by a drunken man? It is wrong to think that feeling is everything. In the arts, it is nothing without form.

GUSTAVE FLAUBERT

At a few wonderful, always unexpected times the writing flows so fast the draft seems to unroll ahead of you like a highway at night. If this happens to you, keep driving at top speed, follow the highway and allow the writing to write itself.

Most of the time, however, it is hard to decide which highway to take; or the car won't start; or, after starting, it bucks and stalls. You have a focus, a destination, an idea of what you want to say but . . .

It is time to plan.

A writing plan is an artist's sketch, a carpenter's plan scratched on a board, a cook's recipe that will be changed during the cooking. A writing plan is not an order or a binding contract. It is an educated guess, a hunch, a suggestion—"Hey, let's head for the beach." When you write you may not get to the beach, you may stop along the way, decide to go to the mountains, run into some interesting people and spend time with them. Food may be eaten in a restaurant or the restaurant food taken out to a picnic area. But you would not achieve the surprise without the plan.

▪ STARTING WITH A BASIC PLAN ▪

When I feel the need to make a plan, my favorite one has the following elements:

TITLE
LEAD
TRAIL
END

Title

During my apprentice years I drafted as many as 150 titles while I researched and thought about an article I planned to write. I scribbled titles in my day-book during TV commercial breaks, while waiting for my wife at the store, when a friend was late for lunch, while taking a break from another writing project.

Each title helps me:

- Refine the focus
- Establish the voice of the draft
- Target a reader

I might, for example, work on an essay on football, a game I both enjoy and despise. Notice how my draft titles refine the focus, contain a voice, appeal to a reader:

- **To Hurt Is the Name of the Game**
- **Football: America's War Game**
- **Symbol of U.S. Militarism: Football**
- **What I Learned by Playing Football**
- **Hurt or Be Hurt**
- **The Maim Game**
- **Balance the University Budget: Junk Football**
- **How to Exploit Students**
- **Have You Ever Met a Scholar/Athlete?**
- **My Knee 50 Years After the Kick-off**
- **Do You Want Your Leg Straight or Bent?**
- **Play with Pain**
- **Hours of Commercials; Seconds of Action**
- **Why I Love\Hate Football**

None of these quite work but you can see how each is a pre-draft of the text and each demands a *different* draft.

Lead

The lead—the beginning or the promise of the opening—is the single most important element in my planning. I always begin with a lead: the first sentence, paragraph, or page that will lead the reader into the piece. Here are some leads that pass through my mind or appear on my daybook page:

- I was hit by an illegal, blindside clip on a kick-off in 1942 and my knee still hurts.
- I do not approve of football—a violent, militaristic game—but I have a season ticket.
- Historians may see football as a metaphor for what America became at the end of the twentieth century: a violent, militaristic society.
- Football taught me to hit first, to hit hard, to play while in pain, to get ahead in my career.
- I like watching football because it is metaphor for the macho, corporate society in which we live.
- On the football field I learned to swell up so I looked bigger than I was, to grunt, to hit someone I was not angry at, to shower with dozens of strangers, to become an American male.
- I spent a few years learning to play football; the rest of my life trying to unlearn what it taught me.
- Football prepared me for combat. My coaches were like infantry officers: loud, confident, and often dangerously wrong.

Let's choose that last one. You can see how much is established in a line or two:

- Genre

  It is an essay—perhaps an argument against the militarism and violence of football—in which the author will explore the world of football in the context of his wartime experiences. It is not *a poem, play, short story, news story of a football game, although I might explore this subject in those forms of writing another time.*

- Focus

  The essay will focus on the relationship between football player and coach.

- Context

  The essay will be placed in the context of the beginning of another football season.

- Voice

  The voice is cynical, ironic, anti-authority, critical with a strong flavor of bitter humor.

- Audience

  Football fans are not aware of how players are treated and what is wrong about a sport that encourages that treatment.

- The writer's authority

  The lead establishes the authority of the writer to speak as a former football player and combat veteran.

- Angle of vision

  Coaches will be seen from the perspective of a player who later served in combat.

- Opinion

  Critical but with the possibility that the writing of the essay will make the writer see the issue in a different way.

- Material

  The lead makes the writer aware of the material he has in his inventory: He was a scholarship player, he was kept on the field with injuries that still bother him 50 years later. He also has a mental file full of wartime experiences—the lieutenant who caused his unit to mutiny, the stupid before-battle speech, the colonel who commanded U.S. troops to attack U.S. troops.

- Length

  It's shaping up as a strong opinion piece based on autobiographical evidence, not a take-out or exposé, so better keep it to 800 to 1,200 words if it is to be published and read.

- Pace

  Pace is the speed of the writing, which may accelerate when action is described, slow down when the writer reflects on the action. The voice of my first line tells me the piece should move quickly to keep the reader involved and support the cynical, anti-authority voice. The beat is established in the voice. It is a guerrilla attack, not a long campaign.

- Proportion

  Proportion is the effective balance between the parts in a piece of writing: pro as well as con, dialogue and description, action and reaction, statement and documentation, humor and seriousness. In this case there had better be some objective, contemporary evidence to balance the autobiographical views of an old man.

- Evidence required

  See above, plus detailed anecdotal evidence that puts the reader on the field and in the locker room, perhaps on the battlefield.

- Potential end

  The closing will probably echo the lead and suggest that the writer was prepared for combat but not in the way expected.

I am surprised in spelling this out for you. I do my lead writing instinctively and am newly impressed by how much I depend on the lead, the key part of my basic writing plan.

Trail

Sometimes the lead is enough for me, but I usually mark a trail through the material. I rarely make an outline because it restricts discovery. The sketch of the trail ahead usually contains the three to five points I may cover. I always remember, however, that writing is thinking and the writing may take me where I do not expect to go. The plan does not deny discovery but stimulates it.

In this case my trail might read:

- **football practice**
- **combat practice**
- **reality**

That would be enough to get me through the draft. I would show the confidence of the football coach and the game plan, the confidence of the infantry officer and military tactics, and then the reality: game confusion and combat confusion.

End

Many writers—Toni Morrison, John McPhee, Katherine Anne Porter, John Irving—claim they know the end first. I didn't believe them until I found in my daybook a lot of "Ks" for kicker, my code word for end. I, too, had a destination, a place where I thought I would end.

In this case my ending or kicker might read:

- **K—echo back to coach, was prepared**

Implied in that line is the idea I was not inspired in the way the propaganda about football predicts—heroic deeds and exalted patriotism—but I was prepared for the stupidity of war and those who conduct wars.

This quick outline prepares me to write a draft. Many of the problems I will face in its writing have been solved by my basic plan. And another advantage: Once the plan is written, it doesn't matter if I am kept from writing for a few days or a week. I can go back to the plan at any time and begin a draft.

■ PLANNING THE PROMISING OPENING ■

Effective writing opens with a promise to the reader. Writers usually think of the opening—beginning or lead—of a piece of writing in terms of the reader. Readers are in a hurry, they have many distractions, writers have seconds—no more—in which to catch and hold the reader's attention.

The opening promises information that the reader wants or needs. It promises clarity and grace; it hopes to surprise. The lead promises to satisfy the reader's expectations: A narrative tells a story, an argument argues. The opening provides a tension that produces the energy that drives the story forward. The beginning promises a closing, a sense of completion.

The writer must be aware of the promises made in the opening if they are to be fulfilled. Joan Didion reports, "What's so hard about the first sentence is that you're stuck with it. Everything else is going to flow out of that sentence. And by the time you've laid down the first *two* sentences, your options are all gone." Elie Wiesel adds, "With novels it's the first line that's important. If I have that, the novel comes easily. The first line determines the form of the whole novel. The first line sets the tone, the melody. If I hear the tone, the melody, then I have the book."

As we established in the basic plan, an effective opening solves most of the problems the writer would face in the first draft and solves them efficiently, ahead of time, when the writer is not trapped in a tangle of prose.

How to Write an Effective Opening

I *never* proceed with an opening unless I think it will produce a good piece of writing. That's the only "never" in my personal toolbox. That opening may not produce a piece of writing that works and I may have to start over; what I discover in the writing may require a new opening; but I know only one place to start: at the beginning.

The search for the opening begins when I receive the assignment or when I realize I have a piece of writing that must be brought to paper. Sometimes the idea for a piece of writing comes to me in the form of the line or sentence or paragraph that is the opening.

In every case I play with potential openings all during the research and planning process. I note possible openings in my head, in my daybook, in my computer file for that topic. When it is time to write I play with openings. Play is important. I must be free to make discoveries, free enough to allow what I am writing to tell me what I need to say and how I need to say it. I used to write at least 50 to 75 openings for each article or book I wrote. After 50 years of writing I am not that compulsive and don't keep count. Once every couple of years an opening will come to me that seems just right the first time, but most of the time, my openings are a product of word—and sentence and paragraph—play.

When I write openings I am consciously trying to get at the essence of the story. I keep standing back and saying to myself: What is the central tension? What's new? What is changed? How is the reader affected? What do I or the reader need to know? What is the key problem? What surprises me? What question does the story answer? What do I expect the reader to think, feel, do after reading it? I have been involved in researching the details of the topic, now I have to stand back and see its significance.

Use the checklist to find some effective ways to play with your own possible beginnings.

Checklist

After you have written your final opening, read it again to be sure your opening is:

- *Quick.* The reader will decide to read on or not to read on in a matter of seconds.
- *Accurate.* The reader who spots even a tiny error will refuse to believe anything you write.
- *Honest.* Don't hype an opening to tease the reader because you must deliver what you promise.
- *Simple.* Cut back the underbrush. Use proper nouns, active verbs, and concrete details whenever possible.
- *Packed with information.* The effective opening gives the reader information, and that information makes the reader want to read on.
- *Heard.* The reader should hear an individual writer speaking directly to the reader.

Categories of Effective Openings

It may be helpful to take a piece of paper and list the kind of openings you have in your writer's toolbox. Most writers have many more ways of beginning a piece of writing than they realize. Some of the openings in my toolbox are:

- *News.* Tell the reader what the reader needs to know in the order the reader needs to know it. Check the five Ws—who, what, when, where, why—especially why.

The computer system at Western State University crashed when 2,500 students signed up for the same section of Freshman English yesterday to protest new adviser-free, computer registration procedures.

- *Anecdote.* This is a brief story that captures the essence of what you will be dealing with. It is the most popular magazine article opening, but watch out—if it's a good story but doesn't aim the reader in the direction you want the reader to go, the whole piece may be lost.

  When Lorraine B. Well, registrar at Western State University turned on her computer yesterday morning she was surprised by a message in huge letters on her screen: "Tidal Wave."

  She didn't know what it meant until the university computer system crashed. More than 2,500 students had registered for the same section of Freshman English to protest the adviser-free, computer registration program designed by Registrar Well.

- *Quotation.* A quote is a good device because it gives additional authority and an extra voice to the piece. Like the anecdotal opening, however, it must be right on target.

  "This human being heard the students," said Lorraine B. Well, Western State University registrar who developed adviser-free computer registration procedures. A student computer protest shut down all university computers.

  More than 2,500 students registered. . . .

- *Umbrella.* This is an opening that covers several equal, or almost equal, elements in the story.

  Registration procedures at Western State University are bring reconsidered in an emergency meeting this morning after students— by computer—protested new adviser-free computer registration procedures.

- *Descriptive.* The writer sets the scene for the story. Use specifics.

  Students at Western State University went online last night from the school's computer centers, from dorm rooms, from workstations, from their homes, from the library, even from bars and student hang-outs where they could plug their laptops into a phone line.

  They all registered for Section 13 of Freshman English to protest new adviser-free, computer registration. . . .

- *Voice.* Voice establishes the tone of communication between reader and writer. Read aloud and be sure that the voice is communicating information in the tone appropriate to that information.

Civil war broke out on the campus of Western State University when computer fought computer.

Angry at an adviser-free computer registration system, students mobilized their computers and commanded them to attack.

- *Announcement.* This lead tells the reader what you are going to say.

Registration will be delayed at Western State University until a traditional faculty advising system is re-created. It will take the place of a computer registration system attacked by students armed with their own computers as well as university ones.

- *Tension.* This opening reveals the forces in the story in action. They are coming together on a collision course, or pulling against each other. The opening contains the forces, and makes the reader feel the tension between them.

"Human Beings 2,500; Computer 0." That was the headline in the Western State University newspaper today when a protest shut down a new computer registration system.

Philosophy Professor Owen Scanlan was not sure it was victory for human beings. "They had to use computers to attack the university computer," Scanlan pointed out.

- *Problem.* The opening establishes the problem that will be solved, or not solved, in the piece.

How could students protest an impersonal computer registration system at Western State University? By computer.

- *Background.* The writer first gives the reader the background of an event, argument, conflict, issue, or action.

Students at Western State University have complained for years about their difficulties in making appointments with their faculty adviser. When Lorraine B. Well was appointed registrar last year she was told to solve that problem.

Registrar Well designed an adviser-free computer system that made students demand a return to the bad old days. More than 2,500 . . .

- *Narrative.* This opening establishes that the story will be told in narrative form. Be careful not to start too early. Start as near to the end as possible to involve the reader in the story. Background information should not be delivered to the reader ahead of the story. The reader needs to be involved in the story first to know what information is needed—then the experienced writer delivers it.

When Lorraine B. Well was a student at Western State University 20 years ago she had to stand in line from 7 A.M. until after 4 P.M. each year to register for courses.

In the years since then she has been a graduate student, a corporate executive, a college professor. When she was appointed registrar last year, Dr. Well believed that since all students had access to computers she could design a humane, human-being-free registration system that would eliminate standing in line.

- *Question.* This sounds like it should work, but it rarely does. The writer usually knows the answer to the question and so it sounds patronizing, like the nurse who says, "Now we would like to take our medicine, wouldn't we?"

How can registration lines at Western State University be eliminated? Not by computer, not yet.

- *Point of view.* The writer establishes the position from which the reader will be shown the subject.

I am a computer major, a hacker to be honest. I love computers but am writing this letter to protest the new computer registration system at Western State. I need a human being, not a computer, to give me advice on the courses I should take to study computers.

- *Reader identification.* The writer anticipates the reader's concerns and responds to them immediately.

Western State University computerized registration saying that students today are all used to computers. They did not consider that students still would like to be advised by a human being. "Students won't use the computer advising system," predicted junior Minnie Mahler. "I'm a computer major and I'm going to talk to my professors face to face about what courses to take."

- *Face.* A character is revealed in action. The reader becomes interested in the person and then the issue.

Stanley Hunan was the first to hear the beeps and notice the blinking screens that signaled a major attack on the new Western State University computer adviser system.

A work–study student at the computer center, his job was to monitor a registration system he resented.

- *Scene.* The writer establishes a scene that is central to the meaning of the piece.

A Western State University student with a baseball hat on backward rushed into Harry's bar last night, looking around wildly, "Need the men's room?" Harry asked.

"No. A telephone," the student said, waving a laptop at the puzzled barkeep.

- *Dialogue.* The reader hears one person speak and another react. It's not often you can use this opening, but when it's appropriate it is dramatic and provides a lot of energy.

"I wanted to eliminate lines," Registrar Lorraine B. Well told a Western State University sophomore yesterday.

"You did," answered the student. "But you eliminated a human being as well. I need a conversation, not 'if you are a liberal arts student, click on 5,' 'write your major on line three.' I'm a dual biochem and forestry major and the computer doesn't recognize that."

- *Process.* A process central to the story is shown in action, and the reader is carried forward into the story.

Students at Western State University who want registration advice have to boot a computer, click on "Regist," and hope their problem or conflict is one that has been programmed into the system.

The following commands—a student pointed out that the word seems to contradict advice—reveal what it feels like to be a Western State student in need of registration counsel.

These are not all the ways to write openings. They are samples from my own toolbox. Make a list of the openings you like to write, look through periodicals and books to see other ways of writing them, and then adopt the technique. Create your own museum of openings.

My museum of leads has an obvious one right inside the front door: *"In the beginning God created Heaven and earth"* (Genesis 1:1). I learn from the leads by expert writers that I have collected. Here, for example, are many leads with the same subject: New York City.

At the height of Harlem's nighttime fury a white police officer stood in the litter of glass and garbage that had come crashing down from the darkened rooftops and raised a bullhorn to his mouth. "Go home," he pleaded with the glowering Negro mobs that clustered along Seventh Avenue and atop the shabby tenements. "Go home," "Go home." From a man in the mob came a shout: "We are home, Baby."

Time, July 31, 1964

I often feel drawn to the Hudson River, and I have spent a lot of time through the years poking around the part of it that flows past the city. I never get tired of looking at it; it hypnotizes me. I like to look at it in midsummer, when it is warm and dirty and drowsy, and I like to look at it when it is stirred up, when a northeast wind is blowing and a strong tide is running—a new-moon tide or a full-moon tide—and I like to look at it when it is slack. It is exciting to me on weekdays, when it is crowded with ocean craft, harbor craft, and river craft, but it is the river itself that draws me, and not the shipping, and I guess I like it best on Sundays, when there are lulls that sometimes last as long as half an hour, during which, all the way from the Battery to the George Washington Bridge, nothing moves upon it, not even a ferry, not even a tug, and it becomes as hushed and dark and secret and remote and unreal as a river in a dream.

Joseph Mitchell, "The River Men," *The New Yorker,* April 4, 1959

For more than half an hour thirty-eight respectable, law-abiding citizens in Queens watched a killer stalk and stab a woman in three separate attacks in Kew Gardens. Twice the sound of their voices and the sudden glow of their bedroom lights interrupted him and frightened him off. Each time he returned, sought her out, and stabbed her again. Not one person telephoned the police during the assault; one witness called after the woman was dead.

Martin Gansberg, *The New York Times,* March 27, 1964

The New York Giants, who overwhelmed two opponents at football last year, underwhelmed ten and whelmed two . . .

Red Smith, *New York Herald Tribune*

On any person who desires such queer prizes, New York will bestow the gift of loneliness and the gift of privacy. It is this largess that accounts for the presence within the city's walls of a considerable section of the population; for the residents of Manhattan are to a large extent strangers who have pulled up stakes somewhere and come to town, seeking sanctuary or fulfillment or some greater or lesser grail. The capacity to make such dubious gifts is a mysterious quality of New York. It can destroy an individual, or it can fulfill him, depending a good deal on luck. No one should come to New York to live unless he is willing to be lucky.

E. B. White, "Here is New York," *Holiday,* April 1949

All on the same subject, but what a variety of approaches—and voices. Create your own museum for inspiration and instruction.

▪ ALTERNATIVE WAYS OF PLANNING ▪

Many times the way I planned the last piece of writing doesn't work on the next one. I have developed many planning techniques. Here are some of them.

Titles

Most writers don't write titles. They let editors do that, and then complain that the title doesn't fit the article. I never wrote titles until, as a junior editorial writer, I got to work by myself on Sunday. I was my own editor, and I was able to write my own titles. Then I started writing the titles first, and found it greatly improved my writing.

In writing the title I captured the direction of the story, a glimpse of its limitations and pace. Most of all, I discovered its tone. Now when I write an article I take the time to brainstorm many titles. The one I settle on may be the second or third or thirteenth title, but I don't know it's the right one until I see the others that don't work.

When I begin to brainstorm titles some are just labels—"War"; "A Day at the Beach"; "A High School Flunk-out"; "A Book on Writing." Others are too long or vague or weak. A good title has a strong sense of voice; it's specific; it catches the reader and draws the reader into the article—"It Was Easy to Kill"; "Bikinis, Sand Fleas, and the Undertow"; "The Revenge of a High School Flunk-out"; "Write to Learn."

But to find those good titles I have to write a lot of bad ones. I don't like doing it, but it seems to be part of the process for me, and I know that the time spent fishing for titles will make it possible for me to write a draft that works in a much shorter period of time than if I didn't mess around with titles first.

I start by brainstorming titles, putting down any combination of words that might become a title, making the censor stand over in the corner while I am silly, stupid, dumb, clumsy, awkward because I usually have to be all of those to become articulate. When I finish brainstorming titles I often feel a sense of disappointment, even failure. Sometimes a really exciting title leaps off the page, but usually I have a rather ordinary list and have to look back to see if anything is happening.

I play with my list, circling a few that seem to have possibility, connecting ones that are related with arrows, editing titles into new forms, adding new ones, fooling around with the central ideas in the piece of writing, and, of course, in doing that I begin to see the piece of writing more clearly.

I'll keep coming back to these titles and putting new ones into my daybook. The title I'll end with may look spontaneous, but it probably will be worried into place. As Phyllis McGinley said:

> There is such a thing as inspiration (lowercase) but it is no miracle. It is the reward handed to a writer for hard work and good conduct. It is the felicitous word sliding, after hours of evasion, obediently into place. It is a sudden comprehension of how to manufacture an effect, finish off a line or stanza. At the triumphant moment this gift may seem like magic but

actually it is the result of effort, practice, and the slight temperature a sulky brain is apt to run when it is pushed beyond its usual exertions.

When the title does, magically (and usually after hard work), seem just right, notice how much it helps you control and direct the piece of writing. The title leads to the opening and becomes the focus for the piece of writing. It reveals its tone, limits, direction. Titles can be the greatest help you will have in finding your way toward an effective piece of writing.

Closings

The end is a beginning.

John Irving says, "I don't know how far away the end is—only what it is. I know the last sentence, but I'm very much in the dark concerning how to get to it." "If I didn't know the end of a story, I wouldn't begin," says Katherine Anne Porter. "I always write my last line, my last paragraph, my last page first," Eudora Welty agrees. "I think the end is implicit in the beginning. It must be. If that isn't there in the beginning, you don't know what you're working toward. You should have a sense of a story's shape and form and its destination, all of which is like a flower inside a seed."

Many good writers know where they want to end before they begin to write. It gives them a sense of destination. Sometimes they just have the closing in mind, but often they write the end first. They know, of course, that the closing may change after the rest of the piece is written, but it still helps during the writing to have a closing in sight.

In effective writing the closing is rarely a formal summary or conclusion in which the writer repeats in general or abstract terms what has already been said. The most effective closings are usually the same devices that make effective openings: specific detail, quotation, anecdote, scene, and all those other tools listed in the section on openings. They do not command readers, telling them how to think, but inspire readers to think about the subject long after they have left the page.

Answering the Reader's Questions

There's a myth that popular writers write "down" to the reader, that the reader is a slob with a fifth-grade education who picks his teeth with a beer can. Not so. The reader is an intelligent person who may not know the subject, but is no dope. The reader will ask intelligent questions of any piece of writing that must be heard and answered by the writer.

Sometimes it helps me to imagine the reader sitting across from my desk, sprawled in an armchair, a skeptical, surly doubting Thomas. I make a statement, and my reader snarls, "Who says?" And I stick in an attribution. I say something else, and the reader asks, "How come?" I stop and tell the reader how come. I write another paragraph and the reader says, "What's that mean?" I tell the reader what it means. The reader snarls, "Who cares?" And I make sure the reader knows the importance of what I'm saying. Other times I imagine a specific person, an individual who is not at all impressed by me or what I know about the subject. And by writing to that person I make my draft clear.

Sometimes I have to write for several very different readers. In that case, I choose one and write for that person. In the revision process I will read and revise for each of the other readers. But I must focus on a single reader at a time.

Good writing is a conversation between an individual writer and an individual reader. The writer has to anticipate where the reader is in that conversation and deliver the information the reader needs when the reader needs it.

Sometimes the reader asks so many nasty questions I can no longer write. I get mad at this surly, overly critical baboon who makes me feel dumb and inadequate. When that happens I send him out of the room. I'll deal with him later, after the draft is done, during the last stage of the writing process, when I have to invite him in anyway. He isn't polite about leaving. Sometimes he even makes obscene gestures, and wears that all-knowing sneer that says, "I'll get you later." Fair enough. I'll have to deal with him later, but when I do there will be a draft we can read together. If I don't get him out of the room there will be no draft at all.

After I have drafted the questions the reader will ask, I put them in the order the reader will ask them. That's always predictable and I have begun to outline my article.

Outlines

Outline is a nasty word to many students, and I was one of them, for it is often taught in such a rigid manner that it doesn't work. An outline is not a formal blueprint that has to be followed precisely; it is not a contract, and you can't be sued if you break it. An outline is a sketch, a guess, a scribbled map that may lead to a treasure. Writers may create outlines and then not refer to them during the writing because what they learned by making the outline allows them to get on with the writing. Sometimes it is also helpful to make outlines in the middle of the writing to see where you've gone and where you might go, and at the end of the draft to see what you have discovered through the writing and how you have organized your material.

There are many ways to outline. Here are eleven possible types. None of these is *the* way to outline. Develop your own system of outlining. Outline only if it helps you, and then outline in a way that provides that help.

I will demonstrate each outline on an assignment given by several Freshman English instructors at the University of New Hampshire: Describe your hometown. The case history of a student, Sarah Hansen, who did an excellent job of describing her hometown, is reprinted in Chapter 8.

Outline 1

This is my favorite form of outline that was described on pages 83–87.

Title
Lead
Trail
End

Demonstration of Outline 1

(TITLE)	My Hometown Was a City
(LEAD)	When other people talk of their hometowns they mention lawns, trees that arch over streets, and backyard swimming pools. My hometown was a city. I remember alleys, boarded-up stores, and vacant lots.
(TRAIL)	• But where I lived was neighborhood • Geography of neighborhood • Who lived there • Games we played
(END)	When I visited my roommate's hometown, it was like a movie set. I thought I'd be envious, but the streets were empty, I never saw his neighbors, I wondered how he could stand the quiet that kept me awake half the night.

Outline 2

My next favorite form of outlining is the one I use in my textbooks. It is the one I would most likely adapt in writing an academic research or term paper.

1. I write the chapter or section titles, playing with them until I get it right, until a see a clear line through the material.

2. I write the headings for each section within the chapter, the headings that appear in the middle of the page playing with them until I see a trail through the chapter.

3. I write the subheads for each section within the major section, ordering and reordering them.

4. I draft the text for each section, changing heads as the material dictates. Writing is thinking; the order will change in the writing.

This is a good technique for the research paper, the grant proposal, the corporate annual report, the brochure, all sorts of writing that must communicate an abundance of information in an orderly fashion.

Demonstration of Outline 2

1. The title of my sociology paper will be "The Urban Neighborhood as Hometown."

2. The main sections will be:
   - Expanding Horizons
   - Worlds Within Worlds (ethnic diversity)
   - Neighborhood Games
   - Neighborhood Ethics
   - Neighborhood Inheritance (beliefs taken to suburbs)

3. The sections within the section on Expanding Horizons (neighborhood geography) will be:
   - Apartment
   - Stairway
   - Front stoop
   - Block
   - Back alley
   - Across the street and away

4. Draft one section within a section at a time. If one doesn't go easily, skip to the next. When you go back, many sections will not be needed; the rest will be easy to write.

Outline 3

The formal outline may be appropriate for a very structured subject. It uses Arabic and Roman numerals and uppercase and lowercase to break down a subject into categories and subcategories in a logical sequence. There are also numerical outlines that are popular in some disciplines; many computer software programs have a formal outline pattern built in.

The most formal outline requires a full and complete sentence for each entry, but most writers just use fragments, as signals for what will be said. Be careful in using the formal outline because it may inhibit the search and discovery of meaning that should come during the writing.

Demonstration of Outline 3

(One section of sociology paper on urban neighborhoods)

III. Neighborhood Games
  A. Importance of games
    1. Aldrich study
      a. LePage response
    2. History of games
  B. Nature of Games
    1. Hiding
      a. Hide-and-seek
      b. Ring-a-lievo
    2. Sports
      a. Stickball
      b. Basketball
      c. Street hockey
      d. Soccer
    3. Gender Differences
      a. Boys' games
      b. Girls' games
      c. Crossovers
        (1) Boys playing girls' games (rare)
        (2) Girls playing boys' games (often)
    4. Ethnic Differences
      a. White
      b. African American
      c. Latin American
      d. Asian

Outline 4

A writer friend of mine, Donald H. Graves, uses this outline form. He lists everything that might be included in the piece of writing in the left-hand column; then he moves items to the columns marked Beginning, Middle, End.

Some of the things don't get moved, of course, and others come to mind as the outline is being made and go right into the appropriate column. Some things in the left-hand column are not used. It's a brainstorming list, and it becomes an inventory of material that may be used. And some items that are not on the list come to mind when the writer is working on the right-hand columns. The items are ordered—by number—within the columns after the writer has finished. Then the writer is ready to write.

Demonstration of Outline 4

Beginning	Middle	End	Brainstorming List
Hometown urban	Qualities of neighborhood life:	How urban attitudes influence	Stickball
Neighborhood urban unit		How see suburban world through urban values	Latins played soccer
You are defined by your neighborhood	Ethnic comfort/ discomfort		Blacks played basketball
	Diversity comfort/ discomfort		Whites played hockey
	Fears		Don't date X
	Pleasures		Girls' games
	Games		Dress
	Family		Mixed families
	Dating + mating		Loyalty to your own
			Food
			Racial myths
			My values today
			Alleys, loved alleys

Outline 5

A way to use the outline to dramatize the importance of certain parts of the piece of writing to the reader is to make a box outline in which the size of each box represents the importance of each part. The first paragraph, for example, is much more important to the reader than the pages that follow and might be two by four inches. The subject of the next four pages indicated in a phrase contained in a box only a quarter of an inch by two inches. A main turning point might be in a box one by three inches, and then the rest of the piece in another tiny box. Finally the closing might be in a box as large—or larger—than the first paragraph. This can best be done with boxes but it can also be done with typefaces.

This outline really forces me to face up to the importance of the opening and the ending—to the importance of what I'm going to say and how I'm going to say it. It also forces me to see the structure of the piece in stark, efficient terms.

Demonstration of Outline 5 (Using Boxes)

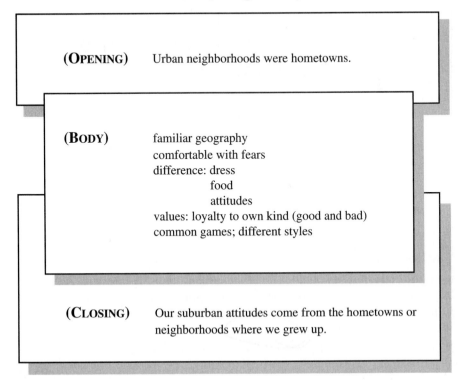

(OPENING)   Urban neighborhoods were hometowns.

(BODY)   familiar geography
             comfortable with fears
             difference: dress
                         food
                         attitudes
             values: loyalty to own kind (good and bad)
             common games; different styles

(CLOSING)   Our suburban attitudes come from the hometowns or
             neighborhoods where we grew up.

Demonstration of Outline 5 (Using Typefaces)

      (OPENING)   Urban neighborhoods were hometowns.

      (BODY)   familiar geography
                    comfortable with fears
                    difference: dress
                                    food
                                    attitudes
                    values: loyalty to own kind
                    (good and bad)
                    common games; different styles

      (CLOSING)   Our suburban attitudes come from the hometowns or neighborhoods where we grew up.

Outline 6

A fine way to outline, especially on a complicated subject, is to brainstorm the questions the reader will ask and then put them in the order the reader will ask them.

There will usually be five questions—sometimes three or four, sometimes six or seven, but most likely five. You don't want to use the questions in the draft, but simply give the answers. The questions are in the reader's mind; the writer anticipates and answers them.

Demonstration of Outline 6

The questions are brainstormed, written down as they come to mind:

- Who were your neighbors? Did you get along with them?
- How can you have a hometown when you lived in a city?
- How is a neighborhood like a small town?
- How does your hometown, your urban neighborhood, influence your life today?
- What attitudes and beliefs did you take away from the neighborhood?
- What was life like in your hometown (neighborhood)?

Now the questions are put in the order the reader will ask them, and sharpened:

- How is a neighborhood like a small town?
- What was daily life like in your city neighborhood?
- Who were your neighbors?
- How did you get along with them?
- What attitudes and beliefs did you take away from the neighborhood?

Outline 7

The writer can adapt outline forms from other disciplines. I often find it helpful to use a flowchart, similar to those used in systems engineering and in business organization study. These charts are designed to show how a factory works, how material flows from a natural resource to a manufactured product, how power flows in a corporation. Using this device I can often spot a movement or force that can order my piece.

Demonstration of Outline 7

When we moved to city I discovered neighborhood was hometown ⟶

Geography of neighborhood ⟶ Streets and blocks ⟶ Ethnic

boundaries ⟶ Playing and living within boundaries ⟶ Attitudes

and beliefs neighborhood taught me

Outline 8

A related outline form I find useful I've borrowed from computers. Computer users have developed a number of different forms of outlining that break down complicated subjects into their sequential parts. Most of these outlines flow from left to right.

At the left I pose the issue: "The hometown in the city is the neighborhood." Then I give two extreme responses, one above the question and over to the right—"physical boundaries"; another below and over to the right—"ethical boundaries." I break down every answer this way until I see a pattern of potential meaning emerging.

Demonstration of Outline 8

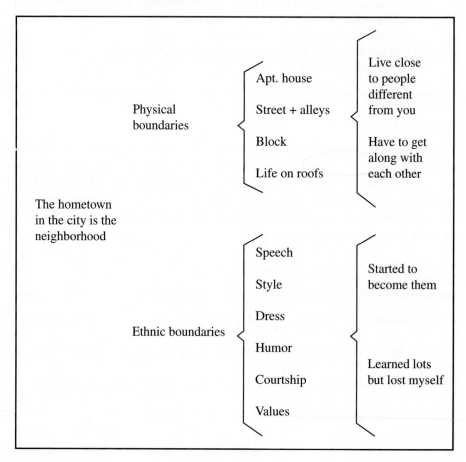

Outline 9

In many effective pieces of writing, fiction as well as nonfiction, each chunk of writing—a paragraph, a page, a scene—answers a question and asks a new question. For example: Will they get married? Yes, but will they be happy? or, Will the product sell? Yes, but will it bring a profit? You can create an outline by anticipating and listing these questions.

Demonstration of Outline 9

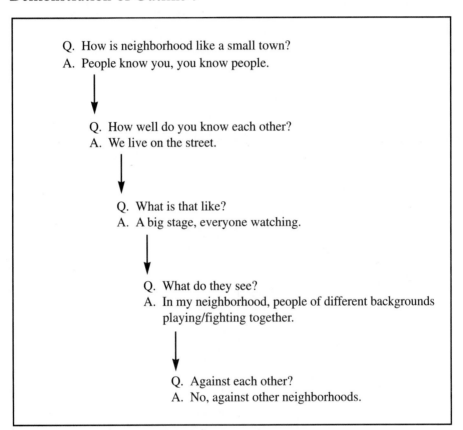

Q. How is neighborhood like a small town?
A. People know you, you know people.

Q. How well do you know each other?
A. We live on the street.

Q. What is that like?
A. A big stage, everyone watching.

Q. What do they see?
A. In my neighborhood, people of different backgrounds playing/fighting together.

Q. Against each other?
A. No, against other neighborhoods.

Outline 10

Many fine writers, such as John McPhee and John Gregory Dunne, use a card technique to outline. This is the most popular technique of movie scriptwriters.

Each scene or key topic in the writing is put on a card, sometimes using cards of different colors for different characters, or different kinds of material in nonfiction. Then the cards are pinned to a cork board and moved around so the writer can see the pattern of the entire piece—book, movie, or article.

Demonstration of Outline 10

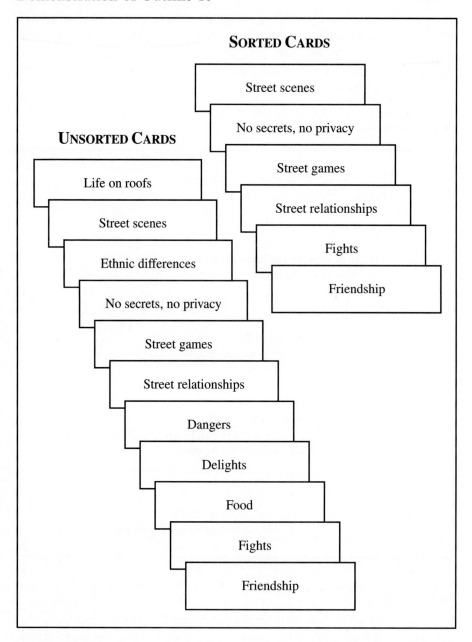

Outline 11

Make file folders for each topic within the piece of writing. This is helpful on a large project. You can renumber and move the file folders around, and you can put all your raw material right into a folder—clips, photocopied articles,

Demonstration of Outline 11

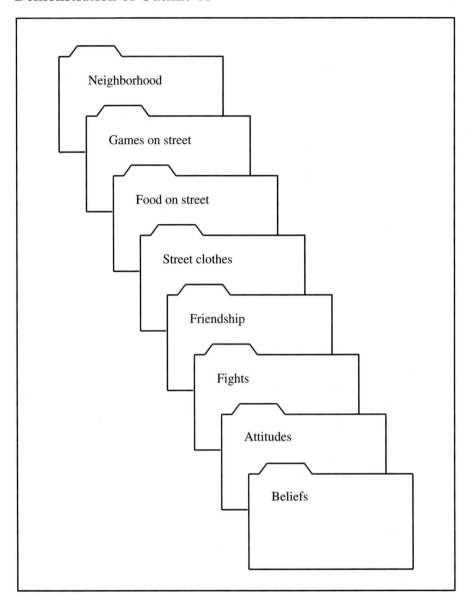

notes, photographs. When a folder is full it may have to be divided. When it has nothing in it you may have to drop that topic, or do more research.

Try out these outline forms, and then make up others that fit the way your mind works. There's no one way to outline, and no eleven ways to outline. But you should find some way of pre-seeing what you may write.

Yes, there are writers who say that they do not outline, but if you interview them, as I have, you find that most of them have outlined in their minds, sometimes without being aware they were doing it. That happens to me sometimes; I just know where the writing is going and how it is going to get there. It seems like a feeling, even though it's probably a very organized intellectual act. When this happens to me, I write. I don't outline unless I feel the need to outline. But I do find that most of the time my drafts collapse unless I have outlines in my mind or on paper.

Of course, when you outline you may realize that you need more information, or that you need a different focus, and you have to go back through one or more of the earlier stages of the writing process. That isn't failure. You haven't made a mistake. That's one of the main reasons to outline, so that you will see the information you need to have before you write the draft. You will see, by outlining, if you have the information to develop the focus.

▪ PLANNING IN THE DAYBOOK ▪

My daybook could be called my planning book. In this notebook I record ideas, draft lines and leads, make the sketches I call outlines, note what I will write the next day. This talking to myself in the daybook stimulates the subconscious and keeps a project working during the majority of hours in the day when I am not sitting at my computer. My daybook is always nearby and when I am walking, in the car, on an airplane, attending a meeting, waiting for my wife, watching television, an idea surfaces from my subconscious and I catch it in my daybook.

The daybook is the place where I perform the play that leads to writing, capturing ideas, connecting them to other ideas, studying the created pattern, rearranging it into another meaning and also playing with language that reveals the surprises essential to writing.

▪ PLANNING USING A COMPUTER ▪

The computer is a wonderful place to play with pattern and language. There are outlining programs, but I prefer to make my own, creating lists, charts, outlines of all forms so that I can see a sketch of what I may write.

When I use Outline 2 the seams between exploring and planning and drafting blur. I may move raw research right into place and I may also write at any place.

I used to write magazine articles in sections and my study floor would be covered with slips of paper of varying sizes and heaps of raw research material. Now I do all that on the screen as I perform the task of the writer: making order from chaos.

• PLANNING FOR THE READER •

The form of a piece of writing—the genre or type of writing it is—serves the reader by being an island of meaning in an ocean of confusion. It provides the reader with an intellectual unit, which represents what the writer has to say. The writer picks a form—an argument, a story, a memo, a literary analysis, a business letter, a review, because it will represent an area of thought the writer and the reader can explore together.

The reader has similar expectations. Each genre implies certain things—a story implies a story, events structured chronologically. The writer can play variations on that expectation, but the writer had better be aware of what the reader expects when choosing a genre.

The order or structure of a piece of writing is designed to lead the reader on a trip of exploration. Sometimes it is effective to arrange what the reader sees or is given to think about in a way such that the reader is unaware of the trail. At other times the reader needs road signs. Some road signs are there all the time—the title, the lead, the end. But it may be helpful to use headings or subheadings; for example, to point out the stages in the evolution of an argument, or the categories of evidence to be presented in a proposal.

One of the most effective tricks of ordering is to anticipate, then order the reader's questions, so that the piece of writing answers those questions as they occur to the reader. If the subject is complicated and important for the reader to understand, for example, a brochure urging people to pay attention to the symptoms of diabetes, or one given to patients after diabetes has been diagnosed, it may be helpful to include the questions in the draft, so that the trail that the reader should follow in exploring this island of meaning is explicit and well marked.

• PLANNING THE VOICE •

Voice is what I am; voice is the person in the writing; voice is what persuades the reader to listen and draws the reader on. We can train ourselves to hear the voice of the finished draft in the fragments with which we plan; we can decide, in advance of the first draft, how we will tune voice to support and communicate the meaning of the writing.

The Personal Voice

Each writer has a personal voice. I can recognize family and friends in another room or on the telephone. People have their own music made up of genes and hormones, regional and ethnic influences, professional training and daily exercise in speaking. Natural tendencies in speech are influenced by other voices and by what draws the best response from those to whom a person speaks. How speech is paced, its pauses and underlined phrases, sense of humor, anger, irony, despair, joy are all communicated by voice. People relate to each other through speech: As the father of daughters I read their relationships by how they spoke on the phone to young men.

We can hear those qualities of our personal voice in the lines we write as we plan and decide which ones should be emphasized and which should be de-emphasized.

The Draft's Voice

Just as I have a voice, so does my draft and the fragments that will lead to the complete draft. Planning involves listening to possible voices in your head and your daybook, then choosing the voice appropriate to the subject and the audience. You draft a statement for a scholarship application in your head, but hear a whining voice that would turn off anyone and discard it. Then you hear the voice of a person so humble and lacking in confidence that the money would be wasted—that person doesn't have enough confidence to graduate. You try another, with confidence, but with so much confidence that the voice sounds arrogant. Then you tone it down and hear the kind of confident-but-not-cocky person the committee would like to support and write the application using that voice.

The Revealing Voice

As we plan, we hear ourselves speak from the page and how we say what we say often reveals the meaning of the draft. The voice tells us what is important—and that often surprises us. You write a paper on alcoholism and realize how angry you are about your parents' drinking and how scared you are for them and for yourself. Voice is a significant element in our learning by writing.

▪ REVISING THE PLAN ▪

Plan is revision at its purest. Planning allows you to abstract many possibilities and describe them simply so that they can be compared and evaluated.

As you make each plan, you are revising potential drafts, solving problems efficiently before they impede the writing of the draft. Many times the revised plan reveals that you need to go back and recast the whole piece—the subject, the genre, the audience is not what we thought. When that happens, you usually have to check with the teacher or employer before you go on. The revised plan allows you to avoid a finished draft that does not meet the teacher or employer's assignment.

And consulting with teacher or employer may produce a newly revised plan. That is central to the process of writing. Writing is discovery and each discovery modifies or develops one's plan.

▪ QUESTIONS ABOUT PLANNING ▪

What if I'm working on an opening and but believe it might make a closing?

Make a note in the margin beside it "close?"; or, make a note in your "closing" file. This often happens, and you shouldn't let the idea get away. Good beginnings often make good endings, and the other way around.

What if the draft openings won't come?

Switch around and try titles or outlines. Try closing. Plunge in and start to write the text. Put someone's name on it and start it as a letter. Try any of the other ordering strategies. You can outline first and then go back and write titles or openings. Closings can come before beginnings. Go with what works.

I do all this stuff in my head—why do I have to write it down?

You don't. If you do it in your head and your writing is well organized, don't do it. There are people who never write down outlines, and others who only do it when they face a new and difficult writing task—writing about a complex, unfamiliar story; trying to appeal to a new audience; writing in a different form than they are used to. If your writing works well, follow the process that is succeeding. If you're having problems writing well, then try some of the techniques proposed in the text.

I had a teacher who taught me to remember CUE as a way of reminding me of coherence, unity, and emphasis. How is that different from the stuff you have on design?

I had a teacher who used the same device, and it is one of the few pieces of teacher advice I remember as I write. It's pretty good stuff. I've gone on to develop it a bit, but in doing that development I've probably paid attention to coherence, unity, and emphasis.

How can I do all this planning when I've got to write the paper tonight?

Planning helps you write more efficiently and more quickly. If you have an hour, take five or ten minutes to collect the information with which you'll be writing. Take a few more minutes to be sure you have the focus, and then a few minutes to put the information in order. If you take ten minutes for each of those tasks, you'll only have invested half an hour. You'll have twenty minutes to write and ten minutes to check over what you've written. The planning will make your draft quicker, often longer, and better.

Do I have to follow the outline?

Of course not. It isn't a legal contract; it's merely a sketch or a plan. It is a tool to help you. Writing isn't completed thought written down; writing is thinking. The draft should change under your hand. It will teach you about the subject. When you're writing best you are often writing what you did not expect to write. Remember John Fowle's counsel: "Follow the accident, fear the fixed plan—that is the rule."

▪ PLANNING ACTIVITIES ▪

1. Scan half a dozen magazines and write down the article titles that made you want to read. Do the same thing with book titles in a library or bookstore. Work alone or in a group to decide what the qualities of a good title are. Decide what elements they have in common.

2. Share your idea for a piece of writing with another person in the class or with a small group; then write titles for each other. Write new titles for textbooks or pieces of literature you are reading.

3. See how many titles you can write for the piece you're working on. List at least twenty. Do them quickly, in small chunks of time.

4. Collect, by yourself or with others, fifty to a hundred good openings and list the different techniques used by these successful opening writers.

5. Write ten new openings, taking no more than five minutes each, for something you've just read.

6. Write at least twenty-five openings for the piece you're working on.

7. Look back at pieces of writing you've read recently or that you consider good and list the PLANNING techniques the writers may have used.

8. Share the idea you're working on with others and draft endings for each other.

9. Take a piece of writing you've read and see how many different ways you can close it.

10. Draft as many closings as you can—at least twenty-five—for the piece of writing you're working on.

11. Take a piece of writing you like and write down the three to five principal points that are made in it.

12. Share your subject with someone else and write down, for each other, the main points that will be made and the order in which they'll have to be made.

13. Sketch out ten different sequences that might be used to get you from one of your leads to one of your endings. (What if the sequence reveals you need a new opening, a new closing, or both? Good. That's one of the reasons to play with sequence.)

14. Design your own outline form and share it with others who are sharing theirs with you.

15. Outline your piece at least five different ways.

16. Say, in one sentence, what you want the reader to do after he or she has read your piece.

17. At the bottom of a page, put what you want the reader to think or feel and then list the steps that will bring the reader to your destination.

18. Write a memo to yourself as new employee, telling yourself what you have to do to complete the next writing job.

19. Draft and redraft the last paragraph of the article you are going to write, then draft and redraft the first paragraph. List how you intend to get from opening to concluding paragraph.

20. Select a favorite piece of writing in the form you are going to write next and create the outline the author may have used.

CHAPTER 5
DRAFT

How do I know what I think until I see what I say?

E. M. FORSTER

Now you are ready to explore your topic with a discovery draft.

No matter how familiar you are with the subject, no matter how well you have thought about and researched the topic, no matter how well you have planned solutions to the problems in the draft, you will be surprised by what appears on the screen or the page.

The draft does not say what you expected. The first draft makes your argument stronger or weaker; it reveals a different problem or solution; it contradicts or deepens your previous beliefs; it reveals a new meaning or changes the old one; it speaks in an unexpected voice or grows into an unintended form. In these ways and others, the draft betrays the writer and the inexperienced writer believes that these surprises are failures.

Just the opposite. Writing is not thinking "thunk," thought completed before the draft and transcribed to the page. Writing is thinking. And as we think, our thoughts change. We use language to discover what we know, what it means, and how we feel about it.

Writers write to see what the blank page reveals. Writers welcome, encourage, cultivate—even force—surprise, contradiction, the unexpected.

Wallace Stevens said, "The tongue is an eye." We speak and we see what we did not see before. Words hold meaning still, sentences clarify and connect, paragraphs develop and place in context, all revealing an evolving meaning that is more than we planned. In writing, two and two add up to seven, eleven, twenty-three.

114

▪ CULTIVATING SURPRISE ▪

The three primary surprises you can hope to experience while writing a discovery draft are as follows:

Contraction

Writing is, first of all, a narrowing down. Before we write, our ideas float, untethered balloons filled with possible meaning. Then we choose a word, connect it with another word, and the meaning is captured and limited. We take the broad, horizonless, not-yet-thought and contract it so that it begins to have a specific meaning.

> It is a ~~beautiful~~ day.
> It is a sunny day.

The broad, vague concept of beauty contracts to one element of beauty, the sun.

Written language—and mathematics is a language—is the most disciplined form of thinking. Words define. Words give thinking precision. Words connected with other words fence in a specific meaning.

In speech we can use words that are not quite on target but qualify them with tone, inflection, facial expression, gesture. "I had a great time with Edmond last night," "The new boss is a dream come true," "My mother just loves Foxy Roxy" can mean that things are better than good or worse than terrible depending on the way the speaker acts out the meaning.

Writing is more difficult. You have to be understood across time and distance. The meaning has to be clear. "Edmond is cheap. He took out a pocket calculator and left an eleven percent tip—to the penny: $1.37—three dimes, one nickel, two pennies." "The new boss asked me how my job should be done. That's a first." "My mother put Roxy in my room and told me I was staying at Aunt Paula's three blocks away."

We write to capture meaning, to limit and qualify, to surprise ourselves by what happens when we control possibility.

Expansion

At the same time, writing expands meaning. We see possibilities we have not seen before. The defined examples above resonate with potential meaning the moment their meaning is limited. This seems a contradiction but it is not: The more specific we are the more possibilities occur. The narrowed concept of beauty expands.

The reader will ask for more documentation and I provide it. I tell the anecdote of the snakes but now it is in a context that makes it significant—I do not let the snake-boy know my fear, I will not let my boss think his new organizational plan will replace confusion with chaos.

I also know the liveliness that results from specifics—63 nights is more dramatic than nine weeks. I also feel free to interrupt the text with the Freudian remark that reminds the reader that an old man is looking back at his camp experience. The reader's point of view is at the side of the old man.

In all such articles, I am trying to write with the ease of a real conversation and the efficiency of an imagined one. The meaning of the piece is in the reflective voice of the writer who is looking back from a distance with good humor and some surprise.

In the last reading I changed the rather free floating "it" at the end of the paragraph to the more specific "my fear."

~~Scholarship boy and had a small taste. . . .~~

When something occurs to me that I may want to mention I make an immediate note within the draft, the way an explorer will mark a map, recording a hill or a bay that may be visited later. In the writing of this column I was aware that many children cannot afford to go to camp and I want to tell everyone I was at camp on scholarship but I cross this out because it does not move the essay forward.

Before I went to camp I had three times almost drownded, as we said, could not swim and was terrified of water above my ankles. Family home movies celebrated my shame each Christmas.

I'm a bad typist and many times my typos lead to good writing. I mistype "drowned" and typed "drownded"; I realize this was just the word I would have used at camp so I kept it.

In writing this paragraph, I'm following the map created earlier when drowning was at the point of emphasis in the paragraph and I set up my fear of the water. And my embarrassment or shame is introduced by the home movies. These things are not thought up, they arrive on their own energy.

One of my ~~most powerful~~ strongest memories of camp was ~~sitting high in the woods~~ hiding in the KYBO—Keep Your Bowels Open—during Beginner's Swim and hearing the hated cheery sounds of boys having fun echoing off the lake.

"Strongest" saves a word; "hiding" does the same thing. "KYBO" and its translation helps establish the male, juvenile, bathroom humor of the environment where no one would be sympathetic to a kid scared of the

water. My alienation and loneliness is, of course, a subtheme that is flowing strongly through the piece.

But I did learn to swim ~~over my head~~ IN WATER OVER MY HEAD, to mess funny food around on my plate so it looked eaten, to accept the punishments I then thought painful and now think cruel and perverse, knuckle punches on the arms from college football players, naked parades in front of camp administrators—and survive.

I change "over my head" to IN WATER OVER MY HEAD in caps to capture a hint of how a young boy would say it. I skip by all the difficulty I had learning to swim, ease off with the food, then find myself mentioning the punishments that were "cruel and perverse."

Chekhov said, "If in the first chapter you say that a gun hung on the wall, in the second or third chapter it must without fail be discharged." If I mention "cruel and perverse," I must document such a strong charge immediately. I insert examples of each right in the middle of the sentence where the reader needs it.

At this point I stop and do a word count on my computer: 389. Like the explorer, I need to know how far I have come and how much farther I have to go within the target limit of 800 words.

My memories of summer camp after more than fifty years [end? wonder about kids coming home this month] surprise me. I am nostalgic for those four summers on Melon [check] Pond~~, grateful~~. I look back with a longing ~~for~~

It was NOT Melon Pond but Millen Pond.

evenings on the lake, the feel of a canoe riding in the water, the lone bugle playing taps at lights out, waking before the others in blankets ~~pinned~~ held together with giant safety pins on Blueberry Hill and seeing the valleys hidden by rivers of mist.

I just described what I remember and then, in the next paragraph returned to what I would have expected. In a final reading I added "for another" before "evening."

I would have expected memories of companionship, stories around a campfire, even memories of practical jokes, perhaps the morning I woke ~~to find~~ nose to nose with the camp goat my tentmates had tucked into bed with me.

I catalogue what I learned and, in writing that list, I categorize them at the end. I also like to inject a little humor in a text that's growing serious. It gives the reader a little room and makes the texture of the essay a bit richer. I also find I put a touch of the serious into humorous columns for the same reasons.

I was an only child who learned to live with boys his own age, to think of others than myself, to accept a world that was not designed to my needs, to make friends of strangers, but my best memories are of those times when I was alone.

The last paragraph tells me what the next one will be: my best memories. I am struck in reading these notes made during writing how easy the writing is, one paragraph growing simply and naturally out of the other. Now I must describe the best memories.

Those were the magic moments when I scouted far ahead in the woods, was allowed to take out a canoe alone, when I spent a day exploring the Asheulot River, when I fell behind the pack and accepted my need for the loneliness I had always been made to feel was wrong, somehow un-American by the parents, teachers, and ministers I tried so hard to please.

Specifics will usually reveal meaning. I have discovered—in the fourteenth paragraph—the meaning of the essay, "accepted my need for the loneliness." But in the word acceptance, *I have to put the need into the context of a culture that resists aloneness, denies the solitary life. In the last reading I added "blueberrying" before "pack" to make it more specific.*

  Now I wind up the essay with a statement of what camp taught me.

Summer camp gave me the ability to swim underwater, ~~the skill of hiding my true feelings, and the acceptance of a strange secret,~~ taught me how to get along with others—live a public life—but it also allowed me to accept my secret—that I often was my own best companion.

And then I have to tie it back to the beginning. I struggle a bit, cut out lines that don't work for me, are not pointed enough, have been said before. In the last reading I added "to" before "live a public life" for musical reasons—it seemed to sound better.

I watch today's campers return lugging strangely sewn leather billfolds, bent hawk feathers, bags of ~~dirty filthy~~ stinky laundry and wonder what they will remember—and treasure—when they are over sixty.

I saw children returning from summer camp and felt powerful emotions I could not name or describe. I wrote to name and understand them and traveling within the landscape of the draft I found those emotions and what they meant.

In going back through this piece for you I was struck by how easy and natural the trip was. One thing—literally—did lead to another. Each paragraph predicted the next paragraph.

I need to know the traditions of my craft; need to hear what other writers, my teachers, and my editors have told me; but I need to shut off all that at the moment of drafting and concentrate all my attention on what is happening at this moment in the draft, solving the problem of the following sentence. I travel light, making the journey a step at a time, rarely looking far ahead or behind, dealing with the situation underfoot. The traditions of language and rhetoric are implied, and all the work is performed in the unraveling context. I don't want to see in this landscape what has been seen in others but to see it anew, with little prediction or intent.

▪ DRAFTING LAYER BY LAYER ▪

The writer who fears saying too much or knows the subject so well that he or she imagines a few general words will give the reader the same full vision they spark in the writer produces copy that is superficial, thin, and undeveloped. Another reason for undeveloped writing is that writing doesn't usually come all at once. It often comes in spurts: Writing produces more writing. I do not know what I will write or how I will write it until I draft. Then the evolving draft instructs me, telling me what I have to say and hinting at how I may say it. And with this comes an increasing awareness of audience as I write in the beginning for myself and, later, for others.

One technique I use is to layer my writing. Once I did quite a bit of oil painting and my pictures were built up, layer after layer of paint, until the scene was revealed to me and a viewer. I've been writing each chapter of some of my books, articles, and poems the same way, starting each day at the beginning of yesterday's draft, reading and writing until my daily stint is finished. Each day I lay down a new layer of writing and when I read it the next day, the new layer reveals more possibility.

There is no one way for writing to develop. As I layer I may start with a sketch, other times the first writing feels complete (next day's reading usually shows it is not); sometimes I race ahead through the draft, other times each paragraph is honed before I go on to the next one. I try to allow the draft to tell me what it needs.

I start reading and when I see—or, more likely, hear—something that needs doing, I do it. One day I'll read through all the written text and move it forward from the last day's writing; another time I'll find myself working on dialogue; the next day I may begin to construct a new scene or argument; one time I'll stumble into a new discovery and later have to set it up or weave references to it through the text; I may build up background description, develop the conflict, make the reader see a character more clearly; I may present more documentation, evidence, or exposition, or hide it in a character's dialogue or action.

Layering is ideally suited for the computer because it is easy to write over what you have written, but it can be done with typewriter or pen and paper as well. Part of the technique involves developing inserts that can be written or pasted within sentences or paragraphs, between paragraphs or sections, at the end, in the middle, or even before the beginning. Remember there are no rules, the draft leads and you follow.

The best way I know to get the feel of layering is to write a paragraph— perhaps of description—then to start again on a new page and write it again without reading the first one or, at least, only reading it loosely. Write easily. Relax. Let the draft lead. Then do it a third time, a fourth, perhaps a fifth. Does that mean you should always do it five times? No. The draft may call for three layers or seventeen. Let me demonstrate and comment as I do:

1.

When I think of North Quincy High School, I think of corridors more than classrooms. I expect to think of classrooms. Say "elementary school" and I think of the huge classroom clocks with Roman numerals and waiting for the last clicks in the afternoon. Three minutes. Two. One. Escape.

I start by writing down my first thoughts about high school.

2.

North Quincy High School. Not classrooms but corridors jammed with the hourly flood of teenagers. Beer jackets and saddle shoes, letter sweaters and girls with mysterious blooming sweaters. Sweater girls. Shouts and laughter, "swell" and "neat," the harsh, ugly south of Boston accent and the fastracingyankeetalk, the slamming of locker doors and the bells summoning the prisoners for lock up.

I try to get into the text faster and, most of all, to develop the scene in my mind, to flesh it out with detail.

3.

I heard myself say, "Everybody's alienated in high school" and was surprised I saw North Quincy High School and long, empty corridors.

I got into it slower so I could put it in context.

I would have expected to remember classrooms, hours that felt like whole lifetimes, clocks with huge Roman numerals with hours between the click of the minute hand, teacher voices that used sarcasm like the flicking end of a bull whip.

I transposed the material from elementary school. We had the same clocks in high school and I waited for their clicks with the same desperation.

Or the flood of students between classes, beer jackets and sweater girls, "swell" and "neat," the slam of locker doors, peanut butter and jelly sandwiches, the perfume of sneakers and gym shorts.

I added detail, paced it a bit differently. All this detail I hoped would take me back to high school and lead me to meaning.

But what I remember, with something close to nostalgia, is the long, empty corridors with the classroom doors closed.

I develop the key image, the picture that haunts my memory.

4.

We were talking about high school the other night and I heard myself say, "Everybody's alienated in high school" and was surprised I saw North Quincy High School, long, empty corridors and something that felt like nostalgia. High school was not a good time for me. I dropped out twice and flunked out at the end. I would have expected anger, perhaps bitterness, even embarrassment, not nostalgia.

In the previous and the following paragraph I continue to develop with more detail, setting up the situation in the first paragraph, revealing the world of the school in the second.

I would have expected to remember classrooms, hours that felt like whole lifetimes, lectures on physics or algebra in which I lost any sense of meaning, clocks with huge Roman numerals with hours between the click of the minute hand, teacher voices that used sarcasm like the flicking end of a bull whip. Or the flood of students between classes, beer jackets and sweater girls, "swell" and "neat," the slam of locker doors, peanut butter and jelly sandwiches, the perfume of sneakers and gym shorts. But what I remember, with something close to nostalgia, is the long, empty corridors with the classroom doors closed.

The floors gleamed with wax and the green locker doors were silent. The walls, I think, were stucco and light fixtures hung from the ceiling. Inside the glass doors of the classrooms I saw the tired gestures of the teachers and numbed faces of the students, faces that seemed drugged by information they did not want to know and would never understand.

Now I have placed myself—and, therefore, the reader—in the lonely corridor. As I distance myself from those locked into the classrooms,

teachers and students alike, I am unknowingly taking a big step toward
the meaning the next layer of text will reveal.

5.

My wife and daughters and I were talking about high school the
other evening—none of us wanted to return—and we laughed at
someone who was still angry at being unappreciated and alienated
in high school and I heard myself say, "Everybody's alienated in
high school." As I spoke I was carried back to North Quincy High
School, long, empty corridors and something that felt like nostalgia.

In the first paragraph I am extending the context a bit, setting the scene
more completely. In these first paragraphs I am instinctively establishing,
mood, tone, pace; tuning my language to the evolving voice of the piece
that will reveal meaning to me and will reveal and support meaning to
the reader.

I was surprised. I have never felt nostalgic about high school before.
It was not a good time for me. I won no letters, retained a virtue I
desperately wanted to lose, dropped out twice, and flunked out in
the end. I would have expected anger, perhaps bitterness, even
shame, not nostalgia.

And I would have expected to remember classrooms, those educational cells to which I had been sentenced with hours that felt like
whole lifetimes, lectures on physics or algebra in which I lost any
sense of meaning, clocks with huge Roman numerals with hours
between the click of the minute hand, teacher voices that used sarcasm like the flicking end of a bull whip. Or the flood of students
between classes, beer jackets and sweater girls, "swell" and "neat,"
the slam of locker doors, peanut butter and jelly sandwiches, the
perfume of sneakers and gym shorts. But what I remember, with
something close to nostalgia, is the long, empty corridors with the
classroom doors closed.

The floors gleamed with wax and the green locker doors were
silent. The walls, I think, were stucco and orange bulbed light fixtures hung from the ceiling. Inside the glass doors of the classrooms
I saw the tired gestures of the teachers and numbed faces of the students, faces that seemed drugged by information they did not want
to know and would never understand. And I was alone in the corridor. I had escaped.

With the word escape, *the draft has revealed the meaning to me.*

Of course, I remember those corridors with nostalgia. Just the other
day I found stacks of forged corridor passes, stored away in case I get

returned to high school. I worked on the newspaper and the year-book; I learned the system and then how to work it. I escaped home-room and study hall, sometimes even class. I possessed the loneliness I had learned at home and the delicious egotism of alienation. I was an outsider, a writer before I knew I would become a writer, an almost-man with forged corridor passes, documentation that I would escape high school, learn new systems and how, as a loner, to ma-nipulate them. Those aged slips of paper were, I now realize, my diploma and oh how I have used that education in the years since, walking so many corridors by myself, alienated and smug.

In the last paragraph I have explored, developed, examined, and extended that meaning, playing with it, turning it over, moving back to the slips, seeing their significance, delighting myself with the surprise of "smug," which gives me an insight about my lifetime of proud alienation. I have maintained the private illusion and arrogance of alienation even when I have earned awards, promotion, title, tenure. I suppose I am smugly alienated, secretly feeling superior to those around me. Too true, at times, not all the time, I hope. This writing I did just to document a point has put me on the couch, revealed myself and made me squirm and made me feel I deserve a couple of good squirms.

And in reading all this over I am struck by my patience. Once I would have wanted to know the meaning right away—or even thought I should have known the meaning before I wrote the first word. I would have sought meaning, panted after it. Now I am patient—and confident. Experience has taught me that if I keep writing, meaning will come. I will not think meaning. I will watch meaning arise from my page. The painter William de Kooning once said, "I can't paint a tree but I can find a tree in my work" and Pablo Picasso testified, "To know what you want to draw, you have to begin drawing. If it turns out to be a man, I draw a man. If it turns out to be a woman, I draw a woman." They are patient and I have learned patience as well. And I have learned it by re-reading these drafts.

That was fun, and totally unexpected. The conversation took place and the image of the empty corridors came to mind but I didn't begin to under-stand them until I completed this hour of layering, putting down text on top of text, revising to produce a first draft.

You will see other things I have done—good or bad—or should have done. And you may make your own discoveries, comfortable and uncomfortable, as you live my drafts. Mark them all down on my draft, then try them on yours.

And what will I do with the version 5? I don't know. Play with it perhaps. See if it grows into a column or a short story. It may pop up in the novel I'm drafting or turn into an academic article on layering, may even be shrunk to a poem. Most likely it will remain what it is: a piece of writing that was fun to do because it captured an important part of my life and allowed me to examine it and come to some understanding I did not have before.

▪ DRAFTING UNIT BY UNIT ▪

The third principal way that I draft is by units. This is the best way for me to write long reports, term papers, or nonfiction books that are not narratives or single long stories.

As I mentioned in the last chapter in the discussion on outlines, I write the chapter heads first, then the primary subheads for each section, then the heads for the sections within the sections. Then I draft a subsection, either in sequence or when one is ready to be written, creating the book as one would create a mosaic, block by block. Of course I may move the blocks around, leave some out and add new ones, as I write the draft and discover what the reader needs.

▪ TWENTY-SIX TREATMENTS FOR WRITER'S BLOCK ▪

It never gets easier to write. All writers are masters of avoidance. If interruptions don't occur, writers create them. They make phone calls, travel far on unnecessary errands, cut wood in July, buy a snow shovel in August. When it is time to write, writers read, attack the correspondence and the filing, sharpen pencils, buy new pens, change the typewriter ribbon, shop for a word processor, make coffee, make tea, rearrange the furniture in the office. When writers get together they often, shamefacedly, share new ways to avoid writing.

But some of that avoidance is good. E. B. White reminds us, "Delay is natural to a writer. He is like a surfer—he bides his time, waits for the perfect wave on which to ride in. Delay is instinctive with him." This waiting is purposeful, for most writers discover that starting a draft prematurely causes a total collapse three, five, or seven pages along, and it's harder to repair a train wreck of a draft than to start one along the right track.

Writers, of course, being writers, are never sure whether they are allowing their subject to ripen properly or are just being lazy. This waiting is often the worst part of writing. It is filled with guilt and doubt, yet it is essential.

And then comes the time—often dictated by the deadline—when there can be no more delay, when the writing must be done. Here are some ways to overcome inertia and start writing:

1. *Nulla dies sine linea.* "Never a day without a line." Make writing a habit. Sit in the same place with the same tools every day and write until it becomes uncomfortable *not* to write. Then writing will come as a matter of course.

2. *Make believe you are writing a letter to a friend.* Put "Dear _____" at the top of the page and start writing. Tom Wolfe did this on one of his first New Journalism pieces. He wrote the editor a letter saying why he couldn't write the piece he'd been assigned. The letter flowed along in such a wonderful, easy fashion that the editor took the salutation off and ran it. It established a new style for contemporary journalism.

3. *Switch your writing tools.* If you normally type, write by hand. If you write by hand, type. Switch from pen to pencil or pencil to pen. Switch from unlined paper to lined paper, or vice versa. Try larger paper or smaller, colored paper or white paper. Use a bound notebook or spiral notebook, a legal pad or a clipboard. Tools are a writer's toys, and effective, easy writing is the product of play.

4. *Talk about the piece of writing with another writer, and pay close attention to what you say.* You may be telling yourself how to write the piece. You may even want to make notes as you talk on the telephone or in person. Pay attention to words or combinations of words that may become a voice and spark a piece of writing.

5. *Write down the reasons you are not writing.* Often when you see the problem you will be able to avoid it. You may realize that your standards are too high, or that you're thinking excessively of how one person will respond to your piece, or that you're trying to include too much. Once you have defined the problem you may be able to dispose of it.

6. *Describe the process you went through when a piece of writing went well.* You may be able to read such an account in your journal. We need to reinforce the writing procedures that produce good writing. A description of what worked before may tell you that you need to delay at this moment, or it may reveal a trick that got you going another time. Keep a careful record of your work habits and the tricks of your trade, so that you have a positive resource to fall back on.

7. *Interview other writers to find out how they get started.* Try your classmates' tricks and see if they work for you.

8. *Switch the time of day.* Sometimes writing at night when you are tired lowers your critical sense in a positive way, and other times you can jump out of bed in the morning and get a start on the writing before your internal critic catches up with you.

9. *Call the draft an experiment or an exercise.* Good writing is always an experiment. Make a run at it. See if it will work. The poet Mekeel McBride is

always writing "exercises" in her journals. Since they are just exercises and not poems, she doesn't get uptight about them, but of course if an exercise turns into a poem she'll accept it.

10. *Dictate a draft.* Use a tape recorder, and then transcribe the draft from it. You may want to transcribe it carefully, or just catch the gist of what you had to say. No matter how experienced you are as a writer you are a million times more experienced as a speaker, and it's often easier to get started writing by talking than by simply writing.

11. *Quit.* Come back later and try again. You can't force writing. You have to keep making runs at it. Come back ten minutes later, or later that day, or the next day. Keep trying until the writing flows so fast you have to run along behind it trying to keep up.

12. *Read.* Some writers read over what they've written, and they may even edit it or recopy it as a way of sliding into the day's writing. I can't do that; I despair too much, and when I read my own writing I feel I have to start over again; it's worthless, hopeless. If you don't feel that way, however, it may be a good device to go over the previous day's work and then push on to the new writing, the way a house painter will paint back into the last brush stroke and then draw the new paint forward.

13. *Write directly to a specific reader.* The too-critical reader can keep you from writing, but you can also get writing by imagining an especially appreciative reader, or a reader who needs the information you have to convey. If you can feel that reader's hunger for what you have to say it will draw you into the text. Sometimes when I write I imagine the enjoyment I expect Don Graves, Chip Scanlan, or Nancie Atwell to feel at an unexpected turn of phrase, a new insight, or a different approach. I read their faces as I write the way you read a friend's face during a conversation.

14. *Take a walk, lift weights, jog, run, dance, swim.* Many writers have found that the best way to get started writing is by getting the blood coursing through the body and the brain. As they get the physical body tuned up the brain moves into high gear. Exercise is also the kind of private activity that allows the mind to free itself of stress and interruption and rehearse what may be written when the exercise is done. Running, walking, bicycling, or swimming are great ways to let the mind wander while the body is working.

15. *Change the place where you write.* I write in my office at home, but I also write on a lap desk in the living room or on the porch. I like to take the car and drive down by Great Bay, where I can look up from my lap desk and watch a heron stalk fish or a sea gull soar—the way I would like to write, without effort. Some writers cover their windows and write to a

wall. I like to write to a different scene. Right now, for example, I'm looking at the green ocean of Indiana farmland and a marvelously angry gray sky as I drive west and write by dictation. In the 1920s, writers thought the cafés of Paris were the best places to write. I don't think I could work on those silly little tables, but my ideal writing place would be in a booth in a busy lunchroom where nobody knows me. Yesterday morning I started writing in a Denny's in a Michigan city; it was a fine place to write. When my writing doesn't go well I move around. I imagine that it must be looking for me, and if it can't find me at home I'll go out to someplace where I may be more visible.

16. *Draw a picture, in your mind or on paper.* Take a photograph. Cut a picture from a magazine and put it on your bulletin board. When small children start writing they usually first draw a picture. They do on paper what writers usually do in their mind: They visualize the subject. Last summer I started my writing sessions by making a sketch of a rubber tree that stands on our porch. I wasn't writing about the rubber tree, but the activity of drawing seemed to help me get started and stimulated the flow of writing.

17. *Free write.* Write as hard and as fast and free as you can. See if language will lead you toward a meaning. As I have said before, free writing isn't very free because the draft starts to develop its own form and direction. But the act of writing freely is one of the techniques that can unleash your mind.

18. *Stop in the middle of a sentence.* This is a good trick when the writing is going well and you are interrupted or come to the end of the day's writing during a long project. Many well-known writers have done this, and I've found that it really helps me at times. If I can pick up the draft and finish an ordinary sentence, then I am immediately back into the writing. If I've stopped at the end of a sentence or a paragraph it's much harder to get going. And if I've stopped at the end of a chapter it may take days or weeks to get the next chapter started.

19. *Write the easy parts first.* If you're stuck on a section or a beginning, skip over it and write the parts of the draft that you are ready to write. Once you've gotten those easy, strong pieces of writing done then you'll be able to build a complete draft by connecting those parts. A variation on this is to write the end first, or to plunge in and grab the beast wherever you can get hold of it. Once you have a working draft, you can extend it backward or forward as it requires.

20. *Be silly.* You're not writing anyway, so you might as well make a fool of yourself. I've numbered the day's quota of pages and then filled them in.

One of my writer neighbors loves cigars, but he won't let himself have a cigar until he has finished his daily quota. Reward yourself with a cup of coffee, a dish of ice cream, or a handful of nuts. It is no accident that some writers are fat; they keep rewarding themselves with food. Do whatever you have to do to keep yourself writing. Jessamyn West writes in bed the first thing in the morning. If the doorbell rings she can't answer it; she isn't up and dressed. Use timers, count pages, count words (you may not be able to say the writing went well, but you'll be able to say "I did 512 words," or "I completed two pages"), play music, write standing up (Thomas Wolfe writes on top of an icebox, Ernest Hemingway put his typewriter on a bureau), start the day writing in the bathtub as Nabokov did. Nothing is silly if it gets you started writing.

21. *Start the writing day by reading writing that inspires you.* This is dangerous for me because I may get so interested in the reading I'll never write, or I'll pick up the voice of another writer. I can't, for example, read William Faulkner when I'm writing fiction: A poor, New Hampshire imitation of that famous Mississippian is not a good way to go. The other day, however, when I couldn't get started writing, I read a short story by Mary Gordon, one of my favorite authors. Reading a really good writer should make you pack up your pen and quit the field, but most of us find reading other writers inspiring. I put down Mary Gordon's short story and was inspired to write.

22. *Read what other writers have written about writing.* I may not write as well as they do, but we work at the same trade, and it helps me to sit around and chat with them. You may want to start a "commonplace book," an eighteenth-century form of self-education in which people made their personal collections of wise or witty sayings. I've collected what writers have said about writing in my own commonplace book, selections from which are now published in my book *Shoptalk* (Boynton/Cook/Heinemann, Portsmouth, New Hampshire, 1990). Some of my favorite quotes from that collection appear before each chapter in this book as well as in the text. I find it comforting to hear that the best writers have many of the same problems I do and browse through these quotes as a way of starting.

23. *Break down the writing task into reasonable goals.* A few years ago I watched on TV as the first woman to climb a spectacular rock face in California made it to the top. It had taken her days and, as soon as she got over the edge, a TV reporter stuck a microphone in her face and asked her what she'd thought of as she kept working her way up the cliff. She said she kept reminding herself that you eat an elephant one bite at a time. You also write a long piece of writing one page, or one paragraph, at a time. John

Steinbeck said, "When I face the desolate impossibility of writing 500 pages a sick sense of failure falls on me and I know I can never do it. Then I gradually write one page and then another. One day's work is all I can permit myself to contemplate." If you contemplate a book you'll never write it, but if you write just a page a day you'll have a 365-page draft at the end of a year. If you're stuck, you may be trying to eat an entire elephant at one gulp. It may be wiser to tell yourself that you'll get just the first page, or perhaps just the lead done that day. That may seem possible, and you'll start writing.

24. *Put someone else's name on it.* I've been hired as a ghostwriter to create texts for politicians or industrialists. I've had little trouble writing when someone else's name is on the work. Most of the time when I can't write I'm excessively self-conscious. Sometimes I've put a pseudonym on a piece of work and the writing has taken off.

25. *Delegate the writing to your subconscious.* Often I will tell my subconscious what I'm working on, and then I'll do something that doesn't take intense concentration and allows my subconscious mind to work. I walk around bookstores or a library, watch a dull baseball game or movie on TV, take a nap, go for a walk or a drive. Some people putter around the house or work in the garden. Whatever you do, you're allowing your mind to work on the problem. Every once in a while a thought, an approach, a lead, a phrase, a line, or a structure will float up to the conscious mind. If it looks workable, then go to your writing desk; if it doesn't, shove it back down under water and continue whatever you're doing until something new surfaces.

26. *Listen.* Alice Walker says, "If you're silent for a long time, people just arrive in your mind." As Americans we are afraid of silence, and I'm guilty, too. I tend to turn on the car radio if I'm moving the car twenty feet from the end of the driveway to into the garage. One of the best ways to get started writing is to do nothing. Waste time. Stare out the window. Try to let your mind go blank. This isn't easy, as those who have tried meditation know. But many times your mind, distracted by trivia, is too busy to write. Good writing comes out of silence, as Charles Simic says. "In the end, I'm always at the beginning. Silence—an endless mythical condition. I think of explorers setting out over an unknown ocean. . . . " Cultivate a quietness, resist the panic that the writing won't come, and allow yourself to sink back into the emptiness. If you don't fight the silence, but accept it, then usually, without being aware of it, the writing will start to come.

These are some ways to get started writing. You will come up with others if you make a list of techniques from other parts of your life that may apply here. A theater major may have all sorts of exercises and theater games that can spark writing. A scientist will be able to apply experimental techniques to writing. Art majors know how to attack a white canvas, and ski team members know how to shove off at the top of a steep slope. Keep a record of methods of starting writing that work for you.

▪ DRAFTING IN THE DAYBOOK ▪

The daybook is a secret place where I can write badly to write well, be silly, attempt crazy experiments, play with words and ideas. When this play is completed and I go to my writing desk the draft always goes more easily.

I also print out pre-drafts from my computer so that I carry them with me and, when I am waiting for someone at lunch or sitting in the car or watching the Boston Bruins, I can pick up the draft and fiddle around with it, noting what might be added, cut out, moved around. Again, this makes the next day's writing go easily.

▪ DRAFTING USING A COMPUTER ▪

The computer and the daybook overlap. I have a small notebook computer that sits by my chair in the living room. Often I use that computer while I am watching television or listening to music, to try new drafts or to keep a draft going. I have traveled to Greece, Scotland, twice to England, to each corner of the United States and over much of Canada with this notebook computer. It makes it possible to write a draft wherever I am—in a car or bus, on train or plane, on a ferry or a boat, in a hotel room or a stateroom.

The computer forgives. More than that, the computer doesn't give a damn if I write well or not. It doesn't care if I spell properly, have them double negatives, syntax up the mix, tipe stoopuityly sos i kanhrkdlee reda itt. You think I'm kidding? Seventy-five percent of my misspelled words cannot be recognized by my computer's spell check. I'm not proud of that but the computer allows me to achieve a draft.

The computer allows me to write fast, it allows me to write faster than my censor can read, and it allows me to write faster than my critical mind can think. I can draft what I do not yet know I have to say. I can draw in background material, move parts of the draft all over the book, write trial drafts, pre-drafts, sketches, experiments in language and meaning that are central to creativity.

I can write a draft on the left and another on the right of the screen. I can make a copy and tear it apart. I can use all sorts of typographical and other design changes to let me see how the text can be clarified. It is the basic drafting tool of writers today.

▪ DRAFTING FOR THE READER ▪

The draft is a conversation with the reader. As I write I hear the reader saying:

- "What do you mean?"
- "Where'd you get that fact?"
- "I'd like to know more about this."
- "Why should I keep reading?"
- "I'm going to sleep, wake me up."
- "Specific details please."
- "Define that word."
- "Clarify."
- "Document."
- "How does this affect me?"
- "Could you be a bit more interesting?"
- "Slow down, I'm confused."
- "Make me see."
- "Make me understand."

And on and on. I answer the reader's concerns the same way you listen to a friend when you are telling what happened Saturday night, reading his or her nods and frowns, smiles and gestures, grunts and laughs to see what they need to know. Never underestimate the hunger of the reader. People read, above all, for information and the business memo, the poem, the engineering report, the essay, the letter, the examination answer are all more effective if the writer anticipates the reader's hunger and satisfies it.

The form of that satisfaction depends on the purpose of the writing and the particular reader you are serving. Sometimes fast foods are just what the reader needs and lists, indented paragraphs, lines capitalized or underlined, tables of statistics are just right. Other times the reader wants to eat a leisurely meal, to taste and chew over what is served. Then the writer can proceed in a more discursive manner, documenting a point in a thoughtful manner, giving the reader adequate time to think over each piece of evidence and its relationship to other points in the draft.

The writer you enjoy reading is generally sneaky. Information may be delivered in large hunks of description, thought, evidence, or documentation, but it is often slid into a paragraph or a sentence so that the reader is not even aware of swallowing information.

Some of the tricks of the sneaky writer:

- The *verb*. "He *walked* into the room." Marched, strode, stumbled will deliver more information to the reader.
- The *noun*. "He carried a *weapon*." Rifle, slingshot, bow and arrow, hand grenade, broken beer bottle, hunting knife tell us more.

- The *clause*. "He carried a broken beer bottle, already caked with blood, in his right hand as if he were ready to use it."
- The immediate *definition*. "He carried a cross-bow, a medieval weapon that shot an arrow with terrifying force, when he came to the reading of the will."
- The immediate *documentation*. "He was a cross-bow marksman; each Sunday morning he shot at the cat, always clipping a few hairs from her tail, never drawing blood."
- The *specific*. "The cat hid in the back of the Mercedes sports car he drove with the top down every Sunday afternoon. When old cross-bow got to Hitchin's curve the cat leaped on his head and scratched at his eyes. As the car sailed off the cliff, the cat jumped free, shook himself, and strolled home without a backward glance."

The more you write and study the most effective writers in your class and the writers you read in magazines and books, the more ways you will find to sneak information into your writing, line by line.

■ HEARING THE DRAFT'S VOICE ■

I have drafted pages with the computer screen turned off. I look at the keys when I draft, or out the window at the squirrel circus that never ends. I *hear* the evolving text and the music of the draft often tells me how I feel about the subject: hate, nostalgia, sadness, rage, anger, detachment, concern. I draft with my ear to understand the meaning of what I am saying. I want to re-create the music that will support that meaning as well as reveal it.

I also write with my ear because I have had much more experience with oral language than with written language even if I am a writer. I may write a thousand words or more a day and read many times that but I speak 10,000 words a day or more and hear even more than that. I want the language experience of my ear involved in the making of the draft.

Good writing is not speech written down but it creates, in the reader's mind, the illusion of speech. The writing readers most enjoy reading has the sound of a good conversation, the one you wish you had created at the party.

■ REVISING WHILE DRAFTING ■

Draft implies revision: Each line, each word, each space between words is an experiment in meaning. As I draft I write the word I do not expect to write, keep it, qualify it, change it, revise it.

Often this revision is almost instantaneous. Brain delivers message and hand changes message. Words qualify what I have said before and predict what

I may say in the future. The draft is an evolution of that: What I write, then read, changes what I will say next. It is a dynamic process, never static, constantly undergoing change as vision and word try to come together.

These days I often revise and even edit as I write, stopping after four paragraphs or more, to revise before going on. Layering combines immediate revision technique with drafting.

▪ QUESTIONS ABOUT DRAFTING ▪

What if the writing doesn't come? What if there's absolutely nothing in my head when I start to write?

I always feel that way—and many times it's true, there's nothing but space between my ears. I don't try to force the writing. I back up, stop, do something else, and try again, perhaps in ten minutes, perhaps the next morning. I'm a morning writer, and I find that if the writing doesn't come one time it will come the next.

But what if it doesn't?

Then I haven't planned well enough. I go back and wallow in the information, mess around with focusing activities, or do some ordering or outlining. If the writing isn't ready to come then I haven't prepared it well.

But won't I get writer's block?

The columnist Roger Simon says, "There is no such thing as writer's block. My father drove a truck for 40 years. And never once did he wake up in the morning and say: 'I have truck driver's block today. I am not going to work.'"

Writer's block is a convenient term to use when you haven't gotten yourself into the chair and waited for writing. John McPhee used to tie himself into the chair the first thing in the morning with his bathrobe cord. Getting into the chair and waiting for writing is the hardest thing to do.

Stick some mottoes or quotations from writers above your writing desk. A few of mine:

> I have to write every day because, the way I work, the writing generates the writing.
>
> E. L. Doctorow

> Two simple rules. (A) You don't have to write. (B) You can't do anything else. The rest comes of itself.
>
> Raymond Chandler

> If you keep working, inspiration comes.
>
> Alexander Calder

Most cases of writer's block are the direct result of inappropriate standards. The writer is trying to write better than is possible for this writer to write at this particular time. Just write; worry about how well it works after you have finished the draft.

My writing changes. I mean, I have all these outlines and stuff, and then it takes off and goes on its own.

Good. Writing is thinking, not just reporting what you've thought. Writing is a dynamic, forward-moving force, and when the writing is going well most writers feel they are following the writing.

But what if it's really out of control, I mean, doesn't make any sense at all?

You have two choices: Go back and start over again, or edit with a firm hand and get it under control.

My piece doesn't so much get out of control as run off in a dozen directions, like when I take my beagle for a walk and she follows her nose, chases cats, investigates garbage pails, chases shadows, keeps circling around. She isn't out of control—we get home—but she walks ten miles more than I do.

I used to write like a beagle myself. Then the late Hannah Lees suggested I write each paragraph on a separate page. For years I did just that, using half pieces of paper—eight by five inch. When I got the piece done I spread all the paragraphs on a large table or on the floor and rearranged them into an efficient pattern. Some of the trails I had followed belonged in the piece; others didn't, and they had to go.

But sometimes I have to write right on deadline.

So do I, and for years, I was a newspaper rewrite person spending five nights a week writing fifteen to fifty stories a night, on deadline. When you write under that pressure you have to follow the patterns of writing laid down in long-term memory. The experience of writing when you had time—the lessons you learned—is on call when you have to write in a hurry.

I know the subject so well, I can't tell what someone else needs to know. How do I know what the reader knows?

Role-play that reader, making yourself become a particular person you know and respect but who doesn't know the subjects; and read as that person would read. Show the draft to test readers, asking them to tell you places where they would like more information.

Can I give the reader too much stuff?

Sure, but its unlikely. Reading a flood of students papers every year, I see 99 percent that are underdeveloped. The writer knows the subject so well that he or she underestimates the reader's need for more information.

• DRAFTING ACTIVITIES •

1. Try a different tool. If you usually write by hand, write directly on the typewriter, or dictate into a tape recorder and then copy down what you've said. Different ways of writing can help capture a working draft.

2. Write a discovery draft, writing as fast as you can to find out what you're going to say.

3. Tell the story to someone else to hear what you say when you have an audience; read the person's reactions by paying attention to body language, interest, and so forth. Don't do this if you think you'll lose the piece. Some writers find this very helpful, but others find that if they have told the piece to someone they won't write it.

4. Write single paragraphs, each describing a place, defining an idea, introducing a person, presenting an argument, revealing a process; then write a second paragraph for each in which you show instead of tell.

5. List the questions the reader will ask about your piece of writing and put them in the order the reader will use to ask them.

6. Read aloud something you've written before and make notes about what reading aloud reveals to you. One significant thing it may reveal is that it's hard to make notes—you hear the flow of the piece of writing and want to be carried on by that flow; in other words, reading aloud is the best way of testing to see if a piece of writing flows.

7. Take a significant piece of information from the writing you're working on and list all of the ways it can be documented: quotation, statistic, description, anecdote, and so on.

8. Go back and use one of the techniques of collecting, focusing, or ordering to see if it will help you get a draft flowing.

9. Imagine a person you feel comfortable with and write the draft to that person, speaking as you would in a conversation. You may even want to start the draft as a letter to that person.

10. Imagine that you are a ghostwriter writing the piece for someone else. Put your "client's" name at the top to see how the piece would go if you were writing it in that voice. Make believe you're James Baldwin, Joan Didion, George Orwell. Try on another style as a way of seeing how that style works and as a way of getting into a text that you can make your own.

11. Write the draft backward, writing the end first, the next to the end next, until you've worked your way back to the beginning.

12. Write the section that is easiest for you to write, then the next easiest, and so forth until you get all of the parts written and can fit it together into a working draft.

13. Give yourself a time quota (an hour, an hour and a half, two hours) or page quota (one page, or three, or five), and then write to fill the time or the number of pages. Don't worry for the moment about the whole piece and its final quality; just deal with the chunk of writing time or the number of pages you have assigned yourself.

14. Revise another student's draft, developing it for a different audience or in a different way.

15. Take a piece of writing you like and layer it, writing over it as you change it, making it your own. You will better understand how it was made and learn some of your own writing strengths.

16. Take a piece of your writing or someone else's and do what I have done, describing how each paragraph grows from the last ones as I did on pages 119–25.

17. Do what Sandra Cisneros suggests: "Imagine yourself at your kitchen table, in your pajamas. Imagine one person you'd allow to see you that way, and write in the voice you'd use to that friend."

18. Write each section or paragraph of your article on a separate piece of paper—or cut up a printout—then assemble the units into a draft that carries the reader toward meaning.

19. If you know another language draft the beginning in that language and then translate it to discover new ways of writing that reveal.

20. Write a new draft as fast as you can WITHOUT LOOKING AT THE PREVIOUS DRAFT to see what you remember, what may be left out, what new material you discover.

CHAPTER 6
CLARIFY

What makes me happy is rewriting. In the first draft you get your ideas and your theme clear, if you are using some kind of metaphor you get that established, and certainly you have to know where you're coming out. But the next time through it's like cleaning house, getting rid of all the junk, getting things in the right order, tightening things up. I like the process of making writing neat.

ELLEN GOODMAN

Now that you have written a draft, you become a reader—a very special kind of reader because you can change the printed text. It is not final; it can be fine tuned. But as you read remember to answer these key questions in this order:

1. WHAT WORKS?
2. WHAT NEEDS WORK?

▪ HOW TO READ THE FIRST DRAFT ▪

To revise effectively, you need to find the potential in the discovery draft. The first draft is an act of thinking, more than communication; the writer is exploring the subject—and the writer's opinion of the subject. With your first draft, follow these steps:

- Read the draft aloud and mark where the voice is strong and clear, where the music of your language informs and supports the meaning of the draft.
- Scan the draft and note the words, sentences, paragraphs, details, connections, opinions that surprised you.
- Underline the most specific pieces of information in the draft.
- Check the most convincing pieces of evidence that document and support the meaning of the draft.
- Note the places where the draft flows most strongly toward meaning.
- Star the words, lines, and passages that secretly please you.

You have not yet evaluated the draft. It may be worth an A or an F, good writing or bad, publishable or not; none of that matters at the moment. What matters is that you have found something worth saying and a way of saying it.

▪ REVISING TO DEVELOP THE DRAFT'S POTENTIAL ▪

Now that you have discovered the possibilities in the draft, you revise to develop them. Revision is not so much a matter of turning failure into success or correcting error—although both those things will happen—as it is a matter of making the strengths of a draft stronger.

If the focus of the draft is on target, sharpen the focus; if the documentation seems to carry the piece, make the documentation as powerful as possible; if the logic and structure of the draft are sturdy, reinforce them; if you have reached an audience, be sure you convince them; if the language is good, make it better; if the meaning and its context is important, dramatize that importance.

If you work first on what is good in your draft—or potentially good—you will find that many of the problems in the draft disappear. Meaning, documentation, structure, voice correct themselves and each other as you work to improve the positive.

The process of developing the potential may, of course, lead to a second draft, a third, more. None of the drafts is a failure; each is a stage necessary to your final draft. Sometimes there will be many drafts, sometimes revision of the first draft is enough. There is nothing virtuous about writing many drafts. If you need to write another draft, do it; if not, don't.

The Revision Checklist

Revision is not editing. They are two separate activities and keeping them apart makes the task of preparing a text for publication in a course or in the world much easier.

The following diagram shows how the emphasis changes from revision to editing:

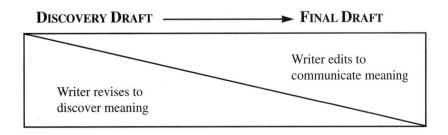

DISCOVERY DRAFT ⟶ **FINAL DRAFT**

Writer edits to communicate meaning

Writer revises to discover meaning

Revision is re-seeing the entire draft so that the writer can deal with the large issues that must be resolved before the writer deals with line-by-line, word-by-word issues involved in editing.

In reading for revision, it is important to step back and scan the draft so that you can see it is a whole, noticing such things as the relationship between the section of the draft that you cannot see when you are concentrating on the relationship between a particular verb and an individual noun.

Make your own revision checklist. Here's mine. The list is long but many of the questions can be answered in an instant. Because you have focused, explored, planned, and drafted, you have solved most of these problems in advance. This is a checklist to see if there are problems that must be solved before the editing that produces the final draft:

Checklist for Revising

Subject
- Do I have something I need to say?
- Are there readers who need to hear what I have to say?

Focus
- Does the draft have a clear, dominant point?
- Are there clear, appropriate limits to the draft that include what needs to be included, exclude what is unnecessary?
- Do writer and reader stand at the appropriate distance from the material?

Authority
- Are the writer's credentials to write this draft established and clear?

Context
- Is the context of the draft clear, the world in which the story exists?

Voice
- Does the draft have an individual voice?
- Is the voice appropriate to the subject?
- Does the voice support and extend the meaning of the draft?

Reader
- Can you identify a reader who will need to read the draft?
- Can you see a reader who will want to read the draft?
- Are the reader's questions answered where they will be asked?

Genre
- Is the form of the story the best one to carry the meaning to the reader?
- Does the draft fulfill the reader's expectations of that form?

Structure
- Will the lead attract and hold a reader?
- Does the ending resolve the issues raised in the draft?
- Is there a clear trail through the draft?
- Does each point lead to the next point?
- Does each section support and advance the meaning?

Information
- Is the reader's hunger for specific information satisfied?

Documentation
- Does the reader have the evidence to believe each point in the draft?

Pace
- Is the reader carried forward toward the meaning by the flow of the draft?
- Are there points where the draft needs to be speeded up to keep the reader from abandoning the draft?
- Are there points where the draft needs to be slowed down so the reader has time to comprehend the meaning of what is being written?

Proportion
- Are the sections in appropriate proportion to one another to advance and support the meaning of the draft?

Quantity
- Where does the draft need to be developed?
- Where does it need to be cut?

Move through the checklist quickly, scanning the draft and then revising part or all of the draft as necessary until you have done all you can do—or until the deadline is upon you. Then begin editing the final draft.

▪ EDITING TO CLARIFY THE DRAFT'S MEANING ▪

I have worked for the past few years with editors on some of the best newspapers in the country, and have found these editors make the same mistake most teachers—and their students—make. The mistake is to plunge in and start editing language first, working from the written line back to form and then to meaning. It simply doesn't work.

Proofreading

Proofreading is what most people think of when editing is mentioned, but it is only a small part of editing. It is important you correct spelling, to check facts and names and quotations, to conform to certain stylistic standards of mechanics and usage, to clean up typographical errors, but editing is that and much more.

Editing is the honing of thinking, making meaning rational and clear, accurate and graceful. Editing is the final clarification of meaning. You choose one word and reject another word in relation to meaning. If the meaning isn't clear the choice will be arbitrary and often wrong. There are no rules for word choice unrelated to meaning. And when you choose to write a short sentence or a short paragraph it is usually for emphasis, and unless you know what you want to emphasize you won't know whether to make the sentence or the paragraph long or short.

When you edit there are repetitions from the revision checklist, but your reading is different. When you revise, you read to see what needs to be done in the next draft; when you edit you are the reader's advocate, preparing the final draft for your readers.

Editing Priorities

Effective editing is usually the result of three separate and distinct readings, each with its own pace, strategies, and techniques.

The highly skillful editor or writer may be able to perform all three readings simultaneously, moving from the large global questions of meaning to structural questions of order, and to line-by-line questions of voice. But those interrelated skills are best developed by separating the reading—reading first for meaning, next for order, and third for voice.

And of course in each case the writer has to keep an eye open for the audience, standing back and making sure that what is being said and resaid on the page is clear to the reader.

This seems to be a slow process, but *the first reading* is usually a very fast reading—a quick flyover of the territory to make sure that there is a single dominant meaning and an abundant inventory of information to support that meaning.

If there is no subject, no dominant meaning, no inventory of information, it is a waste of time to do more revising and editing. Stop immediately. Find a subject. Find its meaning. Find the facts to support that meaning.

The second reading is for form and structure. It is a bit slower, but not much. The piece is still read in chunks to see if the sections support the main point and appear when the reader needs them.

If there is no form to the writing, no order within that form that leads the reader to meaning, read no further. It will be a waste of time. Stop. Choose a form and establish an order within that form.

At the end there is *the third reading,* a slow, careful, line-by-line editing of the draft to be sure that it is ready for a final proofreading. Here the writer cuts, adds, and reorders, paragraph by paragraph, sentence by sentence, word by word.

The process of three readings may sound tedious, but it shouldn't be. In each case you'll have the excitement of discovery, of finding a meaning that you did not expect to find and having a change to make it become clear. Writing gives you the satisfaction of craft, the feeling you have when you lean your weight into the corner and make your bicycle swing gracefully where you want it to go. Writing is similar to hitting a tennis ball, baking bread, building a sturdy shelf, sewing a dress, planting a garden. It is a process of making, and it is fun to make something well, to handcraft a piece of prose that will carry meaning and feeling to another person.

Editing Marks

Most computer editing is invisible, but those who work with typewriter and pen or pencil will find it helpful to mark up the copy according to the traditions of the editor's trade:

During the first two readings I sit away from the desk, if I

am not using a computer, in an easy chair and use a

clipboard or a bean bag lap desk. I read the draft quickly, as

a reader will, and do not mark anything within the text. I

do not correct spelling or typos, change words, revise, or

edit. Instead, I make marks in the left margin:

✓   A check for something that works,

✱   a star for something that works well,

C   a C for something that needs cutting,

⌐→   an arrow that suggests movement,

↗↘   a two-headed arrow to indicate the need for expansion,

→◄— two arrows pointing at each other to show what needs to be

tightened,

?   and a question mark for further consideration.

These marks allow me to move through the text quickly.

On the following page are some of the most helpful editing marks for the third, careful line-by-line reading. If you are reading "hard copy" (manuscript pages, not a computer screen) you will find these marks helpful in editing your drafts or the drafts of a classmate in a peer-editing session:

paragraph	The craft of editing depends on reading aloud.
capital	the craft of editing depends on reading aloud.
lowercase	The craft of editing depends on reading aloud.
close	The craft of edit ing depends on reading aloud.
separate	The craft of editing depends on reading aloud.
transpose	The editing craft of depends on reading aloud.
punctuate	The craft of editing depends on reading aloud
insert	The craft of editing depends on reading aloud.
take out	The craft of editing depends on reading aloud.
cut	~~The craft of~~ editing depends on reading aloud.
restore	~~The craft of~~ editing depends on reading aloud.
move	Insert The craft of editing depends on reading aloud.

Large inserts should be numbered or lettered and an arrow should be marked in the margin of the text where it is to be placed.

→ (move Insert A here)

Editing Checklists

The following checklists are built on the editing system that uses three readings—one for the topic, one for development of the topic, and one for language that communicates the topic. Of course the process of revising and editing will not be so neatly contained. Change of focus leads to change of language and change of language can change the topic, but the master list is a way of proceeding logically and efficiently through a serious of confusing writing problems.

Each writer has his or her own writing strengths and weaknesses. Eventually you should adapt my checklist to your own style, problems, and solutions.

Many times writers edit on deadline, without time to do a careful job of revising and editing. Remember that you have to deal with the first item before going on to the second and the second before the third. Here is a checklist for that situation:

The Quick Checklist

- State the single, most important message you have for the reader in one sentence.
- List the points that support that message in the order the reader needs to receive them.
- Read the draft aloud to be sure the text is accurate, fair, and that the music of the language supports the message you are sending to the reader.

When you learn that the first draft is not at the end of the writing process, you will plan so that there is time—at least as much as comes before the first draft—for reading, revising, and editing. The checklist is designed to help in the three readings for subject, structure, and language. But don't be surprised when you have to move back and forth through the checklist as solutions breed problems and new problems demand new solutions.

The list is long but remember that many of your answers will come rapidly, in a second or less. You are scanning the text to catch the problems that have survived the writing process and must be solved before the draft is final, ready to face a reader.

Checklist for Editing

- *State the single, most important message you have for the reader in one sentence.*
  - Does the draft deliver on the promise of the title and lead?
  - Does your message have significant meaning you can make clear to the reader?
  - Is the message important, worth the reader's time?
  - Does your message contain the tension that will provide the energy to drive the reader forward?
  - Is your message focused? Do you have a clear point of view toward the subject?

- Is the message placed in a significant context? Will that context be clear to the reader?
- Does the message have limitations that help you control and deliver the information?
- Do you have an abundance of information upon which to build the draft? Can you answer the questions the reader will certainly ask?
- Is that information accurate and fair?

- *List the points that support that message in the order the reader needs to receive them.*

  - Is the form, the genre, of the draft appropriate to deliver the message to the reader? Will it contain and support the meaning of the draft?
  - Does the structure within the draft support and advance the principal message?
  - Does the order in the piece make the reader move forward, anticipating and answering the reader's questions?
  - Is the structure logical? Does each point lead to the next in a sensible sequence? Is there a narrative thread that carries the reader forward? Will the sequence or narrative stand up to a doubting reader?
  - Is the draft too long? Too short?
  - Are the proportions within the draft appropriate to the information they deliver? Are there sections that are too long? Too short?
  - Is the draft effectively paced? Does the draft move fast enough to keep the reader reading, slow enough to allow the reader to absorb what is being read?
  - Does the draft go off on tangents that take the reader away from the principal message of the text? Are there good pieces of writing that do not support this message but may be developed on their own later?
  - Is each point supported with evidence that will convince the reader?
  - Is the draft at a distance that will involve the reader but also allow the reader to consider the significance of the message?

- *Read the draft aloud to be sure it is accurate, fair, and that the music of the language supports the message you are sending to the reader.*

  - Does the title catch the reader's attention and does it make a promise to the reader that can be delivered by the draft?
  - Does the opening accomplish the same thing?
  - Is each piece of information accurate and fair and in context?
  - Does the reader need more information? Less? Can anything be cut? Must anything be added?
  - Does the reader finish each sentence with more information than when the reader started?

- Can the draft be heard by the reader? Does the music of the draft support and advance the meaning of the message?
- Does the draft reveal rather than tell whenever possible? Does the draft call attention to the message rather than the reader?
- Does each paragraph and each sentence have the appropriate information emphasized?
- Does the sentence length vary in relation to the meaning being communicated with shorter sentences at the most important points?
- Does the draft depend, at important points, on the subject–verb–object sentence?
- Is the draft written in the active voice whenever possible?
- Is each word the right word?
- Has all sexist and racist language been eliminated?
- Has private language—jargon—been replaced with public language the reader can understand?
- Has worn-out language—clichés and stereotypes—been replaced with language that carries specific meaning to the reader?
- Is the draft primarily constructed with verbs and nouns rather than adverbs and adjectives?
- Has the verb "to be" in all its forms been eliminated whenever possible? And excess "woulds," "thats," and "ings"?
- Is the simplest tense possible used?
- Are the tenses consistent?
- Are any words misspelled?
- Are the traditions of language and mechanics followed except when they are ungraceful or change the meaning of the draft?
- Is the draft attractively presented so that nothing gets between the reader and the message?
- Does the closing give the reader a feeling of closure and completeness yet stimulate the reader to continue to think about the message that has been delivered?

Develop your own list, build on your own strengths and weaknesses in writing. And do not forget that this final stage of writing is still a matter of discovery of meaning; as you edit you will learn more about your topic and will make what you have to say come clear to the reader—so clear and easy to read the reader may believe the writing was spontaneous.

▪ CLARIFYING IN THE DAYBOOK ▪

The daybook becomes, in this last stage of the writing process, a lab book in which I make notes on references and facts I have to check in the library or by phone call. I also note problems I have in writing that should go on my checklist.

The most important thing I do in the daybook at this stage is to make notes on what I might write next. As this draft is finished, I want to begin another writing project immediately.

▪ CLARIFYING USING A COMPUTER ▪

The computer is of enormous help in editing, making it possible to read the draft and fix spelling, punctuation, diction, usage as you read.

Some software programs check the spelling in a document but will pass any correctly spelled word. If I mistype "top" for "to" the program does not recognize that as the wrong word. It will say OK to any real word. Other programs identify problems in mechanics and usage but be careful with those as well. No software program can institutionalize George Orwell's wise advice in "Politics and the English Language":

   (i) Never use a metaphor, simile or other figure of speech which you are used to seeing in print.
   (ii) Never use a long word where a short one will do.
  (iii) If it is possible to cut a word out, always cut it out.
  (iv) Never use the passive where you can use the active.
   (v) Never use a foreign phrase, a scientific word or jargon word if you can think of an everyday English equivalent.
  (vi) Break any of these rules sooner than say anything barbarous.

Pay special attention to that last rule.

▪ LISTENING TO TEST READERS ▪

With care. We all need good test readers but they are rare. The writer has to search for friends, coworkers, classmates, teachers, editors who can test what you have written. Good test readers usually share similar qualities:

- *They write themselves.* They know the territory emotionally and intellectually and can appreciate how the writer is thinking and feeling.
- *They listen to what the draft is saying without preconception of what the writer should say and how the writer should say it.* I once had a well-known poet read my short poems and tell me that since I was a big guy I should write big poems. He didn't seem to understand that the poet in me is a short, secretive *little* guy. The criticism wasn't helpful. The effective test reader is a colleague who helps you, the writer, see what is evolving, which is unexpected and worth keeping. This reader delights in surprises, in variation, in diversity, and helps evaluate the text on its own terms.

whereas the style of a freshman economics text might be central in a book review for teachers.

Use quotations to document each point. The reader wants evidence to support what the reviewer says.

Compare. In the context of other books that have been published on the same subject, evaluate the strong and weak points of the book you're reporting on. Writers do not publish in isolation. Writers build on the writers that have gone before; readers build on what they have read before. The review places the book within the tradition, showing how they follow and depart from the tradition, telling what reconfirms the tradition and what takes it a step forward. This is just as true for the horror novel as it is for a book with a new theory of corporate management or philosophical inquiry.

Include biographical information. Only if it will help the reader to understand or question the basis of the writer's authority, then include biographical information.

The Reflective Essay

The **reflective essay** is a more sophisticated form of analysis. It often begins with a personal experience—the death of a grandmother, the coach's instructions to cheat to win a game, the decision to get or not get an abortion—and finds meaning in it.

It is a common misconception that analysis is a cold, detached, scientific process in which writers analyze the thoughts, experiences, writing of others. And, of course, it often is; but in the reflective essay, writers analyze their own thoughts, feelings, reactions. A classic case of such an essay is George Orwell's short story "A Hanging" in which the real subject is Orwell's reflection upon his reaction to the event.

The personal experience is analyzed in much the same way as the academic paper but is written about in a much more reflective manner as the writer focuses on a personal experience and finds meaning in it. The finding of meaning or significance is important. People who tell stories often just ramble on. The writer of the effective essay reflects, ruminates, considers, reconsiders, and takes the reader along on the adventure of thought.

That meaning may be thought out in considerable detail before the first draft is written. This is likely to happen when the writer attempts to explore a traumatic subject, such as the death of a loved one, because that topic has been rehearsed: thought over and over in the writer's mind.

The meaning, however, may be entirely discovered in the writing. The writer may be obsessed with a subject and have no understanding of it until the shape of the draft, what is in the act of being said and how it is in the act of being said, reveals the meaning to the reader. This often happens to me. I plunge hoping that meaning lies on the blank page—or the blank screen—and it usually is, revealed in the words I do not expect to write. Most times meanings come in a combination of pre-thinking and drafting. I have a hint, a clue, a sense of what I *may* discover and then the writing defines and redefines, qualifies and clarifies that idea, gives it fullness and meaning.

In writing the reflective essay, you discover and develop the skills of critical thinking. You move in close and then stand back. There is immediacy and detachment, close examination and the placing of events in perspective, there is compassion and judgment, feeling and thought.

An effective reflective essay is often personal but it is not private. The reflective essay allows the reader to discover the subject—and the meaning of that subject—with the writer. The reader is invited to think along with the writer and to think against the writer, discovering in the act of reading the reader's own meaning in the essay.

Tips on Writing the Reflective Essay

Be personal. The more personal you are the more universal your readership. You should speak to the human condition in specific terms. Your strength is your difference, your own peculiar vision of the world.

Allow your mind to run free. Write rapidly so that you will discover what you didn't know you remembered, what you didn't know you thought and felt, what patterns and connections lay hidden in the experience.

Be critical. The function of writing the personal or reflective essay is to find meaning in experience, not just to record experience. Be skeptical and critical, challenge your own prejudices, beliefs, your own knowing.

Put your vision in context. Describe your vision of the world then place it in a context: historical, scientific, sociological, psychological, political. The personal experience should connect with a larger meaning.

Take the reader along. Invite the reader to accompany you as you reflect upon experience, allow the experience and the meaning that arises from it to unfold.

▪ WRITING TO INFORM ▪

One of the reasons to write is to report, to make others understand our knowing and our living, to explain. As the old hunter came back to the cave and described the mastodon, where it could be found, how it could be trapped, so we as citizens and scholars report back to the community, so that what we each learn is shared with others, and the community knowing exceeds the knowledge of each individual.

To inform we have to attract listeners by quickly showing them how what we have to say affects them. We have to make a connection with readers so that they have a personal stake in hearing what we have to say.

This is a tricky business because if we are too sure of ourselves, too full of our own knowing, we will offend and put off potential listeners. We will call attention to ourselves, not to what we have to say. On the other hand, if we are too modest, too shy, too unsure of what we have to say, no one will pay attention.

The best ways to steer a middle course is not to say too much about ourselves and not to say too much directly to the reader, telling the reader how valuable what the reader is to hear may be for him or her. Rather, deliver the message, focus on the material itself, allowing its importance to grow in the reader's mind as he or she is informed by the facts.

Humans enjoy learning, and perhaps as much enjoy being an authority and informing others. You will be well-read if you give the reader information the reader can put to use and can share with others.

Tips on Writing to Inform

Write with information. Give specific, revealing details, concrete facts, and accurate information. Build the piece of writing from information not language. Be direct, informative.

Anticipate your reader's questions. Role-play your reader and imagine what you would need and want to know, and when you would want to know it. Good writing is a conversation with the reader in which the writer hears the reader's unspoken questions: "How come?"; "What do you mean?"; "So what?"

Answer your reader's questions. In writing the reader has no stupid questions. The reader must be accepted where the reader is. It is the task of the informing writer to serve the reader who does not know.

Connect the information with the readers' experience. Give readers information in a form and context they can use in their thinking, in their lives, in their work.

Write in an inviting voice. Do not preach, condescend, patronize, talk up or down to the reader. Just share your delight in the information with the reader in a voice that focuses on the information to be shared.

The Research Paper

One common way of informing is to write a **research paper**. In writing, revising, and editing the research paper, you must conform to the style in which research is reported in each discipline. Each scholarly discipline has its own form for the research paper. Not only are there significant differences in the way the physicists, literary scholars, sociologists, historians, botanists report their findings, a single discipline such as psychology may have a differing within-field style for clinical psychologists, social psychologists, laboratory psychologists, each conforming to a different tradition. Discover the traditions and forms of the research paper appropriate to the discipline in which you write a research paper.

There are, however, important similarities in all research papers.

The Research Question

Good research is usually the product of a well-focused question. The experienced researcher spends time narrowing that question until it is one that can be answered within the limited time of a course or a grant, and with the resources available to the researcher. Research is a discipline of accumulation, with each researcher adding to the increasing knowledge within a field of study.

Research Note Taking

The researcher must have a consistent system of note taking appropriate to the discipline. Note cards of all sizes are still popular because each card can be ordered and reordered during research as the scholar explores the subject.

The biggest problem for the inexperienced researcher is knowing and recognizing the difference between direct quotation and paraphrase. A direct quote is precisely what is said or written. It is enclosed in "quotation marks." Paraphrase is the technique of putting what you have read or heard into your own words and it must never be put in quotation marks.

As a card is reordered, the information on the source of the information travels with the note. Write down *ALL* the details on where you found the information, for example, the title of the book, the author's name, the person quoted, the publisher of the book and the city where it was published, the edition or printing, the year of publication, the library where the material is stored, the chapter, page, paragraph, and line so that you can check the source and so that other scholars can go to the source of your information.

Plagiarism

If you use another writer's words as your own, you have committed a major— perhaps *the* major—intellectual crime. I have been plagiarized, and I know what it feels like. A high school student won a national writing contest with a short story of mine until someone recognized it; a nun who ran workshops for writing teachers used almost 100 pages of one of my books, distributing it as her own text, until another nun read it and identified it as mine. In both cases, the plagiarists had not changed a word. I felt as though they had broken into my mind and stolen my ideas and my language.

Plagiarism is a felony. Where I taught, students who plagiarized were given an F and made to take the course over. *I* thought they should be driven from the campus and banned from ever returning; or hung by their writing hand from the university flagpole for a month; or put in stocks in front of a dining hall so students could pelt them with old salad parts; or used as human football tackling dummies; or charged with theft in a court of law, as they would be if they stole the computer or typewriter on which they had plagiarized.

The responsible writer—student or professional—gives credit for the specific words, information, and ideas that belong to someone else.

The Form of the Research Paper

As I said at the beginning of this section, you must conform to the style required by your discipline. This is not a time for creativity. The form is designed to serve readers who want to find the information they need in the form and place they expect it.

Footnotes

The research paper serves other researchers and so you provide the source of specific information *at the time you use that information* through a footnote system that tells the reader where you discovered the fact or quote you are using at the moment the reader reads it. This is easy if your notes are in order.

Bibliography

At the end of research paper, you should provide other scholars with a list of your sources according to the style of the field in which you are working. Your note cards, if properly kept, make this a simple task.

Follow the golden rule: Serve your reader as you would want to be served yourself.

Tips on Writing the Research Paper

Attribute. ATTRIBUTE. **ATTRIBUTE.** The reader of a research paper not only wants to know the evidence you have to back up each point but also wants to know where it came from. You should have a system of footnotes and bibliography that the reader can use to research the same area.

Define your terms. Each discipline or profession has its own language or jargon that others may not understand. It is important to define any term that the reader may not understand, that others in a different branch of the same discipline may not understand, or that has a different meaning in normal, nonprofessional speech.

Use graphics. Make charts, maps, illustrations that will clarify your research. Use typographical designs and type that emphasize what you have to say. If you have a list, you may want to use a list as I have here rather than have it run along in normal sentences.

Explain your methods. Other researchers will want to know the procedures you followed to arrive at your results. This may involve a review of the literature or that review may be a separate section of the paper in which you reveal what you read and comment on how helpful particular articles or books were.

There are many forms we use to inform: speeches and presentations, letters and brochures, advertisements and book reports. Each form has a similar purpose: to teach the reader the subject.

▪ WRITING TO PERSUADE ▪

One of the principal reasons we write is to persuade. In the academic world this form of writing is often called argument but most students hear that title and envision a fight. I use the term *persuasion,* which more accurately describes the form—and voice—of appropriate intellectual discourse in which writers attempt to persuade readers to reconsider their views on a topic through a process of reason.

In fact, I believe, academic argument is a term and a process leftover from the days when the academic world was exclusively male. The training I received from my male professors—and all my professors were men—was similar to the training I received on the football field and in the paratroops. Truth was found by two men taking completely opposite sides and trying to destroy the other. It must be a direct descendant from the tournament practice of two knights trying to knock each other off their horses.

When I taught a course in argument, I found the male students comfortable with this term to describe a form of writing that is designed to cause the reader to rethink a position. They had been socialized on the playground or hockey rink to appear as if they enjoyed battle: hurt and do not reveal your own hurt.

But the majority of the class were women, most of whom were far brighter than the male students and the male who taught the class. And the women hated argument. I think we need far more development of forms of persuasion, which are not built on the concept of the knights with lances hurtling toward each other on horseback. I reject the term *argument* and use *persuasion* to describe the form of writing in which the writer attempts to make readers reconsider their views on a topic.

Persuasion is the basic form of intellectual discourse; it is the way that new ideas are introduced, that old ideas are discarded, and how old ideas are adapted to new trends of thought.

Tips on Writing Persuasion

State your position. This is no place for suspense. Make it clear what you intend to advocate. Define and establish your own issues and the context in which they are to be discussed.

Establish your credentials. Let the reader know up front what experience you have had, what research you have done; that should convince the reader to listen to your position.

Anticipate your reader's points. You should be able to empathize with your opponent, read that person's mind by imagining you are taking the other side, then make the best persuasive points you can.

Disarm your opponent. Know that you know your opponent's views, you can counter them right away, taking them away, and presenting your own.

Appeal to reason. Readers are rarely persuaded—at least in the intellectual world—by emotion. Appeal to reason; base your position on documented evidence presented in a logical order.

The Job Application

There are many other forms of persuasion. A **letter applying for a job** tries to persuade someone that you should be given a job. Again you should role-play that person so that you will know what appeals to him or her, what questions will be asked, what information will be required, what tone of voice will persuade.

Tips on Writing a Job Application Letter

Research the application process. Talk to your college placement office for counsel in writing job-seeking letters. Study books and articles that describe the strategies and techniques of successful job-seekers.

Research the company. Look up the company in the business reference sources in the library, read the company's annual report and brochures, interview people who work and have worked there, who supply the company and are supplied by the company. Be sure you know what they do: provide advertising services or manufacture ball bearings—and how they do it: specialize in mail-order advertising or sell ball bearings in the international market.

Say specifically what skills you offer a potential employer. "I'm willing to do anything" doesn't entice an employer but "I learned to get along with a great variety of people working as a waiter, then as head waiter, at a resort that attracted many tourists from overseas" or "I tested my courses in accounting against my experience in summer jobs, in serving as treasurer of the student union, and in spending a semester internship with the U.S. Internal Revenue Service."

Be specific about your goals. Tell the employer what you hope to learn from the job, what additional skills you hope to develop so that you may better serve your employer.

Anticipate and answer the employer's questions. Remember that the reader is looking for someone who fills his or her needs. Read the advertisement or announcement carefully and respond to the specifics of the job.

Sound professional. Write in a professional manner that demonstrates that you are someone who will do a good job and represent the company well.

You will discover that in using your experience with the writing process that you know how to define the writing job to be done and adapt or design a form of writing that will communicate your meaning to your reader with graceful efficiency.

▪ QUESTIONS ON FITTING YOUR PROCESS TO YOUR TASK ▪

How can I be sure I understand just what the teacher or employer expects when he or she assigns a writing task?

Ask for an example or look up how the person who gave the assignment has completed the task. If you can't do that, look for a model from the library or the files.

Read it carefully, making an outline of each part, writing out what is done in that section and describing the voice in which it is written.

Then adapt the blueprint so it is true to your topic, your purpose, your reader, and yourself.

What if the form of my writing just grows naturally from what I have to say?

Wonderful. That is what should happen. Writers call those forms *organic;* they grow from the subject itself. We can make writing hard by rejecting what comes naturally but there is no need to make writing hard: Don't fix what is working.

I asked my instructor to tell me precisely how he wanted me to complete the assignment and he said, "I want to be surprised." Did he mean it?

Take a chance. Figure out how you, not someone else, should write the paper. There is no single right or wrong way to complete a writing assignment but many effective and ineffective ways.

I asked my students to surprise me and they taught me ways of writing I had never read or imagined. They taught me. Teach your teacher.

On a recent assignment I found I was taking part of one form, then another and still another, fitting them together in a sort of patchwork quilt. Was that all right?

Did it work? Did the reader understand what you had to say?

Yes.

Then it was all right.

Writing is too complex a process to be constrained by a rule or always fitted into a single form. We often use parts of familiar forms to put together one that does a particular job.

You haven't talked about length. Isn't that part of form?

It is. As you study the traditional forms used to solve specific writing tasks you will get a sense of the expected length but that doesn't mean you have to meet it. You should give the reader all the information the reader needs and no more.

And remember: Short is better. I have never had to cut a piece of writing without making it better. One famous writer said to "kill all your darlings." I don't entirely agree. Some of the writing you especially like may be effective but there is a danger that many of the paragraphs we like really don't carry their weight of meaning to the reader. When that occurs, cut them.

This is just as true of literary writing as business writing. Poetry is the highest form of literary art in part because it says the most with the fewest words.

Peter de Vries said, "When I see a paragraph shrinking under my eyes like a strip of bacon in a skillet, I know I'm on the right track."

I have a lot of good stuff that doesn't fit. What should I do with it?

Good. You can tell a good piece of writing by the amount of good stuff that's left over. And if it is really great stuff, place it on a shelf in inventory to use when you are writing something else.

Sometimes I do most of the writing in my head. I get an assignment and see just how I'm going to do it and other times I have to keep making notes, outlining, trying drafts. When am I going to have this writing process down so I'll just do every piece of writing the same way?

Never. You will have a basic writing process—I generally rehearse until I have a line that contains the tension within the piece, write fast to discover what I have to say, revise, and edit—but all that may change with a new writing task. And the time I spent on each stage of the writing process changes. The writing process approach helps by allowing you to break down a writing job into a sequence of smaller tasks that make each step possible until the final draft is completed.

Sometimes I have the form all set and then as I write it doesn't fit what I have to say. Is this a common problem?

Of course. Writing is thinking and the form that fits the final thought cannot be predicted. As we write we think and as we think we write. As our meaning evolves so will the form that best expresses it.

Each time I begin a new writing task, it's like having to start over learning to write. Will it get easier?

Easier but not easy. Our writing process changes according to the task at hand, and our experience with that task. A new task means new learning—and we do know what has worked best for us in the past—but after we have completed a writing task successfully several times, the process of solving the problems of that particular writing task become familiar and easier.

▪ ACTIVITIES TO FIT YOUR PROCESS TO YOUR TASK ▪

1. Take a piece of writing you admire and write down the task the writer faced. Then write down the steps the writer probably took to complete the task.

2. List all the different writing tasks you have completed and then, under each one, write out the process you used to complete the job.

3. Take a piece of writing you like that was written by a classmate, colleague, or friend and interview that person to discover what the assignment was and just how it was done.

4. Think of subject you'd like to explore, then give yourself a writing assignment. List the steps you will take to complete the assignment.

5. Take a task that you are familiar with on the job, in a sport, or in another course and list the steps in the process you use to complete the task.

Compare that with how you write to see if there are ways you can apply those familiar, successful methods to the writing task.

6. Interview someone who uses writing on the job—a newspaper reporter, engineer, professor, nurse, police officer, insurance adjuster, social worker, lawyer, children's book writer—to see what writing tasks they face on the job and how they solve them.

7. Create a situation in which you have to write—to apply for a scholarship, to have your boss change a procedure at work, to create a news release for a concert—and list the steps you would take to do it.

8. Find someone who has a writing task to complete and teach them how to use the writing process approach.

9. Keep a journal noting all the writing tasks you and those around you faced in a month and how they were completed.

10. Choose another discipline and read to see the problems faced by an environmental engineer, a criminal lawyer, a screenwriter, political ghostwriter, literary scholar, composer, historian, artist were solved. Apply the lessons you learned to the writing you do.

11. Study what the ancient Greeks said about writing. A good book is Edward P. J. Corbett's *Classical Rhetoric for the Modern Student,* Oxford University Press, 1965. Then apply those lessons to your writing tasks.

12. Interview someone who teaches public speaking or the member of the debate team to discover their problems and how they solve them. Adapt their methods to your writing tasks.

CHAPTER 8

GO INTO THE WRITER'S WORKSHOP

If you want to be a tuba player you get a tuba, and some tuba music. And you ask the neighbors to move away or put cotton in their ears. And you probably get a tuba teacher, because there are a lot of objective rules and techniques to both written music and to tuba performance. And then you sit down and you play the tuba, every day, every week, every month, year after year, until you are good at playing the tuba; until you can—if you desire—play the truth on the tuba.

It is exactly the same with writing. You sit down, and you do it, and you do it, and you do it, until you have learned how to do it.

URSULA K. LE GUIN

The best way to learn to write is to write.

But the learning by practice can be reinforced and understood by going into the workshops of writers: reading the autobiographies and biographies of writers, their collected letters and published notebooks, their case histories and the reproductions of their manuscript pages, the interviews with writers such as those published in the *Paris Review* and collected in the series *Writers at Work*.

The student writers also have other resources close at hand: the case histories of fellow classmates and the case histories of their own writing.

In the case histories we work back from the finished text to see the problems the writer faced and the solutions the writer used to solve them. Too many people see writing as a matter of talent. They have never had the opportunity to attend a play or symphony rehearsal, watch an artist or sculptor at work in a studio, and, most of all, since writing is ordinarily a secret art, see a writer alone with the page. When Ernest Hemingway was asked where he worked, he reportedly said, "In my head."

We can't open up the skull of writers, but we can go into the writer's workroom and observe the process of "making" writing. The case histories follow the order of writing tasks we introduced in Chapter 7, to describe, analyze, inform, persuade.

In the first case history, Sarah Hansen reveals how she developed a fine descriptive essay.

▪ WRITING TO DESCRIBE: A STUDENT CASE HISTORY ▪

Students have access to their own case histories and those of their classmates. Writing a case history forces each of us to articulate what we may have done instinctively and, in doing that, we both learn and reinforce our learning.

Sarah Hansen has written an excellent student case history that covers the entire writing process from finding a topic to completing a final draft. Her piece grew out of an assignment to write, with abundant detail, about a familiar place. Here is Sarah's commentary on the writing of her essay:

This descriptive essay is the result of eight drafts, conferencing, workshopping, journal writing, thinking, and sharing. It was hard work—sometimes frustrating but mostly rewarding. I have learned to have confidence in my own writing. But I still have not tackled procrastination, and wonder if I ever will.

To come up with a topic, I brainstormed places and people that I would like to describe and that I know a lot about. I picked my hometown, Birch Grove, Illinois, because I have a lot to say about it and at that point I was confused about my feelings for Birch Grove. My English teacher, Bruce Ballenger, says confusing topics are the best to write about because by writing about them a discovery might be made that will help to end the confusion.

Before I began a first draft, I brainstormed another list of Birch Grove people, places, and events. The list I made ended up in two piles: one bad and one good. This was something I hadn't expected.

I circled the most controversial and the weirdest things on the list. Directly after this, I began to freewrite about the circled things.

I thought about the paper for a few days then went to the computer to type what I had written during the freewrite. I added more stuff to it that had been in my head and took the first draft to my conference with Bruce. He liked it. But the point I was trying to make was not clear because I didn't really know exactly what the point was. Ideas about a hometown are complex. This was the most difficult part of writing this essay: trying to find the point.

Also, my first draft had too much description. I had to find the places where the description didn't fit the purpose of the essay. I actually used scissors and tape on the first draft to cut out unnecessary description. The second draft had less description but was no closer to realizing a point than the first. I was frustrated.

Our writing class had group workshops where we shared our pieces with three or four other students. I read the Birch Grove paper to my workshop group because I needed fresh perspectives. I also needed some positive reinforcement. All three students liked my paper—that made me feel more motivated to work on it. One woman in my workshop agreed with Bruce and me that the point of the essay needed to be clearer. The most valuable thing I learned from the workshop was that the topic of the essay wasn't clear until the middle. They suggested starting the essay with a paragraph or idea from the middle.

With this in mind, I changed the first paragraph and fiddled around with various parts of the essay. But I was still frustrated with the meaning. I knew that the essay was slowly progressing with each draft, but from drafts two to six I made little progress finding exactly what it was I wanted to say without sounding boring, clichéd or obvious. I started to share the essay with a lot of different people. Most close friends tend to like just about anything you do and aren't objective enough and don't give much criticism. Older English majors and my parents and their friends, people that read a good amount of writing, turned out to be the most helpful.

With each successive draft, the second to the sixth, my English teacher and I became more and more discouraged. I couldn't reach exactly what it was about Birch Grove I wanted to say. Did I want to say how I felt, did I want to say something to the people of Birch Grove, did I want to make a point about all hometowns, did I want to make a statement about the world by talking about one hometown? My biggest mistake was not writing in my journal enough. I procrastinated writing about my feelings for Birch Grove because it was too frustrating.

Around draft four or five, I couldn't look at the paper with objectivity anymore. I was too close to my subject and practically had the words memorized, as did my English teacher. Finally, after draft five, Bruce gave the draft back to me with questions written all over it about what it was I was trying to say. In my journal I wrote answers to his questions. It was this way, by talking to myself in my journal, and by answering questions, that I nearly found what I wanted to say.

I wrote that the good in Birch Grove I had realized by going away far outweighed the bad. The energy of the good things is what makes Birch Grove all right. When people realize this, then Birch Grove will be safe. We decided that this would be the final draft. I thought I was done.

But when my father read the essay out loud that night I realized what I had wanted to come across did not. In the sixth draft it seemed I had forgotten the racism and the close-mindedness. I intended just the opposite. I wanted to say that I have realized the good in Birch Grove but that the bad needs to be changed.

The biggest problem I had writing this essay was attempting to find exactly what the meaning was. I also needed to spend more time talking to myself about the essay in my journal. In hand with this, I needed to spend more time writing than thinking about the essay. A good idea can sometimes surprise me as I write, but that rarely happens when I think about my writing without a pen in my hand.

I learned to share my work with as many people as I could who were willing to take the time to read it and give their responses. It is motivating to hear fresh and new ideas. The conferences helped in that Bruce and I would talk about what it was I was trying to say. The discussions helped each draft to come closer and closer. It was also good to hear someone give positive comments about my writing.

Writing a descriptive essay can help with any other kind of writing. It is not only a creative type of essay. Description is about saying things so that other people can see, feel, hear, and smell what you have. These things are revealed through specific details. It is exactly the same concrete writing that is needed to critique a novel or write a term paper.

Sarah's daybook started out with the following entry:

I have to write a paper for a book—a descriptive essay—to be published. I have no idea what to write about—just knowing it's for a book makes me nervous. I've even been avoiding thinking about it. Dad—Heather—East H—— —commune— —— —expectations—

~~God~~-grandma—Birch Grove—Berry Farm—trip to France—2nd semester at UNH.

She starts out with a writer's apprehension and makes a list of possible topics. She did put a mark like a rising sun after Birch Grove, and then she wrote a draft that plunged into the subject: *"The round and friendly minister of the Methodist Church of Birch Grove, Illinois, was found in Sanderson's three-story department store stealing a large pair of light brown corduroys."*

In her daybook Sarah writes:

> I showed my first draft of the essay for the book today. Bruce liked it. I was so relieved. He's really helped me to be more confident about my writing. We decided that the point of the paper wasn't too clear. He said that I need to "peel the onion." In class we talked about how the layers of the onion are like layers of ideas and points to an essay or a piece of writing. The deeper into the onion layers you get, the closer you are to your main point. I know a few things that I am pointing out but I don't know exactly how to say them. I think my main point is about how Birch Grove was all bad to me at first, and then, as I went to UNH, I realized the better things about it. But the better things don't excuse the bad things. I'm still confused about it. I don't think this paper is very interesting. I don't think it will keep the reader's interest. We also talked about how there are too many descriptions.

I find this sort of writing to myself important. It helps to put into words what you got from a conference and to identify your feelings about the text and about the process of writing.

The next page in Sarah's daybook shows a typical jumble of doodling and writing. She is listing potential specifics as a form of recovering memories and discovering what she may write.

Later she writes in her daybook:

> I've decided to show my paper on Birch Grove to my workshop group. I don't know where to go with it. I have been thinking a lot about the focus of this paper and it's getting me nowhere. Hopefully, they'll have some insight to it that will get me motivated for revising this paper. I spend too much time just thinking—I should be writing in this journal more but don't have discipline—I procrastinate too much.

• • •

> My workshop group really liked my paper. Lin said it reminded her of her hometown which is cool cause that's sort of a point I'm trying

to make—every hometown for every person is both good and bad—
end up blaming hometown for everything—have bitterness towards
it. A love–hate thing. I don't know that's quite what I want to say
though—seems cliché. Brian and —— both thought that the beginning isn't clear—maybe begin with paragraph that starts, "I moved
to Birch Grove, where life offers more," when I was four. . . ." They
said as it stands now it's a little unclear what I'm talking about. So
I'll try to rework that into the beginning and Brian thought that
my point was perfectly said—that I shouldn't add more but ——
said I should make my point clearer. I agree more with —— cause
at this point I don't even know what my main point is. I asked
them if they thought it was boring and if it caught and kept their
attention. They said it was interesting and kept their attention
well so that made me feel better. Asked if there was too much description and they said no.

In all her daybook entries Sarah reveals the way a writer's mind—and
emotions—work. I certainly feel the same way about my drafts as Sarah does
about hers. To learn to write effectively you need to be open and realize your
feelings and how to deal with them. Later in her daybook Sarah writes:

I'm annoyed with my paper about Birch Grove. I'm sick of it. I'm
too close to it and can't see it correctly any more. It seems so trite
and boring and cliché. Bruce seems to not like it much either. That's
really discouraging. I don't know what exactly I want my point to
be that's creative and fresh. . . .

These excerpts from her account reveal the writer at work, what goes on
backstage that is essential to the creation of an effective piece of writing. Space
limitations here preclude reproducing her drafts, sometimes marked up with
her comments, other times with the comments of her readers, but they document the evolution of her essay. In the third draft, for example, Sarah begins,
*"When I was four, my mother, my dog, ~~and I moved into the upstairs apartment of a~~
~~rundown house in~~ moved to Birch Grove, Illinois. I've spent all my time there minus
the summers which I've spent with my father. Passing the town border a cheap billboard
reads: 'Life offers more in Birch Grove.'"*
By the fifth draft her lead reads, *"Passing over the town border into Birch
Grove, Illinois, a billboard, paint peeling off, reads: 'Life offers more in Birch Grove.'
When I was four years old my mother, my dog, and I moved to this Midwestern town.
As I grew up, I'd pass the fading billboard ~~faded as was along with~~ and my tolerance for
BIRCH GROVE, ~~my bitterness and anger seen in a grimace as I thought: 'Life offers~~
~~less in Birch Grove.'~~ faded along with it."* By the eighth draft the lead was as it

appears below. Writers have to learn by writing and by considering what they have written and how it can be improved.

Here is Sarah's final draft as it was turned in:

Simple Birch Grove

by Sarah Hansen

Passing over the town border into Birch Grove, Illinois, a billboard, paint peeling off, reads: "Life Offers More In Birch Grove." When I was four years old my mother, my dad, and I moved to this Midwestern town. As I grew up, I'd pass the fading billboard, and my tolerance for Birch Grove faded along with it.

The owner of Sanderson's three-story department store found the round and friendly minister, Donald Morison, of the Methodist Church of Sycamore stealing a pair of brown corduroys. Most of the bank presidents and company founders and Mercedes Benz owners of Birch Grove belonged to the Methodist Church on the corner of Third and Main. They put up a big fuss about having a kleptomaniac as a minister. There was great pressure on Don to leave. These influential people weren't seen at Sunday service anymore to listen to Don with his brown, shining eyes give the sermon. Only a few members forgave Don, told him so, and asked him to stay. One Sunday, a woman slowly stood up and told the churchgoers that the Bible says to forgive, and that we should forgive Don, and help him out, because his problem is a disease, just as alcoholism is a disease. Don left the Methodist Church two long months after the incident, and the members are now content to sit in the pews and sing out of the worn, red cloth-covered hymnals.

Miss Gooch, the assistant counselor at Birch Grove High School, wears her thin, gray-brown hair in a tight curl perm. I was the student council president my senior year, and we were discussing some upcoming activities. Miss Gooch liked to gossip; she asked me how my friend Peggy was doing. Peggy has fair freckled skin and blond curled hair—like most other girls at Birch Grove High School. Her boyfriend is thin and has beautiful, chocolate brown skin. What Miss Gooch meant was, "How is she dealing with having a black boyfriend?" Miss Gooch said, "I am not prejudiced, but I don't think the races should intermingle . . . and I hate Mexicans." Sixteen black students and forty Mexican students attend Birch Grove High School where Miss Gooch is the counselor and student council advisor.

At age eleven, my sister Traci walked to The Save And Shop, three blocks down Walnut Street from our house, to buy groceries. As she crossed the supermarket parking lot, a little girl, not over seven years old, was left alone in a beat-up station wagon. The girl rolled down the front seat window. "Nigger," she said to Traci, my adopted sister, now one of the sixteen black students at the high school. Traci is startled as she looks in the mirror to see her own black face. Her eyes are so accustomed to whiteness.

Sam Ritchel was salutatorian of my class. Now, when I come home for Christmas or Easter vacation, I see Sam wandering around Birch Grove, or staring off in a booth in the Coffee Shop. He's taken too much acid, refuses to get a job, dropped out of the University of Wisconsin, shaves his eyebrows, wears black lipstick, black eyeliner, and black clothing. He listens to Jim Morrison on his tape recorder, and says nothing but "black, melancholy, darkness, despair . . ." In the Weston Elementary School, Sam's nickname was Happy.

I hated everything about Birch Grove. I hated its conservatism, its hypocrisy, its ignorance, its racism, its close-mindedness, and its ugliness. I hated what it did to bright, open-minded people who could not escape. In Birch Grove, I could only think about itchy, depressing, angering things. Times when snotty Claire Saunders knocked over my newly painted three-speed bike in the fifth grade, when the whole of Birch Grove watched <u>Top Gun</u> perpetually for weeks after it came out on video, when high school students egged our house five times in two months because my stepfather is the assistant principal of the high school—a fair, kind man who must punish students for skipping a study hall, for smoking in the music wing.

But since I've been at college, far away from my hometown, I can remember eating macaroni and cheese on Kiersten's sunny, white porch with her mother and mine, enjoying the lunch hour before returning back to the third grade. I can remember the annual January snow sculpture competition in front of Prince's Restaurant across from Birch Grove Park. I remember my very first valentine in seventh grade from my very first boyfriend: shy, curly white-haired Jim Morse, a farm boy. The homemade card was caringly shaped and cut out of red, pink, and white construction paper. Two white rabbits kissed on the front; inside, pencil cursive writing read, "I'm glad that you're my valentine, Sarah."

I remember the annual Birch Grove Pumpkin Festival where all of Birch Grove competes in a pumpkin competition, decorating them as a scary monster with orange peels for hair and gourds for arms and legs or a pumpkinphone for goblins and ghosts to use. The Miller family won the grand prize one year and got to go on the Bozo Show. There was a pumpkin princess or prince award to the best essay in the junior high, and the grade-schooler with the best scary picture got to ride on the fire engine at the front of the Sunday Pumpkin Parade. I watched the parade from the Abbens' house on Somonauk Street with people from our church, eating warm carameled apples, and drinking hot apple cider sitting on fold-out chairs along the street. The huge oak, maple, and sycamore trees lining the street screamed autumn with their yellows, golds, reds, and oranges.

I remember Mrs. Munter, my junior and senior year English teacher, my most influential teacher, sneaking chocolate M&Ms out of the second drawer down. I remember her strong, clear, enunciated voice demanding and challenging us to accomplish more in her class than we ever had before.

I remember driving along the smooth and winding North River Road just after dusk on a hot summer day, windows rolled down and arms out waving, watching the thousands of tiny blinking lights of the fireflies just above the soybeans and wheat fields. Although I used to hate the flatness of the land, now as I return I appreciate the great big sky and lie in the middle of a cornfield with Steven and Pam, watching the silver-white shooting stars stream across the blue-black expanse.

I see Sean Allen in the store window of Ben Franklin, the five and dime, and wave back knowing he's still the same friendly, simple person he always was and will be. I know that every summer the woman with the wrinkled face will bring out her popcorn stand, and my mother and I'll buy sweet caramelcorn and eat the whole bag as we walk slowly home in the hot night air.

Mom says Birch Grove is a good place to bring up children. Maybe it is in some ways. Friendly Sean Allen, the sun on a white porch that makes the skin hum, and Mrs. Munter's deep, resounding voice are as pure and warm as the wealthy churchgoers and close-minded Miss Gooch are tarnished and cold. But even as the sweet-smelling fields, the wide Midwest sky, the leaves of screaming colors that crackle under foot seek to balance this out, I know that Birch Grove still is no place to bring up my children.

Look back at the "Tips on Writing Effective Description" on pages 164–65 in the last chapter. Notice how Sarah packed her description with specific details and made them all advance a single, dominant impression of her hometown. Her angle of vision—a student looking back at her hometown—is steady and she keeps an appropriate distance, not moving in so close the reader loses sight of what she is trying to do or moving back so far the reader doesn't care if she does it.

In the next case history I write an essay of analysis. You may want to refer back to the "Tips on Writing Analysis" on pages 167–68 in the previous chapter. My essay, however, is not a traditional, detached analysis of an objective issue that only involves my intellect but an analysis of my feelings as I attempt to deal with the most terrible experience in my life.

▪ WRITING TO ANALYZE: A PROFESSIONAL CASE HISTORY ▪

I didn't want to write this article. My daughter's death is the worst thing that has happened to us; nothing in my life compares to it. Eighteen years have passed—almost as many as she lived—and the pain is immediate when I remember her as I do many times every day. But I received a letter from a reader discussing his pain at losing a son and asking for any help I could give him from my experience.

I tried—and tried and retried—to write him a letter. I couldn't. I couldn't get any words down that made sense. I wandered all around the subject, mouthed clichés, I couldn't even explore what I wanted to say.

I needed structure. I needed form. I needed discipline. I needed a familiar order. I needed rhetoric. I decided to write a column and told myself I would not publish it. The subject seemed too private but by using the familiar structure of the column I might be able to write something I could turn into a letter.

Now my writing task was clear: a column of analysis in which I would try to think back and discover what I had learned from this terrible experience. What had I done? What had I learned? What did it mean? What counsel did I have for someone going down the same road? I was going into emotional territory but I was armed with rhetoric tradition, with the limitations and experience of column writing. I had a discipline that made it possible for me to write.

The writing didn't go easily. The material was too painful for that. It was the hardest thing I had ever written and when it was done I was able to send it to the man who had written to me, along with a letter I found I could now write.

And I decided to publish it. I offered it, tentatively, to my editor, Evelynne Kramer, who found it painful to read but said it was important to publish it and the letters I received after publication from readers justified our decision to publish. Here is the column as it was published along with my reading of it. Reading it, you will see a published writer responding to his own published work.

A reader who noted in a column that we had lost a daughter at 20 writes to ask me for comfort and counsel as he walks the same road.

Not a great opening, but at least it is direct and it sets up the pattern of the essay for the reader—and for me.

Comfort I can offer. The lonely comfort that each of us must suffer in our own way. That each loss is individual. And that we must accept. We have no choice.

Here I state a theme that runs through the piece and it is a theme that makes it clear to the reader that I do not expect everyone to react as I do. It is important to give readers room, especially in a piece such as this, to respond in their own way.

Counsel? I have not looked back at myself to see what I may have learned. Perhaps, as we come up to the 12th anniversary of Lee's sudden leaving it is time. I worry about being too personal at times in this column but the readers' response in the past has reminded me that we can, at times, connect and help each other.

I am allowing the reader to explore the subject with me. I also face the discomfort I feel in being personal, in worrying that I am exploiting my daughter's death, by sharing my discomfort with the reader, by raising the problem I see and responding to it. We can make the reader an accomplice to our writing.

This essay brings up the whole question of writing about personal or painful topics. I have found that the more personal the writer is, the more honest and direct, the more readers identify and are helped by the writing. Also the writer experiences more therapy. Still, I have my doubts.

A few weeks after Lee died, we had to return to the hospital for a session I dreaded but that turned out to be good therapy. The first thing Dr. Shannon, who knew I was a writer, asked was if I was going to write about this. I was horrified and said, "No." I felt guilty because, as a writer, I had been making mental notes and even rehearsing what I might write. He said, "You have to" and my wife, Lee's sisters and her boyfriend agreed.

I do know that those who are Over Sixty who have had a child leave ahead of them experience a special, continuing sense of loss.

I can only speak honestly and +p13directly of what I did and do. I cannot speak of what her mother does and her sisters. We are together—and alone.

The writer can establish his or her authority to write on the subject and place limitations on that authority.

Each of us has to understand and accept each other's individual loneliness. We reach out to comfort each other but we, each in our own way, grieve alone.

I repeat the theme that seemed to be developing as I wrote, a theme that echoes what Dr. Shannon taught in telling me I had to write, that was my way of dealing with this tragedy. And it was all right. It was normal, natural—for me.

I wept openly and frequently. My wife could not—then. She felt guilty at times about that. No reason she should. I did not feel guilty about my manly tears, she should not feel guilty about her womanly silence. There is no measuring stick to grief and should not be.

Here I document what I have been saying. Yes, when I write about my family, I check with them before submitting what I have written for publication.

These are some landmarks in my own landscape of grief and re-membering:

I had not found a simple pattern of development, a clear sequence of what I had to say, so I use this device to bring some order to what I have to say. The items in these notes are not random or presented just as they came in the writing. I have moved them around so as to best serve the reader and finish on a strong note.

I do not forget Lee—and I will not forget Lee. When I am asked how many children I have, I say three. I can remember being crit-ical of people who spoke of the dead as if they were living, who kept pictures on the mantle of those who are gone. It made me un-comfortable.

I confess my own feelings in the past that may also be the reader's feelings in reading this essay. I understand that, I am saying, and that's all right, just as crying or not crying is all right.

I am no longer critical. I will not push her aside or exclude her. I talk of her, and with her. She was with me in intensive care, she sits in the rocker nearby as I write this.

I worry that I am being too sentimental here but it is the way I feel and I stick with it.

Worth repeating. We grieve in our own way. Only by accepting feel-ings and dealing with them, only by accepting our loneliness and dealing with it, can we make ourselves ready to reach out to others.

After Lee's death one of the hardest things I had to do was to drive alone in the car. More than once I stopped by the side of the road and howled. Like an animal in grief and loss. It was a primi-tive and essential comfort.

The reader accepts repetition for purpose especially if you let the reader know you are repeating and if the repetition adds something to the reader's knowledge.

I could never forget that I was not the only one she left. I tried to reach out to my wife, her sisters, her boyfriend (who, with his wife, are our friends today), her friends. It was a comfort to comfort them, to reach out and do for the living what we cannot do for her. In her memory—and for our own needs.

This was a surprise to me: That it was comforting to comfort others.

And my wife, Minnie Mae, and Lee's sisters, Anne and Hannah, in those cruel days at the hospital, the weeks afterwards, and the years since, have taught this combat veteran a hundred lessons in strength and courage.

We need both to give and to receive. It is important to accept help. A transition to the next point.

And I who always want to drive, to be in control, to give, learned something about accepting. The night we came home from the hospital, Phyllis Heilbronner knelt by my chair and fed me, bite by bite. The Lindens held us in their arms as did Hans Heilbronner; the Clarks and others kept walking by the house to make sure there were not too many people visiting; the Graves, Father Joe Desmond, the Swifts, the Robinsons, the Griewanks, the Ladds, the Mertons, the Milnes, and dozens of other friends and neighbors cared for us and still do. Karen Mower's letter, and all the other notes, meant so much. They all taught me to receive as well as give, never to apologize for my needing their love.

Of course I am thanking my friends and neighbors in print, but their acts can tell the reader how to behave as well as reinforce the importance of accepting help.

I had to accept Lee's death from Reye's Syndrome. Most survive; our daughter did not. We had to remove extraordinary means—our beautiful Lee looked as if she were asleep but she was brain dead—and I had to execute her family's decision. I still have day visions and night dreams of her hopping up, laughing, saying it was a joke.

The reader needs to know how Lee died and this seems the natural place to tell the reader since it supports an important point.

It was not. And I have to realize that her death, and my grief, is simply a condition of my life, as much a part of me as the nearsightedness, the funny walk, the sense of humor she and I shared. My grief was not going to go away. It was there, to be lived with, made part of me.

This is one of the most important things I had to say. This grief, this loss stays with you, it becomes part of you. Sometimes people want you "to get over it." Impossible.

And I've learned to avoid. Our favorite instrument was the oboe and we had a large collection of oboe recordings. Lee had just been accepted at the New England Conservatory to study oboe when she died. I know it makes her unhappy, but we cannot listen to those soaring melodies. Not yet.

Admit what you cannot do and don't feel guilty about it.

But we can celebrate life. In fact, my life seems, in some strange way, a gift from Lee. After the days in the hospital, after her burial, after I had begun to get through parts of days instead of parts of hours, I remember walking home from work and realizing that I had done what I had to do, for Lee, for her sisters, for my wife. I was 53 years old and I made, in that moment, the first step in accepting myself. I was far from what I wanted to be, from what I thought the world thought I should be, but I had made it. I wasn't so bad after all.

I do want to have something positive to say and I discovered in writing that I did. Writing of this growth of understanding reinforces it. The writing of this essay, although painful, was constructive and helpful.

Lee's death reminded me not only to accept myself but to appreciate the life I have left. My private memorial, never mentioned to anyone before, is to take pleasure in small things. Perhaps the submarine sandwich with everything on it Lee liked so much, certainly the Handel organ concerto that is playing on the hi-fi this moment, the pattern of sun and shadow on my hands as I write this that is different from yesterday because the leaves have begun to unfold this late spring. She would want me to appreciate such moments of life. When I get busy and forget, Lee reminds me. I stop. I celebrate, for her, the life she celebrated but left so early.

I discovered the depth of this in writing it. I knew it on one level but had not realized how extensive it was. I hope my sharing of this isn't embarrassing to the reader but helpful.
Of course I'll never know. We do not own the text we create. Each person reads such a piece, as you have, with your own autobiography. If you have not suffered the death of anyone you love, you will read it differently from those who have lost a child, a parent, a brother or a sister,

*a friend, a grandparent—and each of those readers will create their own
texts while reading mine.*

*We write to communicate, yes, but just as important, to allow—
inspire—readers to articulate their own unread thoughts and feelings.*

**Lee, I'm sure, was with me the other morning when I whistled at a
bird and it whistled back. For a quarter of a mile the bird and I
continued our conversation. Lee was listening—and laughing.**

*I worried about this. Speaking directly to Lee, although I do it, might
seem hokey or fake to a reader. The editor helped me tone this paragraph
down a bit. I don't have my first draft, but this is the toned-down
version.*

**And I reach out, as I have tried to here, believing that if we are
honest and open to each other, that pain can be shared, and if not
healed, at least accepted and survived.**

*This was added in my early revisions. I still think it might have been
better to drop this paragraph. It seems preachy, to wrap up everything too
neatly. It tells the reader how to think and feel and I don't like to do that.
I prefer to close in a way that will cause the reader to do the thinking and
feeling alone. You decide.*

It was therapeutic for me to write about this subject—painful but helpful—
but I hope that it helped the reader who wrote. The letters of other readers
made it clear that I was able to articulate some of the feelings of others who have
traveled through this lonely country of losing a child. It is the task of the writer
to do that: to speak of what others can not speak, to give words to those who
have no words to express what they feel. I hope I have done that job. You, the
reader, will have to decide. But at least I hope it is helpful to see an experienced
writer at work. Now we will see a less experienced but excellent writer—a
student—at work.

▪ WRITING TO INFORM: A
STUDENT CASE HISTORY ▪

The research paper is the fundamental building block of academic discourse—
and it is the most dreaded composition assignment by the students who have to
write research papers and the instructors who have to read them. Most research
papers are dull because the students have not yet done research on a topic important to them and the form becomes more important than the message.

Yet students need experience in gathering information, building the information into a significant meaning, and presenting it so that the reader does

not only understand the message but has access to the sources of information the writer used.

Tina Winslow demonstrates that a student can not only prove that the student know academic research conventions but also can write a lively, interesting report that places scholarly material in a human context.

Her assignment was to "Inform readers by completing a five- to ten-page [1500–2500 word] research report that will demonstrate your ability to use scholarly techniques to investigate a topic and reveal its significance to them."

She was told to keep a journal that would reveal her writing problems and how she solved them. The student was given time to find a territory, then a topic, sharpening her research question in consultation with the instructor and classmates, then to write several drafts. She was to have at least a dozen sources with footnotes and a bibliography that follows Modern Language Association guidelines. And Tina was referred to the "Tips on Writing to Inform" on page 171.

The case history shows how she moved from the vague and general to the specific, finding a way to combine several aspects of her topic so that the final article had a clear, documented focus. And she moved toward this clarity of vision while achieving an increasing grace. Her work is a demonstration of good thinking as well as good writing, as all effective prose should be.

In her journal she first brainstormed (pp. 19–22) on animal rights looking for a focus line (pp. 47–52) that contained enough tension to spark a research report:

- animal rights—where is the line
- who decides whose rights get to be violated
- the chemical industry at odds with the natural order or is it the natural order?
- would people buy the products if they saw the process it goes through?
- do animals have rights—historical/religious implications
- meat industry—health implications
- pumping poultry, beef, with hormones
- is the meat industry lying about the health requirements and how far down the line does it go
- feel passionately about not eating meat without bias, why?
- no meat has helped achieve my goals to trim down—why? What does meat do psychologically or physiologically that slims people
- moods are evened out—hormones in meat?
- no guilt with eating healthy, cheaper
- in small way have stopped poor treatment of animals
- read a book that describes the process

- people live too much of their life with spurts of unrealistic violence or softened reality
- would you enjoy chicken if you watched the man rip his feet off because the nails had grown around the bars of the cage back into his feet

This is an excellent way to begin. Tina doesn't worry about the writing, she is scouting the territory to find a way into her subject and the reader can see her ranging across the whole area, looking for the most important material—the material she needs to explore and that her reader needs to know. Her final topic is deeply hidden in her list and the approach that makes her final paper distinctive does not appear. But this step was essential to her thinking process.

Now let us listen in as she talks to herself in her journal. Remember that the direction in which she thinks she is headed is not the direction in which she will go. Elizabeth Bowen said: "The writer . . . sees what he did not expect to see . . . Inattentive learner in the schoolroom of life, he keeps some faculty free to hear and wonder. His is the roving eye. By that roving eye is his subject found. The glance, at first only vaguely caught, goes on to concentrate, deepen; becomes the vision." In Tina's journal we catch a rare but important glimpse of the writing in the act of thought, catching her unexpected vision.

Journal

When I think about animal rights many issues shoot through my head. My two kitties waiting on my bed, waking up with a lazy stare that pretty much lays out the law—"You have the right to scratch my ears and why you are at it the bowl in the other room is a bit empty." Those are their rights but they are lucky cause I'm a sucker for a good mew and milk breath. Society's definition of animal rights extends more into our comfort zone as human beings. Not only my comfort zone about what I will use on my body but what goes into my body and the realities that went into mundane things I take for granted. My true experience in this issue began when my roommates a year or so ago were very much into the movement of animal rights. They were adamant about how cruel vivisection was and that it should cease immediately for all products. While I struggle as a compassionate human who has done volunteer work with animals to comprehend the exact reality of vivisection, which in essence needs a proper definition this issue becomes one of limits. Flipping in the handy Miriam-Webster the definition alone of vivisection bothers me inside—"the cutting of or operation on a living animal usually for physiological or pathological investigation" or worse, definition two, "animal experimentation especially if considered to cause distress to the subject." Who gave us the power to take that animal's life? Or worse keeping it alive to test it's reactions. I understand the theory that it's an us or them kind of world but in reality where people are just vain creatures how much does it matter if the deodorant and the makeup don't look just right or don't exist especially when everyone will not be wearing it. It's just a layer of protection anyway.

Her final paper will not focus on animal rights but she needs to start here to find her ultimate focus. Her journal reveals the writer talking to herself and what some people might describe as bad or sloppy writing is good writing here, appropriate to the task. It is courageous of Tina to allow us to see a good writer doing the rough pre-draft writing that is essential but not usually revealed to a reader.

Let's listen to Tina talking to herself. She is at once the appropriately floundering writer allowing her evolving text to carry her toward meaning and the craftsperson standing back and watching herself working. This split vision—being in the writing act and observing and standing back watching herself in the act—is essential for good writing.

The paper I want to write needs a focus line. Something that creates a tension. I think if you take the normal person who wasn't attacked by vicious dogs as a child and who was socialized with animals normally and show them the process from start to finish they will understand the brutality of the process. To take something living and breathing and warp it for our needs doesn't seem right. Do the end results, a juicy piece of chicken or tube of lipstick, really make the process OK? In a world filled with lawsuits on product liability, companies are scrambling to find proof that this product when accidently swallowed, poked in an eye or applied incorrectly won't adversely affect humans. If there is so much concern with humans why aren't humans used to test these results and why is there such a lack of concern with humans when their food is concerned. If they don't want to harm people why would they pump pesticides onto the eventual food of cows and poultry, pump hormones into animals for better growth, keep them in deplorable conditions and then wonder why Americans are getting fatter, madder and sicker. It all comes back to a basic respect for other things.

This paper will be about the realities involved in everyday products that involve animals. It could go two ways right now. With vivisection you have the brutality of pictures and there is a plenty of tension about it with animal righters and research industry. When

I visited a pharmaceutical company my friend worked in she told me not to even joke about freeing the animals. They had them locked up in a special room you had to have 4 keys to get into. When I asked her why she didn't mind testing on them she was like well they throw poop on me and are mean but ultimately her argument was humans first, everything else "bah." She didn't realize that if someone put me in a cage and shot me full of drugs I would have a very similar reaction. Mean as spit and proud of it. The other direction of the paper could be on when we eat, what is the process of the food. The chickens and cows we eat aren't exactly running around the yard, they are chemicals through and through from the minute they are born.

Focus lines—potential:

> Chemical food—what are we eating?
> Whose rights are they anyway
> Food industry—provider or killer?

In consultation with her classmates and a conference with her instructor, Tina came to realize she didn't really have anything new to say about animal rights but that she had strong feelings about her new decision to be a vegetarian that was tested on a cruise with her parents and confirmed two weeks later when her mother—a life-long meat eater— suffered a heart attack. Tina felt uncomfortable about using her personal feelings and her personal experience in a research paper but was encouraged to try to find a way to combine objective research information with personal experience.

Writing is often like a tunnel that is wide at the beginning but narrows as you follow it. Here you will see Tina as the tunnel narrows and she finds her focus and begins to work within it.

OK, focus line:

> Solidifying Vegetarianism—the hard way.
> Or why I am still a Vegetarian today.
> Or Taming the Taco Urges.

But really the focus although it doesn't sound focused is that the after shocks of my Mom's heart attack solidified never eating meat again for me. I guess I need to trim it into a more readable state but basically this issue to me is like a spark to gasoline. For the record, when I shared this topic with my parents they were not exactly thrilled. To defend my mother, who really wants to know that an incident in her life scared everyone down to their belief foundations. To defend my father, well he just likes to argue. Basically, he wants to vent that you can't be a vegetarian for purely health reasons because he believes that you can be un-healthy, heartwise, and eat no meat. For instance, chicken and turkey and low fat/cholesterol meats can be eaten and still be healthy or did you hear the one about the vegetarian who died of a heart attack. He maintains you are a vegetarian for ethical—not health reasons. My point for my focus is that although I was a brand new vegetarian before the heart attack (Wait till I tell you the taunts that a week cruise with my family brought me a week and a half before my mother's run in with her arteries), the ma-terial I read after the scare solidified that I will never again put meat in my mouth. I guess the ethical part is there as back up but after what I learned I see meat and the industry as killers and be-yond that totally unnecessary.

(Title)
• Momma, Me and Meat
• Scaring the Meat out of Me
• Meat Stinks
• A Tube in the Nose Is Meat out of Me
• Vegetarians Unite
• You Don't Get a Chest Pain Eating Broccoli (Unless You Swallow a Stalk)
• Reeducation of My Mouth and My Mom
• Liar, Liar Heart on Fire
• If It Had a Mother I Won't Eat It—Mom
• Moo Cow and Then Shoo
• You Don't Have to Beat Me with a Carrot to Make Me Give Up Meat
• Thicken Your Clogged Arteries with Lies

(Lead)
Understand what will stop me from ever putting meat in my mouth again, was my mother in an ICU bed after her heart attack.

• • •

Well that's part of it. But after reading up on heart attacks and what they are about, I realized she didn't have to be in that bed and that keeps me focused in my non-meat eating habits.

• • •

(Lead—2)
Nothing made being a vegetarian easier than realizing that my mother having a heart attack didn't have to be a reality.

(Trail)
• mother has heart attack
• already a vegetarian but very new

- in learning more about heart attacks read book after book which detailed what meat is and what it isn't both from heart aspect as well as healthy living aspect
- realization it's a lie—meat industry
- based on what it does to your body, what is in it and the benefits of other types of protein—meat stinks
- realize this isn't an ethical attack on meat eater's way of life but I personally feel betrayed

(End)

You don't have to not eat meat to be heart healthy but after realizing what goes into the process and how close you are to being a vegetarian why would you eat meat.

(Possible 1st paragraph)

Through the mist that are tears unshed, I look wildeyed at my mother in an ICU bed with slightly green, thick tubes in her nose. ICU has no room for deep personal talks with the doors flung wide open and everyone's heartbeeps beating loud enough for the staff behind the desks to hear. Her nails are purple as well as her lips. She looks an off color like someone walked in and sucked the oxygen out of her skin. Pale and tired, with wide brown eyes, she pleads with me not to be scared—its just a minor life threatening procedure.

Good writing is promiscuous; writers do not write one draft but many. We do not have the space to show each of Tina's drafts but we can listen to her journal as she reacts to completing her first draft.

OK, the first rough draft is out. It's weak in some areas admittedly but I feel better having the thoughts in a rough diving board for better work. I just hate, hate, hate showing other people work that I don't consider finished. The hardest part for me in this critique sessions is admitting that I have to write just like everyone in stages and that the first things out of my typewriter/computer look just like everyone else's. I guess I want to be brilliant and perfect on the first shot. "BULLS EYE!, the crowd roared as they tossed the first draft writer roses." But alas, I need more work on the quotations and the integration of paraphrases not to mention documentation style at this early stage is a enough to make MLA come out and personally tweek me on the nose. But at least I have exorcised the demons onto paper at this point all while on Tylenol for sinus and cold.

Better flow and tighter in beginning paragraphs, Smoother flow in Paragraph 2. More quotes, direct in Paragraph 3, check for logic flow LOGIC FLOW in paragraph 4 with more sources, more sources and another quote or two. Summary needs more bite.

So . . . round two is done but I have to cut cut cut.

• • •

I guess I am going to have to cut the chemicals paragraph but I do this under duress.

It was not cut. She found a way to keep it in the piece by making it support her focus on why vegetarianism is import to health. Later, in her journal, Tina debates a cut her peer readers suggested. Ultimately the decision has to be the writer's but she expresses the insecure response to a critical suggestion that is natural in a writer.

I like that paragraph, I feel it has merit and geez, it grosses me out and I wrote the thing. I was hoping to get my punch in quick and well I guess as a being with somewhat rational thought I realize it doesn't fit in with the mom-had-a-heart-attack motif. I really like the mixture of personal vignettes mixed in with writing of a more research nature. I find it really interesting the process this had been. I started out with animal rights and have it nuzzled, pushed and CUT It down to just vegetarianism.

For next draft:

- Finish getting the references pinned down to MLA style
- Re-arrange the chemical paragraph out of the paper and work out the flow
- Go through with a fine tooth grammar comb and get all of it laying down without obvious cowlicks (pun intended)

A complete case history would reproduce draft after draft and space prohibits reprinting each one of them. And it would probably be boring to all but the most interested student. The important element in the process is expressed by the writer in her journal where she expresses astonishment at what she has written, discovering that writing is not recording previous thoughts but thinking by writing. Her understanding of the subject changes as she captures and clarifies meaning through language. This is the most important lesson of her writing course.

Man, oh, man. Whew! Done, finis, end of papyrus! OK, so I feel guilty at being relieved that I'm done with the paper. It is not what I would have conceived at the beginning but it wound it's way down the paper trail to completedom. I wanted a paper that bit and nickered at lies and then spit it out in a huge cavalcade of burning all consuming truth. What I got was a paper that resembled "What I Did over the Summer" tone with a vegetarian twist.

Now, now, I can hear that voice now. (How come this voice always resembles my mother's voice?) "If you aren't happy with the paper then change it." The truth is I will never be happy with the paper. I can put it in my treasure box and dig it up 10 years from now and say (in my knowing and critical tone, of course) "This seems so pedantic and stiff," "What was I trying to say here?"

"Why did I pick that word or phrase?" Hopefully, buried in that chest is also my good critic who reads it and nods her head and whispers, "Because that's where you were. The paper is done I can look at it and see the legitimate course it took. I started off worried by what I would write, how to say it perfectly, WHERE AM I GOING TO FIND THE TIME and now I can look at it and realize I created something.

─────────────

Each of Tina's drafts clarified what she had to say and allowed her to say it in with increasing liveliness and fluency. At first she wrote each paragraph separately, moving the information to a position that answered the reader's questions, then she had to consider the pace and proportion: How much of her mother? How much research information? Throughout the process she had to listen to her peer readers and her instructor but make her own way.

Compare the drafts of the lead in her journal with the final, disciplined example of good writing. She had to go from the bland statement of her first effort [*Understand what will stop me from ever putting meat in my mouth again, was my mother in an ICU bed after her heart attack.*] to purple prose [*Through the mist that are tears unshed, I look wildeyed at my mother in an ICU bed with slightly green, thick tubes in her nose.*] to the fine, professional beginning that moves the reader [*I look at my mother in the Cardiac Care Unit bed with pale green, plastic tubes in her nose.*]

In her first draft, Tina moved from her mother to this paragraph:

Defining what a heart attack is, how it occurs and how to prevent it/ takes research It's not as cut and dry as eating to much fatty fried stuff, arteries clogging and then the next moment you are grabbing your arm and clutching your chest calling for an ambulance as you go down. In essence, it is an artery clogging that causes heart attacks but as more and more research is done, it's about a whole lifestyle. Several papers can be written on the technical medical reasons behind a heart attack, why meat is morally wrong, what is wrong with the meat industry but the focus for this paper is on why eating meat and dairy products is unhealthy for the body. Every fork of meat and dairy product have harmful chemicals present, a meat and dairyless diet automatically trims weight off people and a vegetarian diet makes having a heart attack hard to do. Accordingly the premise that being a vegetarians while only one aspect of the whole heart attack chain reaction and still a controversial one, is one worth merit and consideration.

As Tina said in her journal, she is embarrassed at readers seeing her early drafts but it is important for students who imagine that others write well the first time observe how real writing emerges, draft after draft, until the final draft has this excellent paragraph:

> The first step is to look at meat and dairy products for what they really are. Meat and dairy are primarily vehicles for fat and cholesterol. Most of the established health organizations, as well as the Surgeon General, recommend reducing the fat in your diet to 30 percent (Robbins, May All 89). Studies indicate that this number should be even lower to prevent cancer, strokes, diabetes, hypertension and heart disease risks, and to eliminate or drastically reduce cholesterol (Robbins, May All 89). But Dr. T. Colin Campbell, director of one of the most comprehensive and informative diet and health studies ever undertaken (Chen et al.) and on the committee that set the 30 percent guideline, states it would have been impractical to recommend less than 30 percent, as most people would have to drop the animal foods from their diet and go vegetarian. (Robbins, May All 90).

Every piece of information, whether it comes from personal experience or library research, moves the meaning of the paper forward. The result is a moving, significant, well-documented research paper that both pleases and educates the reader. Here is her final draft:

Take a Bite of Life

by Tina Winslow

I look at my mother in the Cardiac Care Unit bed with pale green, plastic tubes in her nose. CCU has no room for personal whisperings with the doors flung wide and everyone's heartbeeps beating loud enough for the staff behind the desk to hear. Her nails are purple as well as her lips. She looks an off color as if someone sucked the oxygen out of her skin. Pale and tired, with wide brown eyes, she pleads with me not to be scared: it's just a minor life-threatening illness.

The initial prognosis was a minor heart attack, which calmed everyone until the tests revealed three of her arteries were more than 65 percent blocked. This new prognosis, terrible and threatening, was the one thing that would force change into my Mom's life so dramatically and so thoroughly. Having married a Nebraska "meat and potatoes man" her response from the beginning was not one of compromise but rather pouty resistance to a new way of life forced upon her.

Even with a monitor recording her heartbeat she was upset by the chicken and pasta they gave her for lunch.

"It is so bland."

"Mom, you're in a hospital."

"But you think they could put some cheese on this stuff."

"Mom, you just had a heart attack."

I had just become a vegetarian shortly before my mother's heart attack and I discovered through the research I did—both before becoming a vegetarian and after my mother's heart attack—that a diet with no meat and dairy products automatically trims weight and reduces the chances of a heart attack. I also learned that a vegetarian diet prevents the harmful ingestion of chemicals that are present in meat and dairy products and provides a good defense against disease. With benefits like these, being a vegetarian seems the only logical choice for a healthy life.

The first step is to look at meat and dairy products for what they really are. Meat and dairy are primarily vehicles for fat and cholesterol. Most of the established health organizations, as well as the Surgeon General, recommend reducing the fat in your diet to 30 percent (Robbins, May All 89). Studies indicate that this number should be even lower to prevent cancer, strokes, diabetes, hypertension and heart disease risks, and to eliminate or drastically reduce cholesterol (Robbins, May All 89). But Dr. T. Colin Campbell, director of one of the most comprehensive and informative diet and health studies ever undertaken (Chen et al.) and on the committee that set the 30 percent guideline, states it would have been impractical to recommend less than 30 percent, as most people would have to drop the animal foods from their diet and go vegetarian (Robbins, May All 90).

Even chicken, the most common alternative consumers choose when trying to cut fat from their diet, derives 35 percent of its calories from fat and that's without the skin (PETA Guide 1). Beef, on the high end of the scale, has about 22 grams of saturated fat in an average 8-oz. serving (PETA Guide Compassionate Living 17). And as Dean Ornish points out in his book Reversing Heart Disease, "eating fat makes you fat" (255).

Why does eating vegetarian naturally cut weight and reduce the chances of a heart attack? According to Martin and Tenenbaum, authors of Diet Against Disease, most of the fat we eat is in the form of meat and dairy products, so reducing our fat consumption in these areas will reduce the total fat and saturated fat in our diets (16). Conversely, vegetarian foods are primarily complex carbohydrates and are hard for your body to convert into fat (Ornish 257), so the less cholesterol you eat, the lower your risk of developing coronary heart disease (Ornish 263). As advised by the Physicians Committee for Responsible Medicine, a diet without meat and dairy products makes low cholesterol easy "since cholesterol is found only in animal products such as meat, dairy and eggs" (2). Your body also makes all the cholesterol it needs naturally so "it's the excessive amounts of cholesterol and saturated fat in the diet that lead to coronary heart disease" (Ornish 263).

Two months after becoming a vegetarian and two weeks before my mother's heart attack, my entire family went on a cruise. I guess on a cruise, where every meal is supposed to be about reckless abandon without regard to waist size, waste or what you're eating, a vegetarian feeling uneasy isn't going to be the most popular topic.

"What do you mean the French onion soup made you sick?"

"Mom, once you don't eat meat, your body gets used to not having it and I didn't think about French onion soup being made with beef broth."

"There is no way broth can make you sick."

My mom, looking concerned but unbelieving, eyed me suspiciously and tried to make light of it.

"Look, honey, I just ate a whole side of cow, tail and all and I'm fine. How can a soup broth made of beef make you sick?"

The vegetarian target on my forehead grew as my mother's tone drew my entire family's attention at the dinner table. That week spent with my family trapped on board a floating buffet table, just two weeks before my mother had a heart attack, was a study of open hostility at the mention of not eating meat or cheese. My mother—at the head of that committee—was unbelieving that meat could be so harmful. "My quirky daughter, what's next?" seemed to be the question asked without realizing she was less than fourteen days away from a full-blown heart attack—not realizing that it was also the same thing making us both sick.

But it is not just the fat and cholesterol we need to be aware of in meat and dairy products: "Most of us, with images in our minds of the cows of yesteryear, could hardly believe the extent to which the meat industry today relies on chemicals, hormones, antibiotics and a plethora of other drugs" (Robbins, Diet New America 109). The image of a cow chewing on grass in a field is an image of the past as is the pecking and scratching chicken of the barnyard, and the loving mother cow letting the farmer squeeze milk into the pail. They are all misconceptions of what meat and dairy consumers are actually internalizing each time they consume these products. Today's cows used for meat are fed a diet with the strict purpose of fattening them up the cheapest way possible (Robbins, Diet New America 110). "It is impossible to raise animals in intensive confinement without continual reliance on antibiotics, sulfa drugs and other substances" (Fund Facts 2).

Chickens are also fed a diet of chemicals to produce more fat and thus more profit. With "over 90% of today's chickens" fed arsenic compounds (Mason and Singer 56–58) and virtually every chicken raised in the United States being fed a diet of antibiotics, it is hard to believe chicken is being sold as a health food (Robbins, <u>Diet New America</u> 65). Furthermore, "up to 90% of federally inspected poultry is infected with salmonella bacteria" (<u>PETA Guide</u> I). Chicken is not health food as presented to Americans everyday.

The ad campaign "Milk: It Does A Body Good" is also a lie. With the introduction of the Bovine Growth Hormone (rBGH), milk, cheese, butter, ice cream, yogurt and infant formula are now being contaminated without the U.S. Food and Drug Administration testing the long-term health effects on consumers (<u>Vegetarian Voice</u> 12). Furthermore, the FDA admits that "use of rBGH in cows may lead to increased amounts of pus and bacteria in milk" and that "powerful antibiotics and other drugs used to fight increased disease in rBGH-injected cows may lead to greater antibiotic and chemical contamination of milk and dangerous resistance to antibiotics in the human population" (<u>Vegetarian Voice</u> 12). And because these drugs present in these forms of meat and dairy products "form toxic residues in animal tissue, they pose a harm to human consumers" (<u>Fund Facts</u> 2). In other words, what they eat, you eat.

After her heart attack, I tried to help my mother understand the vegetarian lifestyle—which means no meat and dairy products of any kind.

"Tina, you can pick the chicken out."

"WHAT!? Mom, it's tortilla soup with shredded chicken not to mention it's in a chicken broth."

"Well it's got lots of vegetables in it. Maybe you can pick those out."

"It's OK, Mom, I'll just make a cucumber sandwich and be fine."

"But I did put in extra veggies for you."

"And for you, too, Mom, you get the benefits, too."

Since the heart attack she has resigned herself to retiring the <u>Cooking Beef: A Recipe a Day</u> cookbook and has even had lessons in low-fat cooking, but it hasn't occurred to her that as she moves away from fat and cholesterol she is also moving into vegetarianism. We are making progress, though. After realizing that fat and cholesterol make eating meat and dairy so bad for us, she also understands what makes them a double jeopardy for everyone.

Meat and dairy products add chemicals, saturated fat, and cholesterol to a diet. So what will vegetarian foods add to a diet? Beyond reducing fat and cholesterol as previously discussed, a diet without meat or dairy products will reduce cancer risks, reduce protein levels, and add fiber. A vegetarian diet higher in fiber than meat-based diets "helps to dilute, bind, inactivate, and remove many of the carcinogens and toxic substances found in our food supply" (McDougall 120). Due to these properties and other considerations involving fiber "a diet high in fiber helps prevent colon cancer as well as cancers of other parts of the body" (McDougall 120). "An additional benefit of a [vegetarian diet] is that it contains generous amounts of substances with 'anticancer' properties" (McDougall 128). Some of these include Vitamin A, Vitamin C, Vitamin E, and minerals. Thus a vegetarian diet, "complemented with vegetables and fruits, provides a multitude of overlapping mechanisms for preventing cancer and keeping us healthy" (McDougall 130).

According to Martin and Tenenbaum, "there is no known nutritional need for the amount of protein we eat" (27). Americans typically eat roughly twice the amount of protein as the Recommended Dietary Allowance sets for healthy people (Martin and Tenenbaum 27) and much of this protein comes in the form of meat and dairy products. Too much protein lowers the body's ability to naturally absorb calcium and "as surprising as it sounds, one major culprit in osteoporosis may be protein" (Barnard 19). Furthermore, high protein "intakes have been found to contribute to progressive kidney damage" (Barnard 24). Through eating more whole grains, fruits, and vegetables, which naturally reduces saturated fat—and maintains the same level of protein intake—an alteration in the ratio of animal to vegetable protein inevitably will occur" (Martin and Tenenbaum 26). The shift allows more reasonable protein intake without the fat.

I couldn't believe it. My mother was defending my beliefs to my aunts. It was a humorous and satisfying scene.

"Tell them, Tina, what is that Bovine Hormone thing you were telling me about. GROSS, pus in my milk."

"Well, the milk farmers put . . ."

"And what about McDonald's cows eating the rain forests" she interrupted.

"See to support the cows used in . . ."

"And the chicken, Tina, tell them about cholesterol in chicken. The whole industry of meat has hoodwinked us all. It's all a mass market sell."

I know she hasn't eliminated meat entirely but I have watched her over the past four months gently guide herself and our family from taco salad, hamburgers, and sausage to red beans and rice, lentil soup, and other vegetarian meals as she discovers the hidden benefits of vegetarianism on her own.

The choice of a vegetarian lifestyle with all the perceived sanctimonious philosophy can be traced back to the simple fact that eating meat and dairy products is bad for you. A constant reminder to me is remembering someone I love with a monitor on her heart now sitting across from me laughing as she puts another bite of life into her mouth.

Works Cited

"Altered Bovine Hormone Makes Milk, Dairy Products Even Riskier." Vegetarian Voice 20.3 (1994): 12.

Barnard, Neil, M.D. Food for Life: How the New Four Food Groups Can Save Your Life. New York: Crown, 1993.

Chen, J., et al. Diet, Lifestyle, and Mortality in China: A Study of the Characteristics of 65 Countries. New York: Oxford UP, Cornell UP, and the China People's Medical, 1990.

Fund for Animals, The. Fund Facts: Animal Agriculture Fact Sheet #2. Houston: Fund for Animals, 1992.

Martin, Alice A., and Frances Tenenbaum. Diet Against Disease. Boston: Houghton Mifflin, 1980.

Mason, J., and P. Singer. Animal Factories. New York: Crown, 1980.

McDougall, John, M.D., and Mary McDougall. The McDougall Plan. Piscataway: New Century, 1983.

Ornish, Dean, Dr. Dr. Dean Ornish's Program for Reversing Heart Disease. New York: Ballantine, 1990.

PETA Guide to Animals and the Meat Industry, The. Washington, D.C.: PETA, 1993.

PETA Guide to Compassionate Living, The. Washington, D. C.: PETA, 1993.

Robbins, John. Diet for a New America. Walpole: Stillpoint, 1987.

Robbins, John. May All Be Fed: Diet for a New World. New York: Avon, 1992.

▪ WRITING TO PERSUADE: A STUDENT CASE HISTORY ▪

On the following pages, Debbie Carson-Elwood demonstrates how a writer can persuade by appealing to reason. Her voice and documentation are appropriate to her topic. She handles extremely complex material, the kind of material most readers are not interested in. Her paper on the flat tax was written a few years ago but it was major issue in a primary race as I wrote this edition. It is an idea that will be brought up again and again—and it is typical of the complex fiscal issues that voters need to have explained. She has to understand her subject, simplify it—but not too much—and make the material lively and persuasive. I think she does a magnificent job.

> The idea of writing about a flat tax came to me during one of my classes. It's a subject that I'm interested in and an argument that I thought I could pose. This is one of the most important points when I'm writing an argument paper, I have to care about my topic. If I don't believe what I'm writing, the paper will be twice as hard. It's difficult to sound convincing when you're not convinced yourself.

> I went into this project not knowing a whole lot about the flat tax proposal. I understood the basic concept and agreed with it but didn't have any concrete facts to back my argument. I learned more about the proposal by reading numerous newspaper articles. I made sure to read up on both sides of the issue so I'd know the negative as well as the positive aspects. By being aware of the problems in the proposal I was able to avoid those areas.

> There was one part of the paper that I had to change. I originally wanted to strengthen my point on "bracket creep" and found from re-researching that my concept of it was incorrect. Only minor changes were needed but those small changes made a big difference. If a reader had picked up a false statement, my credibility would have been lost and the rest of the paper would be doubted. An argument paper cannot be successful unless the reader believes that you're a reliable source.

> Most of the revisions that I made were minor, a lot of restating and strengthening. My main goal was to get the reader from beginning to end and to consider my argument seriously.

Note how she organized her schedule:

Writing Schedule

Date	Time	Activity
April 13	45 minutes	newspaper index
April 17	1½ hours	reading newspaper articles
April 17	25 minutes	writing
April 18	3½ hours	writing / re-working first written draft
April 19	1½ hours	typing 1st draft & making more revisions
May 3	15 minutes	revising 1st typed draft
May 7	1 hour 20 min.	typing 2nd draft revising
May 13	10 minutes	making suggestions on draft
May 13	2½ hours	typing 3rd draft revising
May 20	15 minutes	revising
May 21	2 hours	typing & revising 4th draft

Here are some of her notes:

Notes from newspaper articles
- everyone pays same percentage
- no more deductions
- lower than most pay
- ~~couldn't deduct interest payment on house~~
- buying real estate - no tax cut, just like renters
✓ - did this to help build industry & encourage
✓   private home ownership, used tax laws
       tool of gov. ?
     closed to all but rich ? They got cuts!
     anything for tax cut

✓ - Proposed by Donald T. Regan (treasury secretary)
   - opposed: US Chamber of Commerce, real estate,
      oil groups, business interests, big labor
      state gov. Wall Street
✓ - 15, 25, 35% of income
✓ - allow homeowners to continue to deduct
      interest
✓ - close loopholes for wealthy paying few taxes
✓ - restore some corporate taxes largely
      eliminated by R.A.
✓ - less complications filing tax returns
   * possible - 1990 IRS com. Roscoe L. Egger
     if deductions & credits are eliminated, could be
     possible for IRS to do 2 out of 3 taxpayers work

✓ Firm Yankelovish, Skelly & White   1984

✓ + 4 of 5 $\bar{x}$ believe that current system
   benefits rich & is unfair to average
   working person

✓ + almost 1 in 5 admits to cheating (19%)
   Egger says understated

Her first draft shows a highly organized person going through the messy process of discovering what to say and how to say it:

First Draft

In 1984, the Yankelovish, Skelley & White firm conducted a survey ~~to discover~~ *in order to find out* what taxpayers thought of ~~the~~ *our* tax system. The results ~~say little for the system~~ *concluded that* Four out of five taxpayers believe ~~that~~ the present tax system *to* ~~is~~ beneficial to ~~the~~ *for the* rich and ~~is~~ unfair ~~for the~~ *to the* average working person. *Nineteen percent* ~~19%~~ of those surveyed (almost one in five) admitted to cheating on their taxes. The ~~primary reason~~ *justification* ~~for this cheating is because people believe~~ that the system is unfair ~~and they must alter things~~ *believe that* *by the taxes* themselfs ~~to even out the score~~ *they are* just ~~equaling out the burden.~~

→ Secretary of the treasury, Donald T. Regan, (in a report to the President ∧ *Regan* stated ~~the following facts~~ *facts* that further discredited our current tax system. According to treasury estimates in 1983, 9,000 people who earned \$250,000 or more paid no taxes due to tax shelters. ∧ *An additional* 59,000 people at the same income level managed through loopholes to reduce their tax payments by half. The *Thru out the yrs?* government has (used) *managed to use* the progressive tax as a tool to help build industry and to promote private home ownership. With *An* ~~individual renting a home receives no tax breaks~~ ~~renting there are no tax breaks;~~ however, if you buy a home you qualify for tax deductions. The government allows ~~home~~ owners to deduct their ~~interest payments~~ interest payments on ~~their~~ mortgages. ~~of a house.~~ (So in order to receive any breaks, a person must take out a loan.) ~~Not much of a break.~~ (The only way to lessen taxes is tax shelters and expensive lawyers to seek out loopholes.) Unfortunately, the only taxpayers who can afford such measures are the wealthy.

rephrase — strengthen point

circle? CATCH 22?

It's ironic that the one who needs ~~the~~ TO the most is also the one who can't afford to buy in the first ~~case~~.

Shelters → Lawyers | i.e.

The current system also has the problem of "bracket creep." Often times workers will receive a cost of living raise to help them with the ~~raising~~ changing economy. The ~~raise they~~ extra money receive with their raise goes toward the higher taxes they will have to pay. ~~because~~ Sometimes the pay raise will push them into a higher tax bracket.

Does this example explain "bracket creep"?

For example, ~~if you have~~ a worker with a taxable income of $24,600, in the current system, ~~he pays~~ will pay a tax of $3465 — 14% of his salary. Now if this worker received a $5300 cost of living increase, his taxable income becomes $29,900 and he is now in a higher tax bracket.

check numbers again

Here are the teacher's notes on one page for the conference and the student's notes:

applies to ~~all~~ taxpayers*x* *of all income levels.*

There are two main variations of this proposal: a tax simplification proposal by Donald Regan and a Fair tax (also known as the Bradley-Gephardt proposal) by Senator Bill Bradley and Representative Richard Gephardt. Both of these taxes would reduce the tax bracket to three (for instance, 15%, 25%, and 35%), [lower taxes for the poor,] increase the amount of personal exemption and keep deductions for interest on home mortgages (the Treasury department would not, however, allow interest deductions on second homes.)

elaborate on advantages

The flat tax, or a variation of, would close most loopholes and shelters available to the wealthy. The Treasury Secretary also claims that the tax would restore some corporate taxes that have been largely eliminated by the Reagan Administration. It would do away with all discrimination involved with the distribution of taxes, creating a fair system.

Argue why Cheating on taxes would no longer be necessary, *or possible* and people of the lower and middle class would be unable to label the *no listing deductions* system as "unfair."

no way around it. The complicated tax system would simplify (so much) *to such a degree* that many wouldn't even have to do their own returns. IRS commissioner, Roscoe L. Egger, believes that the elimination of most deductions and credits would allow IRS to do two out of every three tax returns. A bill or refund could be sent solely on information received from the IRS by employers, banks, stockbrokers, etc.

With a relatively low rate, the government would be collecting about the same amount of revenue that it is now. The primary difference is that the source of revenue would be economically neutral, coming from all incomes*x* *levels.*

The seventy-one-year-old system is outdated and it's

Now here's a later draft with further clarifications:

Flat Tax — The Sensible Future

(2nd draft revisions)

In 1984, the Yankelovish, Skelly & White firm conducted a survey in order to find out what taxpayers thought of our tax system. The results (concluded) that four out of five taxpayers believe the present tax system to be beneficial to the rich and unfair to the average working person. Nineteen percent of those surveyed, almost one in five, admitted to cheating on their taxes with the justification that the system is unfair. The belief is that by altering the taxes, they are doing their part to equal out the burden.

transition suggests that

Survey suggests

The present tax system is biased, inefficient and in dire need of reform. In a report to the President, Donald T. Regan, Secretary of the Treasury, stated facts that further discredit our current tax system. According to Treasury Department estimates, in 1983, 9,000 people who earned $250,000 or more paid no taxes due to tax shelters. An additional 59,000 people at the same income level managed through loopholes to reduce their taxes by half.

← more back it interpret numbers

Throughout the years, the government has used the progressive tax as a tool to help build industry and to promote private home ownership. An individual renting a home receives no tax breaks; however, if you buy a home you qualify for deductions. The government allows homeowners to deduct the interest payments on their mortgage. ~~Another words;~~ to receive a tax break, you must take out a loan and spend money. It appears to be a vicious circle, the people who are needy of the tax break are the same people who can't afford to buy a house in the first place. In order to save money they must spend money they don't have. One might question if they're really saving any money at all. The only way around heavy taxes is through legal loopholes and ex-

✳ first 7 lines of p. 2 & 3 cut off. Refer to unrevised second draft

The student needs, at this late date, to make further notes to clarify the subject for herself and then her reader:

Figures to explain "bracket creep"

TAX INC	TAX	% TAX	% of TAX INC
24,600	3465	14%	
27 000	4065	15%	17%
29,900	4790	16%	38% Ⓐ
35,200	6274	17%	31% Ⓐ

(TO TAX INC above % TAX)

Ⓐ 4790 ÷ 3465 = 38% OR (4790 − 3465 ÷ 3465)
6274 ÷ 4790 = 31% OR (6274 − 4790 ÷ 4790)

FLAT TAX OF 14%   Ⓐ

TAX INC	FLAT TAX %	TAX	$ INC	% INC
24,600 ×	14	= 3444		
29,900 ×	14	= 4186	742	21%
35,200 ×	14	= 4928	738	17%

Ⓐ 4186 ÷ 3444   4.928 ÷ 41.86

The next-to-last draft and the writer is still working to clarify what she has to say:

Final Draft with revisions

Debbie Carson-Elwood
English 401
Bob Yagelski

Flat Tax--The Sensible Future

In 1984, the Yankelovish, Skelly & White firm conducted a survey in order to find out what taxpayers thought of our tax system. The results showed that four out of five taxpayers believe the present tax system to be beneficial to the rich and unfair to the average working person. Nineteen percent of those surveyed, almost one in five, admitted to cheating on their taxes with the justification that the system is unfair. The belief is that by altering the taxes, they are doing their part to ~~equal~~ *even* out the burden.

This survey suggests that the present tax system is biased and is in need of reform. In a report to the President, Donald T. Regan, Secretary of the Treasury, (stated facts that) *omit* further discredit*ed* our current tax system. According to Treasury Department estimates, in 1983, 9,000 people who earned $250,000 or more paid no taxes due to tax shelters. An additional 59,000 people at the same income level managed through loopholes to reduce their taxes by half: These figures *clearly* illustrate ~~the bias in our~~ *one of the many reasons our* tax system. *is in need of reorganization.* Those with the largest incomes are the ones escaping taxes because [they can afford *of tax breaks & shelters* to put their money into shelters.] *(available to the wealthy)* Most people in the middle class ~~cannot afford to invest money, they need their cash~~ *do not have these outlets available to them and therefore are unable to reduce their taxes.* ~~readily available to pay expenses.~~

? Smoother sentence
re-state general

Now, the final draft:

Flat Tax—The Sensible Future

by Debbie Carson-Elwood

In 1984, the Yankelovish, Skelly & White firm conducted a survey in order to find out what taxpayers thought of our tax system. The results showed that four out of five taxpayers believe the present tax system to be beneficial to the rich and unfair to the average working person. Nineteen percent of those surveyed, almost one in five, admitted to cheating on their taxes with the justification that the system is unfair. The belief is that by altering the taxes, they are doing their part to even out the burden.

This survey suggests that the present tax system is biased and in need of reform. In a report to the President, Donald T. Regan, Secretary of the Treasury, further discredited our current tax system. According to Treasury Department estimates, in 1983, 9,000 people who earned $250,000 or more paid no taxes due to tax shelters. An additional 59,000 people at the same income level managed through loopholes to reduce their taxes by half. These figures clearly illustrate one of the reasons our tax system is in need of reorganization. Those with the largest incomes are the ones escaping taxes because of the tax breaks and shelters. Most people in the middle class do not have these outlets available to them and are therefore unable to reduce their taxes.

Throughout the years, the government has used the progressive tax as a tool to help build industry and promote private home ownership. An individual renting a home receives no tax breaks; however, if you buy a home you qualify for deductions. The government allows homeowners to deduct the interest payments on their mortgage. To receive a tax break, you must take out a loan and spend money. It appears to be a vicious circle: The people who are in need of the tax break are the same people who can't afford to buy a house in the first place. In order to save money they must spend money they don't have. One might question if they're really saving any money at all. The only way around heavy taxes is through legal loopholes and expensive lawyers or accountants who can find them. But if the poor and middle class could afford such measures, they most likely could afford the taxes as well.

The current system also has the problem of "bracket creep." Often workers will receive a cost of living raise to help them adjust to the changing economy. But sometimes the workers end up being pushed into a higher tax bracket. The extra money they're making goes toward the higher taxes they're paying. For instance, consider a worker with a taxable income of $24,600. In the current system he pays a tax of $3465, which is 14% of his salary. Now suppose this worker received a $5300 cost of living raise. His taxable income becomes $29,900 and he is now in a higher tax bracket. His new tax will be $4790—16% of his salary. This is a 38% tax increase. If another $5300 were to be added on to his salary, he would jump into the next bracket and pay 17% of his income in taxes, which would be a 31% tax increase. That is the creep. The higher your salary goes, the more of it you pay in taxes. In a sense, this policy is taking away the incentive to work harder and earn more. The more you work, the more you earn and the more you earn, the more you're taxed. The only way to escape this is if you work your way above the brackets. However, this means you must earn over $162,000—not an easy goal to attain. The tax system even goes as far as discouraging saving. Money in savings accounts is taxed twice—once as income and again as returns on investment.

There is a great deal of controversy over what should be done and there have been several proposals for reform. The most sensible proposal is that of a flat tax. A flat tax would eliminate all deductions and credits and replace the progressive tax with a single rate (for example 25%) that applies to all taxpayers at all income levels.

There are two main variations of this proposal: a tax simplification proposal by Donald Regan and a Fair Tax (also known as the Bradley-Gephardt proposal) by Senator Bill Bradley and Representative Richard Gephardt. Both of these proposals would reduce the tax brackets from fifteen to three (for instance, 15%, 25% and 35%), increase the amount for personal exemption and keep deductions for interest on home mortgages (the Treasury Department would not, however, allow interest deductions on second homes).

Both proposals would not only lower the taxes themselves but also lower the percentage of tax increase. The burden of taxes would be reduced, enabling people to pay a smaller percentage of their salary in taxes. The wealthy would no longer have the advantage of being "above" taxes; they would be required to pay their fair share along with everyone else.

The flat tax, or variation of, would close most loopholes and shelters available to the rich. The Treasury Secretary also claims that the tax would restore some corporate taxes that have been largely eliminated by the Reagan Administration. It would do away with all discrimination involved with the distribution of taxes, creating a fair system. The problem of cheating would be greatly reduced because the tax would be a straight percentage of your income with no deductions except mortgage interest and personal exemptions. The IRS has records of incomes and interest payments and the exemption would be a straight $2000 per person. A false tax return would be detected immediately.

The complicated tax system would be simplified to such a degree that many wouldn't even have to do their own returns. IRS Commissioner Roscoe L. Egger believes that the elimination of most deductions and credits would allow the IRS to do two out of every three tax returns. A bill of refund could be sent solely on information received from the IRS by employers, banks, stock brokers, etc. This would save the taxpayer time, effort, and money. They wouldn't have to spend hours filling out lengthy returns or figuring out the confusing process. It also would save money for those who have their taxes done by tax accountants.

With a relatively low rate, the government would be collecting the same amount of revenue that it is now, if not more. The primary difference is that the source of revenue would be economically neutral, coming from all income levels.

The seventy-one-year-old system is outdated and it's time for something new. The majority sees problems and the taxpayers of this country certainly deserve a change. It's time for the government to stop wasting time and money and start reforming our taxes to provide us with a future that makes economical sense.

Debbie Carson-Elwood has done an excellent job of demonstrating the "Tips on Writing Persuasion" on page 175 of Chapter 7. She makes it clear from the beginning that she does not think the progressive tax system we have works. She demonstrates her authority by the way she uses specific references and authorities to support each point. She anticipates the reader's reaction and responds to it and all the way through she appeals to reason, not attacking those who disagree with her but providing evidence they must consider.

Create your own case history on your next writing project, keeping notes and drafts, and concentrating on what works best for you. We learn to improve our writing by learning from the writing that has gone well.

▪ QUESTIONS ON WRITING A CASE HISTORY ▪

What if I haven't saved my notes, drafts, kept a journal?

Write an account from memory. You will be surprised at how much you remember about the process of writing. And it will help you reinforce what works for you and identify what you need to work on.

On the next piece of writing, keep a notebook account in a daybook, journal, or in a computer file. Save your notes, outlines, research sources, drafts and write a base history at the end that may surprise you with additional insights.

I'm not a writer. Why should I keep a case history?

Yes you are. You are a writer teaching yourself to write better and the case history will reveal what you have learned in the past, what you are learning, what you need to learn in the future.

But what if my case history is a mess and I start and stop, follow false leads, switch my topic, my genre, my language, change my mind, come up with a final draft that is entirely different from what I started to write?

You sound like a writer and you need to know that. Writing is thinking and the case history will show you that thinking in writing is often a confused, complex process. You will also discover ways of thinking and writing that you can follow—and not follow—the next time you write.

I kept notes and wrote a case history but it is nothing like yours or the students'.

Good. We do not think alike or write alike. There is a glorious diversity in how our minds—and our pens—work. In writing case histories, we learn to observe ourselves as writers. As we continue to write, we will discover that our writing changes with the writing task and our experience with a particular writing task. We learn lessons from our case histories and the case histories of others we can apply to future writing tasks.

Can anyone write an honest case history?

Honest? Yes. Scientifically accurate? Perhaps. But if a writer were observed during the writing process, the researcher would see things the writer might not see. Both case histories would be "true" but they might be different.

Are there other ways of writing a case history?

I'd like to see a video of someone writing with the camera set so the observer could read the evolving text. I did a protocol where I talked into a tape recorder as I wrote and a researcher, Dr. Carol Berkenkotter of Michigan Technical University, analyzed it (*College Composition and Communication* 34(2), May 1983, 156–72.) I found that it became natural to talk as I planned, drafted, revised, and edited. In fact, I had been talking to myself all along as I wrote. Now I was doing it aloud. There was, however, blank places on the tape when I would not speak but would return with a writing problem solved. The researcher interviewed me and called these creative breaks "bathroom epiphanies."

▪ CASE HISTORY ACTIVITIES ▪

1. Study a famous author and re-create a case history of a piece of writing from published journals, notebooks, interviews, autobiographies and biographies. Two famous examples of such studies are *Flaubert and Madame Bovary* by Francis Steegmuller, Viking, 1939; and Thomas Mann's *The Story of a Novel,* Knopf, 1961.

2. Write your own case history as has been suggested above.

3. Read the account of a series of dramatic or musical rehearsals and relate what you learn to writing.

4. Interview a writer, composer, artist, scientist, critic, scholar on your campus to discover how they write, then connect their methods and habits to the writing tasks you face.

5. Check your audio/visual library to find interviews with writers and other creative artists as well as films that reveal creative people at work.

6. Study the CD-ROM disks that show all the versions of a famous musical work.

7. Become a composition scientist and observe a classmate drafting, revising, or editing. Write an account of what you discovered, relating it to the forms of writing expected of students.

8. Read medical and sociological case histories to see the elements that might be appropriate to writing a case history.

9. Write a narrative of a narrative to reveal a writer—yourself?—at work.

10. Write the imaginative case history of a famous piece of literature, showing what the writer *may* have gone through to complete the work.

CHAPTER 9
READ AS A WRITER

*I think that one of the things that gives
pleasure in reading—at least gives me
pleasure in reading—is the sense of the
presence of a storyteller, whether it's
fiction or nonfiction. I think we can use
terms like "voice" or "style," but a large
part of it is the sense that there's someone
behind the scenes adroitly pulling the
strings, the reader's realizing with pleasure
that there's someone there. Not that the
narrator, or the storyteller who may stand
behind the narrator, has to be an obtrusive
presence, but the reader's sense of that
presence, the reader's pleasurable sense of
that presence, is something that I feel is
fundamental.*

TRACY KIDDER

When writers read they are aware of the writer at work behind the page.

They share the same craft and therefore understand the problems the published writer faced and applaud when they read a skillful, perhaps unexpected solution. Of course, writers learn from the authors they read, but, even more, they experience a joy in reading writing that is well crafted, that clarifies meaning with grace and the illusion of ease.

The reading writer sees the author's choices underneath the page and learns from them: This problem was solved, this one was not, another was avoided. When reading, the writer scans the landscape of the subject and notices how the fellow writer chose to focus; the writer imagines the scaffolding the text's writer erected to organize the draft and then took down so it would not get in the reader's way; the writer, when reading, hears the language that might have been used as well as what was used.

When I am served a dinner with each course hot or cold, every dish ready on time, I applaud because I understand, firsthand, how difficult it is to do that. I sketch landscapes when I travel and so have a special appreciation of Rembrandt's sketchbooks, where so few lines reveal so much. I played right tackle and when I watch a football game I take pleasure in the quick, well-timed brush back block that gently neutralizes a charging linebacker.

When I hear a writer extend the horizon of language, leaving an abundance of detail out but revealing more with less, shape a worn vision so it becomes new, I cheer and I learn. And, ironically, I often learn more easily from bad writing. When a great writer, such as Shakespeare, captures a human emotion in a phrase, it is magic, all the craft hidden by grace. But with a poor writer, the workings are all exposed. I see what not to do, and, more often than you would think, what to do with more skill.

But I do not use other writers as conscious models, carefully imitating them. Rather I absorb the lessons of other writers by reading. They tune my instinct so that what I do "naturally" or because of "talent" I often learned subconsciously when I was reading.

In this chapter we will read together as writers, taking delight in what other writers have done and perhaps tuning our instincts so that when we face a similar writing problem we will solve it, not knowing where we learned the solution.

▪ READING ANNIE DILLARD ▪

I read Annie Dillard's essay on "Schedules" because I am schedule-obsessive and want to see what this wonderful writer has to say about her working habits. I am particularly interested when she describes her workplace from where so much writing that has given me pleasure has come.

I write these words in my most recent of many studies—a pine shed on Cape Cod. The pine lumber is unfinished inside the study, the pines outside are finished trees. I see the pines from my two windows. Nuthatches spiral around their long, coarse trunks. Sometimes in June a feeding colony of mixed warblers flies through the pines; the warblers make a racket that draws me out the door. The warblers drift loosely through the stiff pine branches, and I follow through the thin long grass between the trunks.

The study—sold as a prefabricated toolshed—is eight feet by ten feet. Like a plane's cockpit, it is crammed with high-tech equipment. There is no quill pen in sight. There is a computer, a printer, and a photocopying machine. My backless chair, a prie-dieu on which I kneel, slides under the desk; I give it a little kick when I leave. There is an air conditioner, a heater, and an electric kettle. There is a low-tech bookshelf, a shelf of gull and whale bones, and a bed. Under the bed I stow paints—a one-pint can of yellow to touch up the window's trim, and five or six tubes of artists' oils. The study affords ample room for one. One who is supposed to be writing books. You can read in the space of a coffin, and you can write in the space of a toolshed meant for mowers and spades . . . Appealing workplaces are to be avoided. One wants a room with no view, so imagination can dance with memory in the dark. When I furnished this study seven years ago, I pushed the long desk against a blank wall, so I could not see from either window.

I do not agree with her rejection of a view. My desk faces one view and when I am at my computer I face another. But then I don't see as Annie Dillard does and I delight in the simple, graceful way the birds pass through her world and am respectively amused by the difference between her romantic view of nature and the sleeves rolled up, practical attitude she has toward her workplace.

▪ READING ROGER C. PARKER AND DAVID A. HOLZGANG ▪

Too much writing in the computer software manuals on which we all depend obscures and confuses when we need clarification. One exception to the rule is Roger C. Parker, a nationally recognized expert on computer graphic design. With David A. Holzgang he has written *WordPerfect 6 Secrets* (IDG Books, 1993) that argues for simplicity and clarity then—miracles of miracles—practices what they preach. Here is an example I admire. The writers' problem was to demonstrate the simplicity they recommend. They achieve George Orwell's goal: "Good writing is like a window pane." Parker and Holzgang do not strut like peacocks, telling us how much they know about computers; they call attention to the subject and I greatly admire such transparent writing, knowing very well how hard it is to be simple.

Simplicity is preferable to complexity. The thousands of typefaces available and the numerous page layout and typographic features in WordPerfect can actually hinder, rather than enhance, your ability to create good-looking, easy-to-read documents. You may have noticed, too, that pages, like products, that pass the test of time are often characterized by a deceptive simplicity. The trendy, the gaudy, and the attention-getting publications often quickly become passé.

The *New Yorker* magazine, for example, has remained virtually unchanged for over fifty years, as has Strunk and White's *The Elements of Style.* The simplicity of their designs allows the message—the ideas expressed in the writing—to emerge unscathed. Trendy magazines like *Rolling Stone,* regional magazines like *Texas Monthly* or *New York,* and the Sunday supplements of most metropolitan newspapers, however, often rely upon short-lived redesigns to maintain reader (and advertiser) enthusiasm. Trendy publications often sacrifice the ease with which readers can understand their articles in a continuing search for impact and novelty.

The issue of efficiency also plays a role in design. A complex document is usually harder and more time-consuming to produce than a simple one and often opens the door to more opportunity for you to make mistakes. Good-looking design often reflects a deceptive simplicity, a transparency that allows the message, not the medium, to emerge.

Simplicity is also preferable to complexity because complexity often has unwanted side effects. . . . Text wraps tend to create narrow columns of type, which are frequently characterized by irregular word spacing and excessive hyphenation, creating a problem where no problem previously existed.

Although Parker and Holzgang are not writing for professionals but beginners they do not write down to their audience. They also clarify and document each point as they make it so their meaning is clear.

▪ READING SEI SHŌNAGON ▪

Writing crosses barriers of culture and time. Sei Shōnagon was a member of the aristocracy; I came from a working-class neighborhood. She was Chinese; I am American. She wrote in the tenth century; I write a millennium, a thousand years later. Yet I delight—and share—her views of our world in the journal she called "Hateful Things."

One is in a hurry to leave, but one's visitor keeps chattering away. If it is someone of no importance, one can get rid of him by saying, "You must tell me all about it next time"; but, should it be the sort of visitor whose presence commands one's best behavior, the situation is hateful indeed.

• • •

Someone has suddenly fallen ill and one summons the exorcist. Since he is not at home, one has to send messengers to look for him. After one has had a long fretful wait, the exorcist finally arrives, and with a sigh of relief one asks him to start his incantations. But perhaps he has been exorcising too many evil spirits recently; for hardly has he installed himself and begun praying when his voice becomes drowsy. Oh, how hateful!

• • •

A man who has nothing in particular to recommend him discusses all sorts of subjects at random as though he knew everything.

• • •

I hate the sight of men in their cups who shout, poke their fingers in their mouths, stroke their beards, and pass on the wine to their neighbours with great cries of "Have some more! Drink up!" They tremble, shake their heads, twist their faces, and gesticulate like children who are singing, "We're off to see the Governor."

I have seen really well-bred people behave like this and I find it most distasteful.

• • •

One has gone to bed and is about to doze off when a mosquito appears, announcing himself in a reedy voice. One can actually feel the wind made by his wings and, slight though it is, one finds it hateful in the extreme.

For exorcist read neurologist—or the ologist of your choice, perhaps a resident who has been on duty for 97 hours. I am struck—again—in reading these simple observations how important it is to capture and examine the ordinariness of life. In the small there is the large—the disinterest of some who care for us when we face life-threatening situations and how much it can hurt those who are suffering, all told in a few simple words.

▪ READING ANNA QUINDLEN ▪

Anna Quindlen has given up her column in the *New York Times* to write novels but here, in one of her last columns, she shows how much she can say within the limitations of journalism—or perhaps because of journalistic training that makes it possible for the reporter/writer to get to the essentials immediately and communicate human events and the emotional reaction to them with short words in brief sentences.

My great journalistic contribution to my family is that I write obituaries. First my mother's, 22 years ago, listing her accomplishments: two daughters, three sons. Then that of my father's second wife, dead of the same disease that killed his first one.

Last week it was my sister-in-law. "Sherry Quindlen, 41," I tapped out on the keyboard, and then it was real, like a last breath. "When you write about me," she said one day in the hospital, "be nice."

For the obit I could only be accurate. The limitations of the form eliminate the more subjective truths: a good heart, a generous soul, who made her living taking care of other people's children. My brother's wife, the mother of a teen-ager and a toddler, who went from a bad cough to what was mistakenly said to be pneumonia to what was correctly diagnosed as lung and liver cancer, from fall to spring, from the day she threw a surprise 40th birthday party for her husband to the day he chose her casket.

I reread each sentence, amazed at how this craftsperson, whose trade I share, can accomplish so much so quickly—and yet I never feel rushed. I have time to reflect, to see my own memories in what she has said of hers. Reread these sentences aloud. For example, read the series of clauses in the not-so-simple last sentence to see how much chronological, medical, and emotional territory she covered in 47 words: "who went from a bad cough to what was mistakenly said to be pneumonia to what was correctly diagnosed as lung and liver cancer, from fall to spring, from the day she threw a surprise 40th birthday party for her husband to the day he chose her casket."

If you want to know how to write with specifics, study these lines.

▪ READING ED LINN ▪

In writing about Ted Williams, the famous baseball player, Ed Linn, in his book *Hitter* (Harcourt Brace, 1993), sets up Williams as an instinctive genius, comparing him to Mozart and others who supposedly had a talent that did not have to be learned, then allows Williams to respond to that concept. This writer is always impressed when a writer can get out of the way and let the subject do the writing. It gives the book liveliness, a change of voice, and a special authority.

When Williams is told he has a natural talent, he answers:

"I can tell you exactly when it started," he says. "It wasn't when I was ten or eleven. It happened when I was twelve. I had never followed major-league baseball. The only players I had ever heard of were Ruth and Gehrig. And then I read that Bill Terry had hit .400, and that really excited me. Four hundred! I don't think I even knew what you had to do to hit .400, but I could tell that it was something wonderful. I knew I wanted to do that, too. Hit .400. I was so excited that even though it was dark out—I've never told this to anybody before—I got my little bat, ran out to our little backyard, and began to swing."

And continued to swing every night. Hour after hour, the little boy, alone at home, out in the tiny backyard, swinging by the light of the moon . . . Over and over and over. Whoooosh . . . whooooosh . . . whooooosh. "There were two things I concentrated on. First, I wanted to have a great-looking swing. That was important to me, everybody wants to look good. Second, I wanted to visualize what I was doing. And I always visualized myself in the Polo Grounds, because that's where Bill Terry played." Men on first and second, two out, high inside fast ball. See the ball, see the swing, see the bat hitting the ball, see the long, high fly arcing out toward the right-field bleachers. Whoooosh . . . whooooosh . . . whooooosh. Whoooosh.

"I was playing in a sandlot game, and I heard a man say, 'Gee, that kid has quick wrists.' And I thought, If you think I'm quick with my wrists now, just wait awhile."

I enjoy the way Linn allows Williams to talk and how Williams, interviewed and edited by Linn, re-creates himself as a boy. Linn is a master interviewer, someone you want to talk to and I imagine how long it took for Williams to tell this story he has never told before to Linn.

▪ READING DOROTHY ALLISON ▪

I remember getting goose bumps the first time I read these lines, the beginning of the Preface to *Trash,* a collection of stories by Dorothy Allison, a writer I had never heard of. I still get goose bumps.

There was a day in my life when I decided to live.

After my childhood, after all that long terrible struggle to simply survive, to escape my stepfather, uncles, speeding Pontiacs, broken glass and rotten floorboards, or that inevitable death by misadventure that claimed so many of my cousins; after watching so many die around me, I had not imagined that I would ever need to make such a choice. I had imagined the hunger for life in me was insatiable, endless, unshakable.

I became an escapee—one of the ones others talked about. I became the one who got away, who got glasses from the Lions Club, a job from Lyndon Johnson's War On Poverty, and finally went to college on a scholarship. There I met the people I had always read about: girls whose fathers loved them—innocently; boys who drove cars they had not stolen; whole armies of the middle and upper classes I had not truly believed to be real; the children to whom I could not help but compare myself. I matched their innocence, their confidence, their capacity to trust, to love, to be generous against the bitterness, the rage, the pure and terrible hatred that consumed me. Like many others who had gone before me, I began to dream longingly of my own death.

I began to court it. Cowardly, traditionally—that is, in the tradition of all those others like me, through drugs and drinking and stubbornly putting myself in the way of other people's violence. Even now, I cannot believe how it was that everything I survived became one more reason to want to die.

Whew! With enormous authority, with extraordinary control of specific information, without anger and without a single whine, she takes us to the center of life. The one-line first paragraph presents us with the human dilemma—to live or not.

The next paragraph gives you her life before she escaped; the next the life after, allowing you to see the scholarship winners from the other side of the tracks or the trailer park as they see themselves and how they compare themselves to those who "belong"; and then the life of self-destruction, which we all have observed if not experienced.

Accomplished in four paragraphs, 273 words. It is interesting to study these sentences to see how she has established a distance that allows her to take the reader into her world yet allows her to comment on it: distance and voice, demonstrated by an enormously skillful writer.

▪ READING THOMAS FRENCH ▪

Thomas French spent a year in a Florida high school—where he saw many in Dorothy Allison's situation—and wrote a superb book, *South of Heaven* (Doubleday, 1993), that captures the world of the high school. An editor once said that a good reporter is "forever astonished by the obvious" and French is a great reporter who sees the drama in the ordinary and reveals the true human condition. He is also a skillful writer who is able to describe what he reports with perception and grace. As a writer, I delight in how he dramatizes a significant situation a less-perceptive reporter would overlook.

Day after day, Karin sits in that class—she sits right in front of Bret Harper, the kid on the quiz team, the one known as Elvis—and listens to Ms. Fish talk on and on about synthetic division and inverse variation and negative reciprocals. She barely understands a word of it.

"Where are we? Wait," she says, frantically trying to keep up. "Please."

Karin might have a chance if only she weren't stuck in the middle of the pack, jammed into crowded rooms like this one. That's the problem. If she were a wonderful student like YY and the others, she'd be in those honor courses, where the classes are usually kept to a reasonable size. And if she were a failing student, she'd probably be down in the pod, where the classes are also small and where individualized attention is always the specialty of the day. But Karin doesn't fit either category. She's average, so she's forced to fight for air inside regular classes, where the rest of teen humanity is assigned. Sometimes, there are more than thirty-five kids jammed into one room, which means that the teacher hardly has time to take the roll, much less answer individual questions. In those classes, it's survival of the fittest.

Lots of times, if Karin has trouble understanding something, she doesn't even bother raising her hand. What's the point? She knows what happens to kids who are lost and try to take up too much class time with questions.

"If you don't get it," some teachers say, "we'll just have to move on."

As Ms. Fish talks "on and on about synthetic division and inverse variation and negative reciprocals. She barely understands a word of it" I am back in the classroom. French specifics put me there.

And as a fellow writer, I want to stand up and shout—perhaps I did—when I read "She's average, so she's forced to fight for air inside regular classes." Look how much he does with the verb, with the image: "fight for air inside regular classes."

■ READING JOAN DIDION ■

The writer's mission is to articulate the experiences, thoughts, feelings of the inarticulate. I keep returning to Joan Didion's "In Bed" because I suffered migraines for years and first read this essay when I was having a migraine. She expressed the feelings I had not been able to express and there was comfort in that—and I could give it to family and friends and say, "You wanta know how it is, read Didion. Here." Didion is the only person I have read who describes the relief and euphoria you feel when you return to life.

At first every small apprehension is magnified, every anxiety a pounding terror. Then the pain comes, and I concentrate only on that. Right there is the usefulness of migraine, there in that imposed yoga, the concentration on the pain. For when the pain recedes, ten or twelve hours later, everything goes with it, all the hidden resentments, all the vain anxieties. The migraine has acted as a circuit breaker, and the fuses have emerged intact.

> There is a pleasant convalescent euphoria. I open the windows and feel the air, eat gratefully, sleep well. I notice the particular nature of a flower in a glass on the stair landing. I count my blessings.

Didion speaks for me and there is therapy in that as when I write of my own anxieties, fears, problems. The naming of the dragon often makes him retreat if not disappear.

▪ READING MICHAEL KELLY ▪

The best book to come out of the Gulf War, in my opinion, is Michael Kelly's *Martyr's Day—Chronicle of a Small War* (Random House, 1993). In the few paragraphs that follow he is able to reveal the robbing of individual personality that is one of the costs of combat. In this brief anecdote, we can feel, if not experience, the terror and inhumanity of war.

> I remember one sharp, small scene. Several prisoners signaled to one of the Egyptian officers that they had to urinate. With a beckoning wave of his pistol, he moved them forward to the edge of the trench that had been theirs to defend. Motioning downward with the pistol he had them kneel in the mud. I thought for a horrible moment that he was going to execute them so that their bodies would tumble into the trench, but the Iraqis knew what he wanted. Together on their knees in line, they unzipped their pants and sent their streams into the ditch.
>
> Behind them, the others of their unit were now, as the Egyptians directed, taking off their boots. It is a difficult thing to take off a shoe with one hand remaining on your head. Some managed to balance on one leg, but most fell into a clumsy sit when they tried it. They pitched their boots into a pile, and the guards motioned them up again and herded them into two groups, the enlisted men in one, the officers in another, and they all sat down in the mud. A few feet away a .50-caliber machine gun had been set up on a tripod to guard them, and the young soldier who manned it watched with eager intent for the first sign of trouble, but he might have been assigned to cover a group of nuns for all the need there was of his services. The prisoners sat silent and unmoving.

Kelly puts us beside him as the expert writer always does so that we see this scene and share his apprehension. Then we have the details, the revealing details. And notice how he lets us see them—and therefore makes imagine we are them: "It is a difficult thing to take off a shoe with one hand remaining on your head. Some managed to balance on one leg, but most fell into a clumsy sit when they tried it."

▪ READING VIRGINIA WOOLF ▪

In her essay "Street Haunting," novelist Virginia Woolf expresses a feeling I have as a city boy. These days it is politically correct to romanticize the country but when I went to college after World War II we all dreamt of the city.

> How beautiful a London street is then, with its islands of light, and its long groves of darkness, and on one side of it perhaps some tree-sprinkled, grass-grown space where night is folding herself to sleep naturally and, as one passes the iron railing, one hears those little cracklings and stirrings of leaf and twig, which seem to suppose the silence of fields all round them, an owl hooting, and far away the rattle of a train in the valley. But this is London, we are reminded; high among the bare trees are hung oblong frames of reddish yellow light-windows; there are points of brilliance burning steadily like low stars—lamps; this empty ground which holds the country in it and its peace, is only a London square, set about by offices and houses where at this hour fierce lights burn over maps, over documents, over desks where clerks sit turning with wetted forefinger the files of endless correspondences; or more suffusedly the firelight wavers and the lamplight falls upon the privacy of some drawing-room, its easy chairs, its papers, its china, its inlaid table, and the figure of a woman, accurately measuring out the precise number of spoons of tea which—She looks at the door as if she heard a ring downstairs and somebody asking, is she in?

It is the eye that writes and Virginia Woolf's observations of city make me see the familiar as if I had never seen it before. And at the end of this excerpt from an essay, I see the novelist as she captures the world of people. I have reproductions of paintings by the Dutch master, Vermeer, who captured an action—a woman opening a letter—that somehow contains all the drama of life.

At the end of this paragraph by Woolf, we feel the drama and mystery in the life of the woman and I wish that Woolf would step through the window, enter into that life, and tell me if someone is at the door, or is it a memory or an apprehension and if there is someone at the door, who is, and what will happen as they face each other. The force of narrative that we talked about on pages 165–66 lies coiled in that last sentence.

▪ READING JOSEPH MITCHELL ▪

Voice is the most magical and important quality in writing and an example of voice I return to hear again and again, is the master writer Joseph Mitchell—another celebrant of the city—as he begins the reportage that also provides the title of his most recent collection, *Up in the Old Hotel* (Pantheon, 1992).

Mitchell is an individual writer speaking to an individual reader. He reveals something of himself in the first lines. The pace is deceptively casual, reflective. He is going to report and he quickly demonstrates his ability to report with startling specifics but the important thing will be his thoughts, his commentary on what he finds. His voice promises that his conversation in type will be interesting and that he will invite readers to have their own thoughts in response to his.

Read this aloud to hear the music of Mitchell's written voice:

> Every now and then, seeking to rid my mind of thoughts of death and doom, I get up early and go down to Fulton Fish Market. I usually arrive around five-thirty, and take a walk through the two huge open-fronted market sheds, the Old Market and the New Market, whose fronts rest on South Street and whose backs rest on piles in the East River. At that time, a little while before the trading begins, the stands in the sheds are heaped high and spilling over with forty to sixty kinds of finfish and shellfish from the East Coast, the West Coast, the Gulf Coast, and half a dozen foreign countries. The smoky riverbank dawn, the racket the fishmongers make, the seaweed's smell, and the sight of this plentifulness always give me a feeling of well-being, and sometimes they elate me. I wander among the stands for an hour or so. Then I go into a cheerful market restaurant named Sloppy Louie's and eat a big, inexpensive, invigorating breakfast— kippered herring and scrambled eggs, or a shad-roe omelet, or split sea scallops and bacon, or some other breakfast specialty of the place.

I am always struck by that beginning followed by the glorious litany of fish, none a cliché, all familiar and somehow exotic and different at the same time.

▪ READING NATALIE GINZBURG ▪

Natalie Ginzburg (who died in 1991) was a major Italian writer whose "He and I" is a deceptively simple celebration of love. When I read it again and again, I am impressed by how much it reveals of human relationships—and I have a rare desire to imitate and write a column about Minnie Mae and myself. Perhaps I will, giving full credit to Natalie Ginzburg.

> He always feels hot. I always feel cold. In the summer when it really is hot he does nothing but complain about how hot he feels. He is irritated if he sees me put a jumper on in the evening.
>
> He speaks several languages well; I do not speak any well. He manages— in his own way—to speak even the languages that he doesn't know.
>
> He has an excellent sense of direction, I have none at all. After one day in a foreign city he can move about in it as thoughtlessly as a butterfly. I get

lost in my own city; I have to ask directions so that I can get back home again. He hates asking directions; when we go by car to a town we don't know he doesn't want to ask directions and tells me to look at the map. I don't know how to read maps and I get confused by all the little red circles and he loses his temper.

He loves the theater, painting, music, especially music. I do not understand music at all, painting doesn't mean much to me and I get bored at the theater. I love and understand one thing in the world and that is poetry.

He loves museums, and I will go if I am forced to but with an unpleasant sense of effort and duty. He loves libraries and I hate them.

He loves travelling, unfamiliar foreign cities, restaurants. I would like to stay at home all the time and never move.

All the same I follow him on his many journeys. I follow him to museums, to churches, to the opera. I even follow him to concerts, where I fall asleep.

It is easier to have a clever idea than to carry it off but she does, all the way through to the end. Note the word choice and the voice that doesn't complain or gripe or grouse or attack but simply celebrates their loving differences.

▪ READING PETER D. KRAMER ▪

The writer has the ability to recover significance from the river of experience and put it in context. Peter D. Kramer did that well in his best-selling book about an antidepressant drug, *Listening to Prozac* (Viking, 1993). In these few lines he exposes a central problem of mind-altering drugs: Is the real person the one without or with a drug?

An indication of the power of medication to reshape a person's identity is contained in the sentence Tess used when, eight months after first stopping Prozac, she telephoned me to ask whether she might resume the medication. She said, "I am not myself."

I found this statement remarkable. After all, Tess had existed in one mental state for twenty or thirty years; she then briefly felt different on medication. Now that the old mental state was threatening to re-emerge—the one she had experienced almost all her adult life—her response was "I am not myself." But who had she been all those years if not herself? Had medication somehow removed a false self and replaced it with a true one? Might Tess, absent the invention of the modern antidepressant, have lived her whole life—a successful life, perhaps, by external standards—and never been herself?

When I asked her to expand on what she meant, Tess said she no longer felt like herself when certain aspects of her ailment—lack of confidence, feelings of vulnerability—returned, even to a small degree. Ordinarily, if we ask a person why she holds back socially, she may say, "That's just who I am," meaning shy or hesitant or melancholy or overly cautious. These characteristics often persist throughout life, and they have a strong influence on career, friendships, marriage, self-image. . . .

On imipramine, no longer depressed but still inhibited and subdued, Tess felt "myself again." But while on Prozac, she underwent a redefinition of self. Off Prozac, when she again became inhibited and subdued—perhaps the identical sensations she had experienced while on imipramine—she now felt "not myself." Prozac redefined Tess's understanding of what was essential to her and what was intrusive and pathological.

Kramer is able to write with the authority of a physician without playing God. He is speculating and he makes contact with the reader, allowing us to speculate along with him. He doesn't suggest an easy answer, perhaps there is no answer, but there certainly is an issue that we should consider for society— and for ourselves.

▪ READING BERNARD CHAET ▪

I always enjoy seeing how different writers approach the same subject: two well-written art books—so well written you do not need the illustration to which the authors refer. Each are writing about the line. In the first, Bernard Chaet discusses the line in his *The Art of Drawing,* 3rd ed. (Holt, Rinehart & Winston, 1983).

By traditional definition, a line is the product of a dot moving across the surface of a support, such as paper. Once put down, the line can establish boundaries and separate areas. It can, by its direction and weight on the page, generate a sense of movement. By applying lines in patterns of parallel and cross-hatched marks, the draftsman can simulate texture on a perfectly smooth paper surface with line alone. Indeed, using line—that simplest and most subtle of graphic means—exclusively, the artist can realize any visual effect desired.

▪ READING CLINT BROWN AND CHERYL McLEAN ▪

Writers know there is no one right way to say anything but many ways that work and many that do not. Chaet worked for me and so do Clint Brown and Cheryl McLean in their *Drawing from Life* (Holt, Rinehart & Winston, 1992).

The power of line lies in its versatility, the myriad ways in which the artist can express personal views or characterize the human figure. In twentieth-century artist Alberto Giacometti's drawing, Walking Man, Figure 1.2, the line itself is a metaphor for the body of the man. Giacometti's line abbreviates the form and concept of a man in motion, recognizing the power line has to imply so much beyond itself. In a more complete narrative, the Oriental master Hokusai uses a brisk, chisel-like line to suggest the tension and action of combative wrestlers, Figure 1.3. Honore Daumier lavishly applies line to build up volumes through a kind of sketchy layering, Figure 1.4. His lines are loaded with energy. Rather than give a clear sense of the body's contour, these lines collectively create an impression of the body as an undulating mass. Each line adds a bit more momentum and synergy to the overall impression of the drawing.

▪ READING JONATHAN SHAY ▪

Jonathan Shay, a psychiatrist who works with combat veterans, saw a connection between the great Greek epics and the combat experience of Vietnam veterans. In his *Achilles in Vietnam* (Athenaeum, 1994) he argues for a different form of treatment for veterans. I always appreciate a clearly wrought thesis that tells the reader what the writer will argue for. After allowing the reader to hear testimony from a veteran, Shay says:

> We shall hear this man's voice and the voices of other combat veterans many times in these pages. I shall argue throughout this book that healing from trauma depends upon communalization of the trauma—being able safely to tell the story to someone who is listening and who can be trusted to retell it truthfully to others in the community. So before analyzing, before classifying, before thinking, before trying to do anything—we should listen. Categories and classifications play a large role in the institutions of mental health care for veterans, in the education of mental health professionals, and as tentative guides to perception. All too often, however, our mode of listening deteriorates into intellectual sorting, with the professional grabbing the veterans' words from the air and sticking them in mental bins. To some degree that is institutionally and educationally necessary, but listening this way destroys trust.

▪ READING ANNE TYLER ▪

Anne Tyler, one of our best novelists, has written brilliantly of being a writer, saying, "I hated childhood, and spent it sitting behind a book waiting for adulthood to arrive. When I ran out of books I made up my own. At night, when I couldn't sleep, I made up stories in the dark. . . . I guess I work from a combination of curiosity and distance. . . . Mostly, it's lies, writing novels. You set out to tell an untrue story and you try to make it believable, even to yourself. Which calls for details; any good lie does. I'm quicker to believe I was once a circus aerialist if I remember that just before every performance, I used to dip my hands in a box of chalk powder that smelled like clean, dry cloth being torn."

> After his wife left him, Macon had thought the house would seem larger. Instead, he felt more crowded. The windows shrank. The ceilings lowered. There was something insistent about the furniture, as if it were pressing in on him. . . . The house itself was medium-sized, unexceptional to look at, standing on a street of such houses in an older part of Baltimore. Heavy oak trees hung over it, shading it from the hot summer sun but also blocking breezes. The rooms inside were square and dim. All that remained in Sarah's closet was a brown silk sash hanging on a hook; in her bureau drawers, lint balls and empty perfume bottles. Their son's old room was neatly made up, as sleek as a room in a Holiday Inn. Some places, the walls gave off a kind of echo. Still, Macon noticed he had a tendency to hold his arms close to his body, to walk past furniture sideways as if he imagined the house could barely accommodate him. He felt too tall. His long, clumsy feet seemed unusually distant. He ducked his head in doorways.

I have always been interested in the beginnings of books, especially novels, because the writer has to do so much without the reader becoming aware of him sawing and drilling, planing and shaping, hammering away.

Think how much a novelist has to establish:

- A central tension or conflict that will carry an entire book forward when it is released
- A character that is believable, complex, interesting, and sympathetic enough for the reader to care what happens to that character
- A place where the story occurs
- A voice that supports its telling with an appropriate and attractive music

All this in a few pages.

▪ READING E. ANNIE PROULX ▪

I have read and reread the beginning of E. Annie Proulx's *Postcards* (Collier, 1993). Read it to see if she grabs you as she grabbed me. To a writer she accomplishes the impossible.

Even before he got up he knew he was on his way. Even in the midst of the involuntary orgasmic jerking he knew. Knew she was dead, knew he was on his way. Even standing there on shaking legs, trying to push the copper buttons through the stiff buttonholes he knew that everything he had done or thought in his life had to be started over again. Even if he got away.

What craft and what unusual and yet appropriate music she makes—how personal and yet accurate. In the very first line the world has changed and he—before we know who "he" is, is on his way. He is the one we soon discover who wanted to stay on the land and his wife, whom he has just murdered, is the one who wanted to go. Talk about a central tension. He is on his way. Seventy-two words and we see his problems with the buttons of her coat as he tries to hide her. And the suspense: *Even if he got away.*

▪ READING JOHN LE CARRE ▪

John Le Carre also immediately draws me into *A Perfect Spy* (Bantam, 1987). Read and reread it to see how much he is doing line by line.

> In the small hours of a blustery October morning in a south Devon coastal town that seemed to have been deserted by its inhabitants, Magnus Pym got out of his elderly country taxi-cab and, having paid the driver and waited till he had left, struck out across the church square. His destination was a terrace of ill-lit Victorian boardinghouses with names like Bel-a-Vista, The Commodore and Eureka. In build he was powerful but stately, a representative of something. His stride was agile, his body forward-sloping in the best tradition of the Anglo-Saxon administrative class. In the same attitude, whether static or in motion, Englishmen have hoisted flags over distant colonies, discovered the sources of great rivers, stood on the decks of sinking ships. He had been travelling in one way or another for sixteen hours but he wore no overcoat or hat. He carried a fat black briefcase of the official kind and in the other hand a green Harrods bag. A strong sea wind lashed at his city suit, salt rain stung his eyes, balls of spume skimmed across his path. Pym ignored them. Reaching the porch of a house marked "No Vacancies" he pressed the bell and waited, first for the outside light to go on, then for the chains to be unfastened from inside . . .
>
> "Why Mr. Canterbury, it's you," an old lady's voice objected sharply as the door opened behind him. "You bad man. You caught the night sleeper again, I can tell. Why ever didn't you telephone?"

Le Carre, master of the spy novel, creates a mysterious place, where a mysterious man acts in a mysterious manner. Notice all the clues that tell you he is leading a double, perhaps a triple life. Read it and you will find out.

▪ READING ALICE WALKER ▪

A writer delights in the glorious diversity of literature. What a change of pace from Le Carre to Alice Walker and the incredible beginning of *The Color Purple* that takes the reader inside the life—and head—of a fourteen-year-old African American living in the rural South shortly after the turn of the century.

> Dear God,
>   I am fourteen years old. I have always been a good girl. Maybe you can give me a sign letting me know what is happening to me.
>   Last spring after little Lucious come I heard them fussing. He was pulling on her arm. She say It too soon, Fonso, I ain't well. Finally he leave her alone. A week go by, he pulling on her arm again. She say Naw, I ain't Donna. Can't you see I'm already half dead, an all of these chilren.
>   She went to visit her sister doctor over Macon. Left me to see after the others. He never had a kine word to say to me. Just say You gonna do what your mummy wouldn't. First he put his thing up gainst my hip and sort of wiggle it around. Then he grab hold my titties. Then he push his thing inside my pussy. When that hurt, I cry. He start to choke me, saying You better shut up and git used to it.
>   But I don't never git used to it. And now I feels sick every time I be the one to cook. My mama she fuss at me an look at me. She happy, cause he good to her now. But too sick to last long.

▪ READING ALICE MUNRO ▪

If I had to choose the best short-story writer today—a choice I would hate to make—I would pick Alice Munro, a Canadian short-story writer who creates worlds and characters in that world that are entire. They are not cardboard flat, but multidimensional people you know and care about. Recently I discovered her first short story and was astonished to see that her talents were all there in "A Basket of Strawberries." Note the power and authority; note how well you know these people and their marriage in a few lines; note the sense of narrative, how the writer has drawn you into the story. Why is she at the window? What does see? What is wrong? What's going to happen next?

> Mr. Torrance had not slept well. The night had been unusually warm for June, and quite still, without the faintest wind. In his light sleep he had had an uneasy sensation of not being able to breathe as deeply as he should, and the darkness above his closed eyelids had seemed to have a reddish tinge, to be aglow with heat, impatience, and anguish of weariness. His wife was fretful, too; he was aware, all night long, of her great soft, heaving

movements and the mumbling, childish noises she made in her sleep. He lay beside her, quite still and motionless, and at dawn there was an ache and heaviness in all his bones; he felt as if he were made of rusty and ill-fitted lengths of iron pipe. He opened his eyes—he would not try to sleep anymore. His wife was standing at the window. She was in her nightgown, with a mauve silk wrapper tied loosely at her soft bulging waist, and her gray dark-streaked hair loose down her back.

▪ READING BARRY LOPEZ ▪

I am attracted to the Arctic for some reason so deep I cannot name it and my favorite book of the Arctic is *Arctic Dreams* (Bantam, 1987), written by one of America's best nature writers, no scratch that, one of our best writers, Barry Lopez. I had mentioned that description, in my opinion, can be high art and is the basic form of writing from which all other writing grows. I reread and reread his descriptions to go to the Arctic, to be inspired and instructed as a writer.

> Like other landscapes that initially appear barren, Arctic tundra can open suddenly, like the corolla of a flower, when any intimacy with it is sought. One begins to notice spots of brilliant red, orange, and green, for example, among the monotonic browns of a tundra tussock. A wolf spider lunges at a glistening beetle. A shred of muskox wool lies inert in the lavender blooms of a saxifrage . . .
>
> The wealth of biological detail on the tundra dispels any feeling that the land is empty; and its likeness to a stage suggests impending events. On a summer walk, the wind-washed air proves deathlessly clear. Time and again you come upon the isolated and succinct evidence of life—animal tracks, the undigested remains of a ptarmigan in an owl's casting, a patch of barren-ground willow nibbled nearly leafless by Arctic hares. You are afforded the companionship of birds which follow after you. (They know you are an animal; sooner or later you will turn up something to eat.) Sandpipers scatter before you, screaming tuituek, an Eskimo name for them. Coming awkwardly down a scree slope of frost-riven limestone you make a glass-tinkling clatter—and at a distance a tundra grizzly rises on its hind legs to study you: the dish-shaped paws of its front legs deathly still, the stance so human it is unnerving.

Lopez creates a poetry of specifics so that I see—feel—care about—the Arctic. He gets out of the way and puts you on the tundra, seeing it with his authoritative eyes—pun very much intended.

▪ READING BROCK DETHIER ▪

The poet Brock Dethier also uses nature to move back and forth in time in a poem in which I find new things to enjoy each time I read it. If you are not familiar with poetry, do not be put off by the funny lines. Read it aloud in the following form, as prose, and then read it aloud with the line breaks, the basic unit of contemporary poetry to see how those pauses and hesitations—beats—enrich the music and the meaning of the poem.

The View from Black Cap

The sun's setting over Cathedral and White Horse, over that new abomination of a hotel leching up on White Horse's neck, over the hardwood green of Moat's skirts, the blueberry bush bronze of Red Ridge's beckoning rocky shin where my parents saw their first pileated woodpecker. There's a road up Cathedral—paved even. We used to ski it. Once in Silvretta bindings and hiking boots I jump-turned it thirties style, thrilled by rhythm and control. Moat was a bear in Granny's day. They'd walk down the hill from the house, ford the Saco, trudge across the valley and hike up to the trailhead at Diana's Baths. That's why they loved Crawford Notch up there to the northwest. They could hop the up-train at the station a quarter-mile from the house, let the steam do the work, get off where they wanted as the train elbowed its way up the grade, climb Willey or Webster or Crawford, sun at the top, plunge sweaty faces into Saco at the bottom, flag down the train with someone's red petticoat. As beloved as it is, Crawford's shape confused us for half a century. From 302 in the Bartlett plains you see a mountain nose peeking above a ridge and Mother and her mother and maybe hers too always said, There's the friendly nose of Crawford, but from the Bear Notch Road vista you can see it's really Nancy, higher and across the Notch from Crawford. Every time I tell Mother that she says Really? in a disappointed voice. Just to the right of Nancy is Bemis where Mother and Granny got lost in the '50s trying to find the old fire tower. I suppose most of the rotting tinkertoys have disappeared but so many remains still stand—one on Carrigain, at the other end of that little range, others at Hale, just a few miles north, and Osceola, just to the south, one right over here on Kearsarge that may still function—at least I've seen people up there working on it. You can see that one from the house, or could before we let all those birches grow up. Last time we went up there, we got buzzed twice—once by a plane, once by a chopper—had to tiptoe around two attack dogs on the way down, eavesdropped three couples arguing about turning back. But from that tower when I was a kid at exactly one o'clock we would aim our tinny mirror towards a knoll in the valley, watch the reflected light sweep down the rock then out towards the house, delight in the answering dots of brightness, the sudden brief flashes from home.

———————

The View from Black Cap

The sun's setting over Cathedral and White Horse,
over that new abomination of a hotel
leching up on White Horse's neck,
over the hardwood green of Moat's skirts,
the blueberry bush bronze of
Red Ridge's beckoning rocky shin
where my parents saw their first pileated woodpecker.

There's a road up Cathedral—
paved even. We used to ski it.
Once in Silvretta bindings and hiking boots
I jump-turned it
thirties style,
thrilled by rhythm and control.
Moat was a bear in Granny's day.
They'd walk down the hill from the house,
ford the Saco,
trudge across the valley and
hike up to the trailhead at Diana's Baths.

That's why they loved Crawford Notch
up there to the northwest.
They could hop the up-train at the station
a quarter-mile from the house,
let the steam do the work,
get off where they wanted
as the train elbowed its way up the grade,
climb Willey or Webster or Crawford,
sun at the top,
plunge sweaty faces into Saco at the bottom,
flag the train down with someone's red petticoat.

As beloved as it is,
Crawford's shape confused us
for half a century.
From 302 in the Bartlett plains
you see a mountain nose peeking above a ridge
and Mother and her mother and maybe hers too
always said, There's the friendly nose of Crawford,
but from the Bear Notch Road vista
you can see it's really Nancy,

higher and across the Notch from Crawford.
Every time I tell Mother that she says
Really? in a disappointed voice.

Just to the right of Nancy is Bemis
where Mother and Granny got lost in the '50s
trying to find the old fire tower.
I suppose most of the rotting tinkertoys have disappeared
but so many remains still stand—
one on Carrigain, at the other end of that little range,
others at Hale, just a few miles north,
and Osceola, just to the south,
one right over here on Kearsarge that may still function—
at least I've seen people up there working on it.

You can see that one from the house,
or could before we let all those birches grow up.
Last time we went up there,
we got buzzed twice—
once by a plane, once by a chopper—
had to tiptoe
around two attack dogs on the way down,
eavesdropped three couples arguing about turning back.
But from that tower when I was a kid
at exactly one o'clock
we would aim our tinny mirror
towards a knoll in the valley,
watch the reflected light sweep down the rock
then out towards the house,
delight in the answering dots of brightness,
the sudden brief flashes from home.

It always surprises me how a writer who is deeply familiar with a world can re-create it with specific names so that we see it or transpose it to a place with which we are familiar. In reading and rereading this poem, I am impressed at how easily he takes us back and forth in time to his grandmother's day, perhaps before, and up to the present so that he—and the reader—see the area and its changes in his lifetime, in his mother's, and his grandmother's and, by implication, his son's and his son's son.

There is something magical and terrifying about the end, when signals across time and space are no longer sent or received. Do I "understand" the poem? As a writer, I read without complete understanding as I live without complete understanding. I understood the poem enough to enter and inhabit the world of the poet. It is writing that becomes part of my experience because there is surprise each time I read it and the promise that no reading will eliminate all its mystery.

Read as writers do to understand our craft, to improve your own craft, to be inspired and, most of all, for delight, celebrate what other writers do that is so difficult but reads so easily when the writer has packed up the tools, swept the workshop floor, and left us a final draft.

▪ QUESTIONS ABOUT READING AS A WRITER ▪

Do I have to like the kind of writing that turns you on?

Certainly not. Sometimes I don't like the writing that "turns me on" and I move on to other kinds of writing. The writing that I think is good keeps changing and your idea of good writing will keep changing. We read to learn what we need to learn about life, we read to hear others confirm and articulate our thoughts and feelings, we read to escape and depending what we are escaping our choice of reading changes, we read to see how other writers solve the problems we face at this stage of our writing development or on a particular writing task. Those tasks and situations keep changing and so what interests us in our reading changes. Follow your own needs.

I don't always see what you see in published writing. In fact, I never see it until after you point it out. But I do see things I do or should do in my writing. Do I have to see what you see?

No. You come to reading with your own autobiography. I read about only children in a different way than my daughters since I was an only child and they were not; I read crime stories in a different way than my neighbors since I have been both a policeman and a police reporter. And when I read as a writer, I usually read to see the writer's solutions to problems that face me at the moment: What would be the advantages of a long line in the poem I'm writing this week? How should I start my next novel? How can I write a column about a conflict when I think both sides are right—or wrong?

Don't you always read as a writer?

Not consciously. I read to see why the teachers in the next town have gone on strike, to become a female private detective in a Sue Grafton novel or a bird artist in Newfoundland in 1911 in a novel by Howard Norman, to see why the Patriots won. I read for information, instruction, entertainment but when I read a page that makes me think or feel or care or laugh or weep, I guess I go back and read, saying, "How did the writer do that?"

Doesn't that take the fun out of it?

No, it increases it. When I watch the replay of a great play by a hockey goalie, I enjoy it more because I played in the goal. That second look—or fourth or fifth—makes it better.

Where do you get that stuff to read? Do you have a reading list?

Not often. Occasionally, I'll write down a couple of titles people have mentioned, or after a TV interview with an author, a book review or some library research, but mostly I follow my nose. I go in a bookstore almost every day and I discover books on the shelves there or in the library. When I was a freelance writer in New Jersey, I had cards from four libraries. And when I read something by a writer that impresses me, I rush to find books by the same author and devour them.

If I read like you do in my English class, I'd get in trouble. Why don't my English teachers read this way?

Some do but many don't because they are not writers. They read as readers. They are critics and scholars. They examine the trends in literature, evaluate the works and their authors, study literature in a context, for example, seeing it as an historical document, a social or political one. They study literature in an aesthetic setting or see a work in cultural, ethic, or gender context. All these are important ways to look at reading and good ways to spend your life. Like most English teachers, I have taught literature as well as composition. But my strengths are in teaching students to write. I read as a maker. They teach how to read more effectively and the purpose of this book is to teach how to write more effectively.

By the way, you can read without writing but you can't write without reading, word by word, line by line, as it appears on the page and is later revised and edited.

Who's your favorite author?

My father was in the fashion business and we ate poorly or well according to what sold at Christmas or Easter. It was a silly game. Literature isn't a silly game. As a literature student I spent a lot of time ranking poems, plays, short stories, essays, novels as works of art but I refuse to play that game any more. A piece of literature has value when it speaks to you of the human condition. By that measure, Lisa Miller is the greatest poet in the English language—for me, today, after I read an as yet unpublished poem of hers that moved my mind and my emotions. Who knows who will be my favorite writer when I pick up a book tonight.

I hear there are lists of books everyone should read. Should I get one and read through the list?

All the lists peddle a point of view. One is white Anglo Saxon male, another is white liberal female, another African American, or Asian or European or Third World or . . . Find your own literature and when you are familiar with it then read the literature of others.

When do you get your reading done? I don't have whole days in which I do nothing but read.

Neither do I. I always have a book with me and I have trained myself to read in fragments of time. I read in the car waiting for my wife, in a hall waiting for a concert or lecture to begin, in bed, on the john, in front of the TV during commercials, in front of the TV during a game or a program, sitting on a rock wall, in the waiting room of a doctor or a car repair shop, on a bench at the mall, in a bath, on the plane, at the beach, in the mountains, in the city park, in a hotel room, when eating alone, on the porch, in my office.

What should I do to start reading like a writer?

Find a writer who is writing on the same subject as you are or in the same genre. Read to see how they performed your task. Find writers who sound like you'd like to sound, who write what you'd like to write, and you'll discover you are reading as a writer.

▪ READING-AS-A-WRITER ACTIVITIES ▪

1. To understand what a favorite writer has done, take a few paragraphs, changing just enough to make it yours. Set the novel or short story in your hometown, write the essay on cooking meat as a vegetarian, write a profile of a parent as the writer wrote of a rock star. Just a few paragraphs will make you see some of what the published writer has done.

2. Read three articles, poems, or short stories on the same topic and list the specific differences or how they approached the task.

3. Read a few paragraphs of a writer aloud and then tune a few paragraphs of your writing to the other writer's music.

4. Reverse the activity above. Read a few paragraphs of something of your own that you liked and then revise a few paragraphs of your favorite author in your voice.

5. Read an interview with a writer, an autobiography, published letters, or journal entries that talk about the making of a work, read the result, and write down how the writer solved the problems discussed by the writer.

6. Take paragraphs that you admire and do what I did, putting what you liked in words, then write a memo to yourself saying how this could be applied to a piece you are writing. Apply it.

7. Write a critical review of a piece of literature as a writer, evaluating the work in terms of what the writer tried to do, how the writer tried to do it, how well the writer succeeded.

8. Using the computer, type in a page or two of a favorite writer, then make a margin as wide as half the page and write a paragraph about what the writer is doing.

9. Take a piece of writing and make a craft outline of the techniques the writer used to open, develop, and close the piece.

10. List the specific editorial decisions a published writer had to make in a single page of writing.

11. Take a piece of writing you respect, then imagine you are an editor who has only space for 25 percent of the original—500 words instead of 2000, 1000 instead of 4000. Cut it and you will discover how it was put together.

12. Take a scene from a novel and make it a scene in a screenplay; take a screenplay and make it into a scene in a novel. In doing either of these you will see what the writer did and did not do.

13. Write an imaginary letter as an editor to a published author making believe a work of literature is *NOT* a final draft. Tell the writer how to make the work publishable. To do that you'll have to understand what the writer did—and needs to do.

14. After reading a writer you admire who has done what you are trying to do, write an editor's letter to yourself, indicating what has to be done to make the draft publishable.

15. Read more of one of the authors I have cited in this chapter, seeing if you agree with what I said and writing out your writer's response to the entire work.

AFTERWORD
The Joy of a Craft That
Can Never Be Learned

You have explored a craft that can never be learned. Be grateful—writing will bring you a lifetime of discovery and surprise. I have been writing for more than fifty years but each morning at my writing desk I am again seventeen. I face the page with just enough fear to make it exciting and little enough expectation to allow me to write what I do not expect.

Writing has allowed my voice to be heard. I have been able to participate in our society, arguing for new ways to teach writing, arguing against old ways of resolving differences and against war, speaking out on the satisfaction and concerns of my generation. At my writing desk, I have been able to discover and explore the mysteries of life and survive the tragedies that enter each life—hurt and loss, sickness and death. I have been able to complain and to celebrate, mourn and laugh, imagine and learn.

Writing has also brought me the gift of concentration as I become lost in my craft, searching for the right word, creating the phrase that gives off sparks of meaning, constructing sentences that flow and paragraphs that satisfy, tuning the music of my voice to my evolving meaning.

Readers have told me that I have articulated their feelings and their thoughts allowing them to feel participating members of the human community.

Writing began as play and it remains play. I hope you will be as fortunate and find a lifetime of play, fooling around with language and finding yourself surprised by a meaning that clarifies your life.

INDEX

To Focus : Prompt #1

> List a few topics you've been thinking about

> pick one + make a deeper list
> pick one + explore a memory it triggers
> pick one word + push it further --
    look for ~~a~~ a central tension.
                        mystery
                        information
                        significance

look for a moment
    an event
    an act
    a cause + effect
    a problem
    a solution

Prompt #2 Try Another Way to focus
    Adjust distance
    Think up an image
    move the reader's angle of vision
    Pose a question
    Write a thesis statement.